Thorsten Gieser
Living with Wolves

I0093191

Thorsten Gieser is a Lecturer in Anthropology at the University of Koblenz and a Research Associate in the ERC project "Veterinarization of Europe? Hunting for Wild Boar Futures in the Time of African Swine Fever (BOAR)" at the Czech Academy of Sciences. He is an environmental anthropologist with a focus on human-wildlife-coexistence in Germany, specialising in the return of wolves and hunting as a form of human-animal relation.

Thorsten Gieser

Living with Wolves

Affects, Feelings and Sentiments in Human-Wolf-Coexistence

[transcript]

The project "The return of the wolf to Germany: mapping extraordinary encounters" (Az. 96446, October 2019–October 2022) was funded by the Volkswagen Foundation.

VolkswagenStiftung

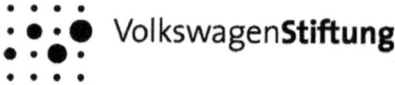

Bibliographic information published by the Deutsche Nationalbibliothek
The Deutsche Nationalbibliothek lists this publication in the Deutsche Nationalbib-liografie; detailed bibliographic data are available in the Internet

First published in 2024 by transcript Verlag, Bielefeld
© Thorsten Gieser

Cover layout: Maria Arndt, Bielefeld
Cover illustration: Thorsten Gieser (photo shows the wolf Odin from the Wolf Center Dörverde)
Copy-editing: Patty A. Gray (rutabagawriter.com)
Translated by: Thorsten Gieser
Print-ISBN: 978-3-8376-7470-5
PDF-ISBN: 978-3-8394-7470-9
ISSN of series: 2702-945X
eISSN of series: 2702-9468

Contents

Foreword

This book is the result of the research project 'The Return of the wolf to Germany: mapping extraordinary affective encounters' (October 2019–October 2022), funded by the initiative 'Originalitätsverdacht? Neue Optionen für die Geistes- und Kulturwissenschaften' of the Volkswagen Foundation, at the Department of Cultural Studies of the University of Koblenz. The initiative aimed to develop innovative research ideas and encourage original and unconventional thinking. I leave it to the reader to decide whether I have produced something original. I enjoyed embarking again on wolf issues after a gap of almost twenty years. As an environmental anthropologist with a focus on human-animal relations, I had started with wolves, ventured astray, and only returned to them many years later.

My studies in social/cultural anthropology, religious studies and environmental sciences at the University of Heidelberg culminated in a master's thesis on human-wolf conflicts in Mongolia. Based on short-term ethnographic fieldwork with Mongolian herders in Tuva, I problematised the prevailing view of wolf biologists working in the area at the time, who saw wolves only as enemies of local herders and a threat to herding and thus to economic livelihoods. While this cultural image of the wolf certainly existed among the Tuva, it turned out to be far more complex and ambiguous. Wolves hunted and killed livestock (or, very rarely, herders themselves); herders hunted and killed wolves. But wolves were also sacred animals, messengers from the sky god, respected and admired for their cunning, endurance and bravery. Wolves living in the neighbourhood were particularly well regarded, not unlike their human neighbours, with whom they formed reciprocal social relationships. The relationship between the Tuva and the wolves thus went far beyond a simple economic relationship and included social and, above all, religious dimensions that made the wolves complex enemies.[1]

Subsequent projects focused on various human-environment relationships—a new religious movement that sees itself as a nature religion, the embodied experiential knowledge in English horticulture—before beginning a long-term project in 2015 on hunting in Germany as a form of human-animal relationship. Conceived as a sensory ethnography, I have since been investigating the sensory training of hunters, their perception of the landscape as a hunting landscape, how their sensory practices are guided by the lives and actions of wild animals, and how the two dominant paradigms in hunting (traditional and ecological) shape their relationships with animals and the environment in general.

Since wolves had also returned to Germany several years before I started my hunting project, I had the opportunity to encounter wolves again, at least thematically. Traditionally, wolves belong to the category of so-called predatory game for hunters, and thus actually also to huntable game, to which hunters used to have privileged access but no longer do, since wolves are now under protection and (except in Saxony and Lower Saxony) are legally no longer game. No wonder, then, that the wolf is a constant topic of discussion among hunters; this was reason enough for me to get on the trail of wolves in Germany and to develop a new research project that would make use of my experience with hunters and wolves. The current wolf project can therefore be seen as part of my many years of research into human-wildlife relationships.

Since autumn 2020, my research on wolves and hunting has continued in a new collaborative and international project funded by the European Research Council (ERC). As a senior researcher, I am working on a project titled, 'Veterinarization of Europe? Hunting for Wild Boar Futures in the Time of African Swine Fever' (BOAR),[2] led by Ludek Broz, at the Department of Ecological Anthropology of the Institute of Ethnology at the Czech Academy of Sciences. Until 2026, I am investigating the relationship between hunters and wildlife (wild boar in particular) in the light of recent changes in hunting practices and technologies in relation to African Swine Fever (ASF), which broke out in eastern Germany in autumn 2020 and has been feared for years. As the ASF area is

---

1   Gieser, Thorsten: 'Beyond Natural Enemies: Wolves and Nomads in Mongolia', in: Heyer, Marlis/Hose, Susanne (eds.), Encounters with wolves: dynamics and futures, Bautzen: Sorbisches Institut 2020, pp. 50–62.

2   https://www.wildboar.cz/ (accessed: 30.03.2024).

also wolf territory, and as the life of wild boar on the ground takes place in the area of tension between human and wolf hunters, wolves will therefore remain part of my research on human-wildlife relations in Germany for several years to come.

At the same time, I will focus on developing new theoretical and methodological approaches to human-wolf encounters in the coming years (until 2027) as a collaborator in the research project 'Sensory Acts: More Than Human Communication in the Circumpolar North' (SACTS),[3] funded by the Social Sciences and Humanities Research Council of Canada (SSHRC), at the University of Regina in Canada and led by Alex Oehler.

Finally, I would like to take this opportunity to thank the people who have contributed to the success of this book. My special thanks go to all those who talked to me about wolves during my research and helped me to better understand the complex relationship between humans and wolves. Among those I would like to (and may) mention by name are: Willi Faber for many monitoring excursions in the Westerwald and for his insights into wolf management in Rhineland-Palatinate and the work of NABU; Frank Wörner for his support and his immense knowledge of wolves in the Westerwald and his insights into the work of the Society for the Protection and Conservation of Wolves; Frank Faß for making me feel so welcome at the Wolf Centre in Dörverden and giving me several days of his time; the team of the LUPUS Institute for Wolf Monitoring and Research, especially Gesa Kluth for many interesting coffee talks and support over the years, and Lea Wirk (with sniffer dog Molly) for what felt like hundreds of kilometres of monitoring excursions in Lusatia, where our conversation never ran out and from whom I was able to learn a lot about wolf management in Saxony; the team of the hotel Zum Hammer in Neustadt/Spreetal, who have hosted me so well over the years that the Hammer and Neustadt have almost become my second home; Stephan Kaasche—simply because you can't get around the best local nature guide if you want to do research on wolves in Lusatia; Joscha Grolms and Laura Gärtner from the wilderness school WildnisWissen, who trained me in the art of tracking for a year and taught me to distinguish wolf tracks from dog tracks (roughly, anyway); Julian Sandrini from the Koordinationszentrum Luchs und Wolf in Rhineland-Palatinate for his support; Garry Marvin and Alex Oehler for their valuable feedback on my book manuscript; the whole BOAR team in Prague for many stimulating discussions on human-animal relations over the past

---

3   http://www.sensoryacts.ca/ (accessed: 30.03.2024).

years; Michaela Fenske, Marlis Heyer, and Irina Arnold from the Würzburg DFG project 'Die Rückkehr der Wölfe: Cultural Anthropological Studies on the Process of Wolf Management in the Federal Republic of Germany' for the good exchange and cooperation on several publications; Bernhard Tschofen, Elisa Frank, and Nico Heinzer from the Zurich SNF project 'Wolves—Knowledge and Practice: Ethnographies on the Return of Wolves in Switzerland' for the stimulating exchange on wolf issues; I also had the opportunity to discuss the German version of my book with the Faculty of Applied Ecology at the Inland Norway University of Applied Sciences at Evenstad. I am grateful to John Linnell, Barbara Zimmermann, Petra Kaczensky, and all the other ecologists there for their insights. At Evenstad, I also profited from conversations and a long walk in the snow with Olve Krange. His sharp sociological mind helped me to see the strengths and weaknesses of my arguments. I presented a paper at the Wolves across borders Conference in Sweden in 2023, based on the German version of Chapter 2 of this book. The many conversations with wolf researchers from all over the world helped me refine the English version of this current book. I am grateful to Andreas Ackermann for the freedom he gives me in Koblenz to pursue my research interests away from teaching. Without the Volkswagen foundation this project would have been impossible, and their flexibility and support were outstanding. My editors Ute Maack (for the German version of this book) and Patty McGray (for the English version) have made this book more readable with their special feel for language. Finally, I would like to thank Erica von Essen, my intellectual sparring partner, who has been with me through the ups and downs of writing this book and who has been a constant source of inspiration.

Figure 1: Wolf territories in Germany in the monitoring year 2020–21

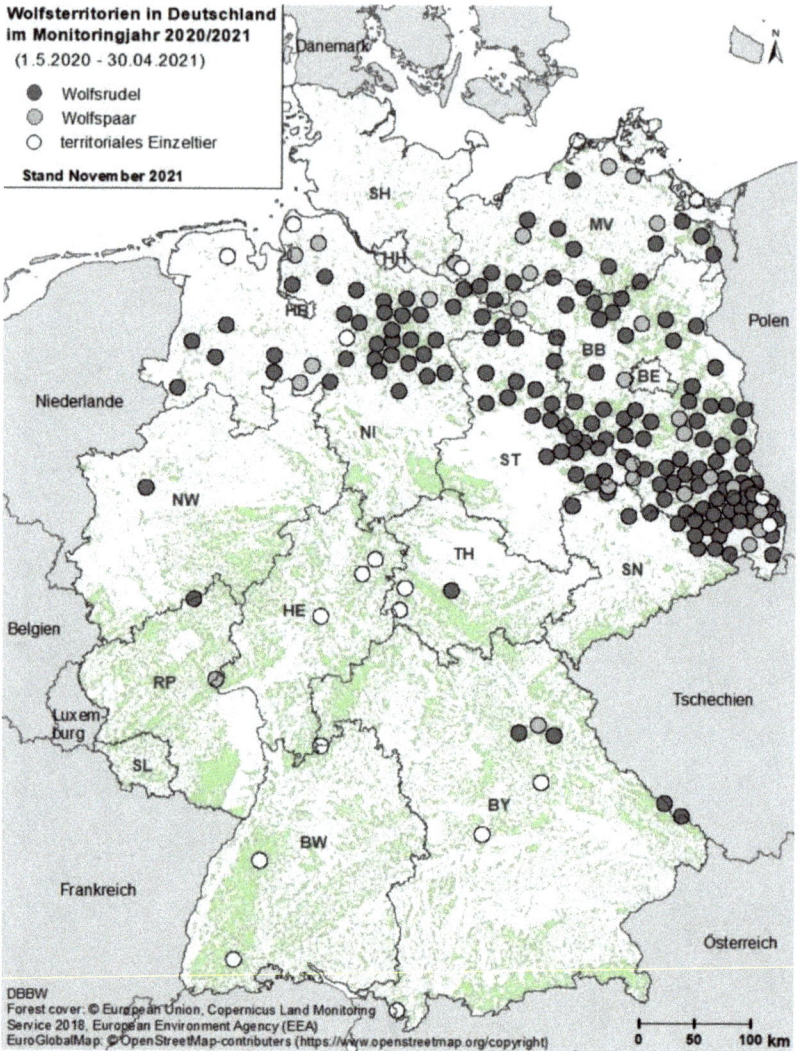

Wolfsterritorien in Deutschland
im Monitoringjahr 2020/2021
(1.5.2020 - 30.04.2021)

● Wolfsrudel
◉ Wolfspaar
○ territoriales Einzeltier

Stand November 2021

Source: Federal Documentation and Advisory Centre on the Wolf (DBBW)

1. Introduction

The return of the wolves to Germany

The last wolf in Germany was shot in the Lausitz region of eastern Germany in 1904, and since then wolves have been considered extinct in the whole country. In fact, wolves made attempts to return throughout the twentieth century. However, as society was unwilling to tolerate them, all wolves were killed (either by humans or in road traffic) shortly after their arrival. As late as the 1990s, six wolves were still being killed, but something had changed in the meantime: wolves had become a protected species. Then, in 2000, two wolves from western Poland had managed to find each other in the Oberlausitz military training area in Saxony and formed the first reproducing wolf pack in almost a hundred years. It took five years for a second pack to be established, and after another five years there were seven packs, seven pairs and six territorial solitary wolves, spread across the states of Saxony, Brandenburg, Saxony-Anhalt, Mecklenburg-Western Pomerania, Hesse and Bavaria. By the 2020–21 monitoring year, the wolf population had increased to 159 packs, thirty-eight pairs, twenty-two territorial solitary wolves and 575 confirmed pups in ten of the sixteen federal states (most of them in Saxony, Brandenburg and Lower Saxony). Germany now has one of the largest wolf populations in Europe, and it continues to grow.[1]

But numbers alone give an incomplete picture. Unlike the return or reintroduction of other wildlife species, such as lynx or beavers, the return of

---

1   For the international status of the species wolf, Canis lupus, see https://www.iucnred list.org/species/3746/144226239#population (accessed: 30.03.2024). For the status of the wolf in Germany, see https://www.dbb-wolf.de/ (accessed: 30.03.2024). In the last monitoring year, 2022/23, the population has grown to 184 packs, forty-eight pairs, and twenty-two territorial solitary wolves and 640 confirmed pups.

wolves seems to have a different quality. Conflicts overshadow the establishment of any kind of coexistence. Wolves enter our lives in many different ways. Wolves are being sighted in new places all the time. Videos and pictures of wolf sightings and encounters circulate on social media. Wolves are establishing new territories. Wolves cross roads and sometimes become victims of traffic accidents. Wolves attack sheep, sometimes horses and cows, overcoming herd protection measures. Wolves are occasionally found to have been illegally killed and buried. People take to the streets to protest against the return of wolves. Public meetings and lectures about wolves are held. People visit wolf exhibitions and wolf parks. In rare cases, wolves mate with dogs and produce hybrids. Sometimes wolves are officially declared 'problem wolves' (after long and heated debates) because they have repeatedly killed farm animals or shown 'unnatural' behaviour. There are media reports that a problem wolf has been killed, or that a wolf could not be killed despite efforts to do so, because it has mysteriously disappeared or moved to a neighbouring state where the original permit for its legal 'removal' (killing) is not valid. Animal rights activists are suing, or threatening to sue, individual politicians or institutions for issuing such permits.[2]

Living with wolves: coexistence as an affective affair

We can see that the return of wolves to Germany is full of potential and real conflicts, and it is no wonder that it has created a highly emotional situation. The parties involved accuse the other side of being too emotional, while they themselves claim to be rational and generally call for a calming of emotions and more objectivity in the debate. And yet emotions always boil up. In parliamentary debates, public speeches and street protests, actors champion their causes and express indignation or outrage. Livestock owners are frustrated and express

---

2   For current attitudes and opinions on wolves in Germany, see Arbieu, Ugo et al.:
     'Attitudes towards returning wolves (Canis lupus) in Germany: Exposure, information sources and trust matter', in: Biological Conservation 234 (2019), pp. 202–210, h
     ttps://doi.org/10.1016/j.biocon.2019.03.027; Lehnen, Lisa/Mueller, Thomas/Reinhardt,
     Ilka/Kaczensky, Petra/Arbieu, Ugo: 'Gesellschaftliche Einstellungen zur Rückkehr des
     Wolfs nach Deutschland', in: Natur und Landschaft 1/2021, pp. 27–33, https://doi.or
     g/ 10.17433/1.2021.50153871.27-33. Pates, Rebecca/Leser, Julia: The wolves are coming
     back. The politics of fear in Eastern Germany, Manchester: Manchester University Press
     2021.

their constant concern for their animals. Wolf critics and supporters meet on-line and offline and get angry or upset with each other. On the one hand, hatred of wolves has led to illegal killings. On the other hand, wolf supporters meet the return of wolves with love and fascination. Meanwhile, most people seem just a little uneasy and don't know what to make of this new situation. They want and need their concerns to be 'taken seriously', as a common phrase in Germany in recent years has gone – especially by politicians and official wolf managers.

The conflicts between humans and wolves are therefore far from being exhausted in the social scientific study of rational debates, the exchange of arguments, or in public knowledge, opinions and attitudes. There seems to be an implicit assumption shared by almost everyone involved that the conflicts can be resolved by 1) more knowledge, 2) more objective ways of dealing with it. Therefore, the role of science and scientific knowledge is paramount in the whole discourse on wolves.[3] While there is certainly a place for studies of knowledge and attitudes in the conflicts, it is clear that they leave significant dimensions of the conflicts unexamined. This is because human-wolf coexistence is not 'emotionally neutral': whether coexistence or conflict, the relationship is deeply emotional.[4] This insight, although often observed, has not yet led to a comprehensive study of the role of emotions in the human-wolf relationship. What is needed, then, is an approach that thinks through emotions in their various manifestations with a nuanced understanding. Two brief examples from my fieldwork give a preliminary idea of where such a perspective might lead.

One of the first hunters I interviewed in Lusatia was introduced to me by a research partner who described him as an opponent of wolves. On the phone, his first question to me was: "Are you one of those wolf fanatics?" He agreed to talk to me (without a recorder), and I visited him in his 'hunting room', which he had set up above his garage: wood-panelled walls hung with trophies and posters of game, and a sticker from the action alliance 'Wolf-Nein Danke!' on the door. At the end of the interview, as I was packing my things, I asked him

---

3   See von Essen, Erica: 'Whose Discourse is it Anyway? Understanding Resistance through the Rise of "Barstool Biology"' in Nature Conservation, in: Environmental Communication 11 (4) (2017), pp. 470–489, https://doi.org/10.1080/17524032.2015.1042986.

4   Thorsten Gieser/von Essen, Erica: 'Wolves, ecologies of fear, and the affective challenges of coexistence', Society and Space, 6 September 2021, https://www.societyandspace.org/articles/wolves-ecologies-of-fear (accessed 18.06.2022).

one last question. Would he consider himself a strong opponent of wolves? "Nooo!" he shouted, visibly agitated and gesticulating wildly. "I just want more rationality in the debate!" An emotional outburst combined with a call for rationality may be paradoxical, but it reveals the characteristics of the public conflicts about human-wolf coexistence.

Although the 'order of discourse' in contemporary society dictates that debates should be conducted according to facts and reason, and that emotions are out of place as a disruptive factor or irritant, emotions cannot be so easily suppressed. This includes the fact that all participants in these debates claim objectivity and rationality for themselves and deny it to the other side. Accordingly, it is always the other side that is emotional. The only group that publicly claims emotionality (and even makes political capital out of it) are the livestock owners. In a public debate, for example, a young female professional shepherd from the Eifel region exclaimed:

[Shepherd:] We live at the existential minimum, like most shepherds. This is a profession with a lot of idealism, and by the way, how are we supposed to enter the debate completely without emotions if the sheep are not wild like game, but they belong to us?

[Moderator:] You don't have to. It's all right [...] Emotions. [loud applause from the audience].[5]

It seems that there is room in the public discourse for a 'justified', positively interpreted emotionality. For the shepherdess, it seems legitimate to express her emotions because they are interpreted as a sign of a positive relationship with her animals. This emotional relationship adds another dimension to the (rational) arguments about the 'ecosystem services' of grazing animals, which are usually presented as objective arguments. But why are shepherds allowed to claim emotions and express them in debates, while others (like hunters or wolf friends) are not? What kind of emotional relationship do they have with their animals? What is the role of the (deliberately played) 'emotional card' in relation to rational arguments in public discourse?

These and several other questions arise from two overarching questions that have guided my research: What role do emotions play in human-wolf relationships, and how are emotions mobilised, performed, encouraged, denied,

---

5   SWR wolf panel discussion, Daaden, 21.11.2019, author's minutes.

withheld, or disciplined in the course of human-wolf coexistence and practices? In this book I address these questions by opening up the concept of emotion to mean more than an internal, subjective and human experience, treating it instead as a phenomenon of more-than-human affect. Colloquially, affect refers to "a temporary excitement or surge of emotion caused by external events or internal psychic processes"[6], although the exact occasion is often unclear and remains undefined. Affect is also associated with an impulse to act that is difficult to control. The working definition used in this book differs somewhat from colloquial usage and is primarily informed by recent developments in interdisciplinary affect theory.[7] By *affectivity* in the broadest sense I mean here:

> [...] a fundamental driving force of [more-than-] human coexistence. Affectivity is, on the one hand, very direct power, movement, intensity, liveliness, and, on the other hand, a thoroughly social, interpersonal event, a mode of being together, a lived and experienced being-in-relation, a multifaceted dynamic 'in-between'. [8]

Affect touches, moves, concerns, influences, excites, irritates and agitates us. Affect thus describes one of the fundamental ways in which bodies are alive, responsive and sensitively engaged with the world. To be alive in this context is to have the capacity to affect and be affected. This relational affective dynamic is also the basis for wolf-human coexistence.

---

6   Wikipedia entry 'Affekt', https://de.wikipedia.org/wiki/Affekt (translated by TG, accessed: 30.04.2024).

7   I refer for the most part to the extensive works of the Berlin Collaborative Research Centre SFB Affective Societies, see e.g. Slaby, Jan/Scheve, Christian v. (eds.): Affective societies. Key concepts (= Routledge studies in affective societies), London/New York: Routledge 2019 as a survey work, as well as the cultural geographer Ben Anderson, see Anderson, Ben: Encountering affect. Capacities, apparatuses, conditions (= An Ashgate Book), London/New York: Routledge 2016.

8   Slaby, Jan/Mühlhoff, Rainer/Wüschner, Philipp: 'Affektive Relationalität. Umrisse eines philosophischen Forschungsprogramms', in: Eberlein, Undine (ed.), Zwischenleiblichkeit und bewegtes Verstehen—Intercorporeity, Movement and Tacit Knowledge, Bielefeld: transcript 2016, pp. 69–108, here p. 69, https://doi.org/10.1515/9783839435793-004.

My basic assumption is that when humans and wolves meet – directly or indirectly – something happens.[9] Individual actors are affectively moved and transformed in many ways: in their phenomenal experience, in their bodily behaviour, in their knowledge and in their values. In order to be able to analyse what is happening in detail, this book uses 'affect' rather loosely as an umbrella term for a variety of related phenomena that arise from such a definition of affect but can take different forms, from feelings and emotions to atmospheres, moods and sentiments. Understood in this way, the term allows us to encompass and bring together pre-subjective, subjective and also intersubjective experiences, spontaneous and sustained affects, stabilising and destabilising affects, human and animal affects. At a basic level, I distinguish between affect, feeling and emotion. In short, while *affect* refers to the interpersonal dynamics between actors, *feeling* refers to the subjective experience of being affected, and emotion refers to the socio-cultural structuring of feelings into categories that can be grasped in language (anger, indignation, envy, love, etc.).

This micro-level analysis of individual actors is complemented by a meso-level analysis in which affects, emotions and feelings are seen as expressions of broader socio-cultural and more-than-human affective structures such as atmospheres, moods and sentiments. In this context, I understand *atmosphere*[10] to be a spatially diffuse quality of feeling that is perceptible to those present, that grips them and affects them by colouring or attuning their momentary state of being according to the atmosphere. It is therefore a kind of 'space of possibility' for affecting and being affected, in which the experience of a certain quality of feeling is made possible without necessarily imposing itself. I understand *mood* as a special case of atmosphere. While not only people, but also spatial environments (architecture, landscape) and other living beings (plants,

---

9   On the importance of wolf encounters in general, see also Arbieu, Ugo et al.: 'The positive experience of encountering wolves in the wild', in: Conservation Science and Practice 2.5 (2020), article e184, https://doi.org/10.1111/csp2.184; Eriksson, Max/Sandström, Camilla/Ericsson, Göran: 'Direct experience and attitude change towards bears and wolves', in: Wildlife Biology 21.3 (2015), pp. 131–137, https://doi.org/10.2981/wlb.0006 2Wam, Hilde Karine: Wolf behaviour towards people. the outcome of 125 monitored encounters. Cand. Scient. thesis. Norwegian Agriculture University, Ås 2002.

10   See Riedel, Friedlind: 'Atmosphere', in: J. Slaby/C. v. Scheve (eds.), Affective societies, pp. 85–95; Slaby, Jan: 'Atmospheres—Schmitz, Massumi and beyond', in: Friedlind Riedel/Juha Torvinen (eds.), Music as Atmosphere: Collective Feelings and Affective Sounds, London: Routledge 2019.

animals) can contribute to the latter, mood is primarily created by and for people in a social situation and thus requires an affective effort (hence the central role of intentionally creating or stirring up moods later). In this book, the term *sentiment* replaces other terms used in the social science literature on wolves, such as opinion or attitude. These terms all refer to primarily cognitive-rational processes, which are then usually supplemented by the separate category of emotion. Sentiments, on the other hand, assume that cognitive and emotional processes occur together. They are an 'evaluative regime of meaning as embedded in and coloured by affective and emotional dynamics'[11] and can find entry in vague emotional experiences as well as in opinions or value judgements.

Finally, these considerations are brought together at the macro level when wolf management regimes are considered as *affective arrangements*, a specific constellation of conditions in which the lives of people and wolves can be intertwined with each other and with broader socio-material forces: from the individual to the societal level, from local to global conditions, from practices to discourses, from ideas and values to the material environment.[12] As a Foucauldian *affective dispositif*, disciplinary regimes of wolf management create and mobilise frames of possible knowledge as well as possible practices, experiences and relations, while constraining and invalidating alternative frames.

Following the sociologist Norbert Elias, this affective dispositif can also be seen as a (social) "order of interweaving human impulses and strivings"[13] that underlies a civilising process, by which he means "how the regulation of the whole instinctual and affective life by steady self-control became more and more stable, more even and more all-embracing"[14]. Each society, then, is endowed with its own particular affective order, which becomes more and more rigorous, more and more regulative, more and more controlled, both by social means and by internalised self-control. The more differentiated a society becomes, the more we rely on more and more people in their various functions and roles in our everyday lives, the greater the need to behave in an affectively restrained manner (as exemplified in particular by norms and rules of behaviour, politeness, manners).

---

11   Bens, Jonas/Zenker, Olaf: 'Sentiment', in: J. Slaby/C. v. Scheve (eds.), Affective societies, p. 96.

12   Slaby, Jan/Mühlhoff, Rainer/Wüschner, Philipp: 'Affective Arrangements', in: Emotion Review 11.1 (2019), pp. 3–12, p. 5, https://doi.org/10.1177/1754073917722214.

13   Elias, Norbert: The Civilising Process, Oxford: Blackwell 2000, p. 366.

14   Ibid: p. 265.

Elias develops his ideas on the civilising process through an examination of German and French history, so it is not surprising to find that Germany is very 'civilised' in terms of norms and rules of affect regulation in public. As one of the leading nations in the development of Enlightenment ideas and the hegemony of reason, it is perhaps not surprising that Germany has a reputation for being a very rational and affect-regulated society. Whether this stereotype was ever true is, of course, debatable. What seems certain, however, is that on the one hand, there has been an increase in even stricter affect regulation in contemporary German society, a new moral sensitivity, especially with regard to discrimination, inequality, racism, classism, etc.[15]

On the other hand, in recent years social scientists have increasingly diagnosed a rise in unregulated public affect. As early as the 1980s, international observers coined the term 'German Angst' to diagnose post-war German society's heightened sensitivity to fear and anxiety.[16] More recently, Germany has been described by various scholars as "the irritated society"[17], "the fear/anxiety society"[18], "the upset society"[19], "the disgruntled democracy"[20], "the agitated Republic" with its *Wutbürger* (enraged citizens)[21]. But it still seems unclear though what is behind these recent changes: is it the rise of social media, the decline of 'traditional' media, a crisis of political parties, economic decline and growing social inequalities?

Whatever the reasons, these paradoxical affective trends form the background to the return of wolves to Germany. In comparison to other European countries, it has been suggested that "despite strong pressure for policy

---

15   Flaßpöhler, Svenja: Sensibel. Über moderne Empfindlichkeit und die Grenzen des Zumutbaren, Leipzig: Lagato Verlag 2021.

16   Pates/Leser: The wolves are coming back, p. 137.

17   Pörksen, Bernhard: Die große Gereiztheit. Wege aus der kollektiven Erregung, Carl Hanser Verlag GmbH & Co. KG 2018.

18   Lübke, Christiane/Delhey, Jan (eds.): Diagnose Angstgesellschaft? Was wir wirklich über die Gefühlslage der Menschen wissen (= Band 51), Bielefeld, Germany: transcript Verlag 2019.

19   Hübl, Philipp: Die aufgeregte Gesellschaft. Wie Emotionen unsere Moral prägen und die Polarisierung verstärken (= Onleihe. E-Book), München: C. Bertelsmann Verlag 2019.

20   Braun, Stephan/Geisler, Alexander (eds.): Die verstimmte Demokratie. Moderne Volksherrschaft zwischen Aufbruch und Frustration (= SpringerLink Bücher), Wiesbaden: VS Verlag für Sozialwissenschaften; Imprint: VS Verlag für Sozialwissenschaften 2012.

21   Bussemer, Thymian: Die erregte Republik: Wutbürger und die Macht der Medien. Stuttgart: Klett-Cotta 2014.

change, wolf governance has remained very stable and dominated by a vision of wolves as an adaptive, self-regulating species that can be accommodated in cultural landscapes with very limited lethal control."[22] In contrast to many Eastern European countries with wolf populations, the wolf is a highly politicised issue and stakeholders have been challenging the protected status of the wolf for years. But unlike in the Nordic countries (Norway, Sweden, Finland), these challenges and public battles over the wolf have not yet led to major changes in wolf policy and management. As it turns out, the 'path dependency' of policies and laws created and institutionalised by Germany when it signed the EU Habitats Directive before the actual return of wolves has withstood all attacks, despite several critical events in the last twenty years (petitions, protests, illegal killings, changes in the derogations). The question, however, is whether this path-dependency will hold up against growing publicly vented anger and resentment, and increasingly organised and professionalised protest and lobbying by anti-wolf activists. Germany now seems to be at a crossroads.

Living with wolves: an etho-ethnological approach

This book is thus an ethnography of the affective dimensions of human-wolf coexistence in Germany at the beginning of the twenty-first century, combining perspectives from anthropology, cultural geography, philosophy, and (wolf) biology. Based on almost three years of ethnographic fieldwork, I examine in particular how wolves actively shape this coexistence and how their lives and actions directly and indirectly affect humans. These are fundamentally ecological questions – provided that ecology is understood as more than the quantitative study of energy and material exchange processes. Jens Soentgen points out that ecology as a relational science has unfortunately largely degenerated into an ecology of objects and has lost sight of the subjects, i.e. it fails to take into account that ecological relationships are lived and experienced by subjects with consciousness and feelings. He therefore argues that a humanistic-hermeneu-

---

22   Niedziałkowski, Krzysztof: 'Between Europeanisation and politicisation: wolf policy and politics in Germany'. Environmental Politics, 32 (2023), 793–814. Here p. 3, https://doi.org/10.1080/09644016.2022.2127646.

tic methodology should be added to the scientific methodology to complement the 'traditional' ecological concern with such an ecology of subjects.[23]

In environmental anthropology, Tim Ingold in particular has developed an ecological approach to life over the last thirty years that unites ecological relations between organisms and socio-cultural relations between 'persons'.[24] For Ingold, both humans and wolves would be considered ecologically situated living beings inhabiting a common lifeworld, which they come to know through practical and habitual interaction with the components of their inanimate environment as well as through encounters with their fellow inhabitants. Such a *dwelling perspective* operates implicitly with what Chris Philo and Chris Wilbert called a '*hesitant* anthropomorphism', i.e. "speculating that some animals may have some qualities akin to humans *alongside* much that will be different, other and unavailable to human ken".[25] What they have in common is that they are sentient and affective beings: "Both humans and non-humans [...] conduct themselves skilfully in and through their surroundings, deploying capacities of attention and response that have been developmentally embodied through practice and experience".[26]

Thus, if we understand both humans and wolves as living beings mutually affecting and being affected by each other through their actions and behaviours in a common, shared lifeworld, then we must also place an ethological approach (broadly defined) alongside an ethnological/anthropological approach and combine both into an etho-ethnological approach. This would assume that humans and wolves share a common lifeworld,[27] in hybrid communities consisting of a multiplicity of human and non-human beings, that is, in a

---

23   Soentgen, Jens: Ökologie der Angst (= Fröhliche Wissenschaft, vol. 117), Berlin: Matthes und Seitz 2018.

24   Ingold, Tim: The perception of the environment: essays on livelihood, dwelling and skill, London/New York: Routledge 2000; Tim Ingold: Being Alive. Essays on Movement, Knowledge and Description, London: Routledge 2011.

25   Philo, Chris/Wilbert, Chris (eds.): Animal spaces, beastly places. New geographies of human-animal relations (= Critical geographies, Vol. 10), London/New York: Routledge 2000, p. 23 (emphasis added); see also Ingold, Tim: What is an animal? (= One World archaeology, vol. 1), Milton Park et al: Routledge 1994.

26   T. Ingold: Being Alive, p. 11.

27   Ohrem, Dominik: '(In)VulnerAbilities: Postanthropozentrische Perspektiven auf Verwundbarkeit, Handlungsmacht und die Ontologie des Körpers', in: S. Wirth et al. (eds.), Das Handeln der Tiere, pp. 67–92, here p. 78, https://doi.org/10.14361/9783839432266-002.

'multispecies world'[28] or a 'nature-culture',[29] in which becoming is always a becoming-with, life is always a living-together. With Dominique Lestel, Florence
Brunois, and Florence Gaunet, we can summarise the coexistence of humans
and wolves as follows:

> Some human societies may upon occasion interact with wolf societies, for
> example, but ethologists and ethnologists generally and implicitly consider
> that human societies and wolf societies are two different kinds of thing
> with separate dynamics, even if the two may interact from time to time. The
> idea that a wolf society and a human society occupying the same ecosystem
> might eventually make up a 'lupo-human' society which should be studied
> in itself is generally not regarded as an option to be envisaged. Yet that is
> precisely what we want to do. It is therefore no longer a question of consid-
> ering one as external to the other but of regarding the two societies, human
> and wolf, as the two poles of a global system that needs to be understood
> as such and its dynamics described, to which should no doubt be added
> societies of dogs and of sheep.[30]

Living with wolves therefore refers to a way of life that is lived in the co-presence
of the other and in which both parties shape their lives in the awareness of this
coexistence. It is important to note that this coexistence does not only consist
of direct encounters. On the contrary, wolves usually keep to themselves and
encounters with humans are rare. However, their bodies linger after they have

---

28   Ameli, Katharina: Multispecies Ethnography, Bielefeld: transcript 2021, https://doi.
      org/10.14361/9783839455326; Hartigan Jr, John: 'Knowing Animals: Multispecies Eth-
      nography and the Scope of Anthropology', in: American Anthropologist 123.4 (2021),
      pp. 846–860, https://doi.org/10.1111/aman.13631; Kirksey, Eben/Helmreich, Stefan: 'The
      emergence of multispecies ethnography', in: Cultural Anthropology 25.4 (2010), pp.
      545–576, https://doi.org/10.1111/j.1548-1360.2010.01069.x.
29   Gesing, Friederike et al. (eds.): NaturenKulturen. Denkräume und Werkzeuge für
      neue politische Ökologien (= Edition Kulturwissenschaft, Vol. 146), Bielefeld: transcript
      2019, https://doi.org/10.14361/9783839440070.
30   Lestel, Dominique/Brunois, Florence/Gaunet, Florence: 'Etho-etnology and ethno-
      ethology', in: Social Science Information 45.2 (2006), pp. 155–177, here p. 157, http
      s://doi.org/10.1177/0539018406063633; Lestel, Dominique/Bussolini, Jeffrey/Chrulew,
      Matthew: 'The Phenomenology of Animal Life', in: Environmental Humanities 5.1
      (2014), pp. 125–148, https://doi.org/10.1215/22011919-3615442; Lescureux, Nicolas: 'To-
      wards the necessity of a new interactive approach integrating ethnology, ecology in the
      study of the relationship between Kyrgyz stockbreeders and wolves', in: Social Science
      Information 45 (2006), pp. 463–478, https://doi.org/10.1177/0539018406066536.

moved on. They leave scent trails as they move through their territory, they leave hair behind as they pass through vegetation, they mark their territory with urine and scat, their howling echoes through the twilight. Likewise, their physical actions and movements inscribe themselves on the landscape when they press tracks into the ground with their paws, when they dig dens, when they scratch the ground and mark their territory, or when they leave the remains of killed animals for others to find.[31] In an affective sense, wolves thus create a potentially *felt presence* that extends their immediate physical location both geographically (across the landscape) and temporally. They are—affectively understood—"territorial engineers".[32]

Humans also create such felt presences through their bodies and bodily actions when they walk, hike, cycle, or drive through a landscape—a landscape that is shaped by its roads, paths, buildings, villages, and towns. At the same time, such presences do not always appear unambiguously, but can present themselves quite differently to different actors. Fences or livestock guarding dogs, for example, are evidence of a human presence to wolves, but evidence of a wolf presence to humans.

Of course, these human and non-human presences are not necessarily perceived by everyone; it depends on people's sensitivity to wolves and their motivation to perceive them. There is also the option of ignoring such presences – unless they force themselves upon you, as is the case if you are a shepherd whose sheep are being killed by wolves. Moreover, it is becoming increasingly difficult to ignore the presence of wolves, as both their population size and geographical distribution increase. Most importantly, the wolf's presence also changes register, moving on in different forms through processes of "transduction", as Stefan Helmreich calls the reshaping and transformation of signals through media.[33] The affective intensities and forces of the physical presence of wolves can be transformed into narratives, social media postings, pho-

---

31   These bodily signs in the landscape can be read as a form of interspecies communication, see Boonman-Berson, S.; Turnhout, E.; Carolan, M.: 'Common sensing: Human-black bear cohabitation practices in Colorado', in: Geoforum 2016, 74, 192–201, https://doi.org/10.1016/j.geoforum.2016.06.010.

32   Hastrup, Kirsten: 'Dogs among others. Inughuit companions in Northwest Greenland', in: Robert J. Losey/Robert P. Wishart/Jan P. L. Loovers (eds.), Dogs in the North. Stories of cooperation and co-domestication, London and New York: Routledge 2018, pp. 212–232, here p. 214.

33   Helmreich, Stefan: 'Listening against Soundscapes', in: Anthropology News 51.9 (2010), p. 10, https://doi.org/10.1111/j.1556-3502.2010.51910.x.

tographs, artworks, etc., where they leave *affective traces* that move the recipients in certain ways and thus gain access to cultural memory. This study differs from others in that it does not start its investigation of the coexistence of humans and wolves with these affective traces—in the terrain commonly called the cultural (human) sphere—but with what humans and wolves *do* in a common 'lupo-human' society.

Methodology: an ethnographic approach to human-wolf coexistence

This lupo-human society is complex. It involves different actors, many institutions at different levels (from local to national to international), different types of legislation, a range of opinions and attitudes as well as representations, experiences, narratives, knowledge and practices. To add to the complexity, Germany's federal political system frames these relationships differently at the state level. Each state has its own wolf management plan, legislation, institutions, etc., so situations can vary greatly even between neighbouring states. Nevertheless, incidents in other states – and even other countries – feed into the human-wolf relationship, as everything related to wolves circulates in the (social) media and becomes entangled with local situations. Finally, the wolves themselves are unevenly distributed across the country, being newcomers in some places and established in others. Pack culture varies between different packs, and even individual wolves – as seen in the lives of the so-called problem wolves – act and behave in their own individual ways, rather than conforming to a supposed standard of 'species-typical behaviour'. In short, this high level of complexity cannot be addressed with a single-method study, but requires a multi-method approach: ethnography.

Ethnography is a qualitative empirical research strategy that aims to explore socio-cultural life where and as it happens, using a variety of methods in a flexible way according to the needs of the field.[34] This multi-method approach allows for the collection, production and interpretation of multiple types of data (field notes, interview transcripts, images and videos, social media postings, official documents, press releases, 'grey literature', etc.) over an extended period of time, which can complement and comment on each other, increasing the complexity of phenomena and thus deepening interpretations and understanding. Although several methods are used (participant observation, inter-

---

34   Pink, Sarah: Doing Sensory Ethnography, London: Sage 2009.

views, textual analysis, visual analysis), there is a strong focus on participant observation, tracing socio-cultural processes of meaning making as, when and where they occur. Ethnographic fieldwork thus enables the researcher to capture the rich complexity of lived reality, rather than reducing it to a particular dimension (such as opinions or attitudes) or perspective (such as that of hunters or animal rights activists). It is underpinned by the ethnographer's experience of continuous engagement and immersion in the field, which enables them to see connections between data and to evaluate them against a range of other data through a recursive research design. Finally, in this process, data production, collection and interpretation alternate constantly, complementing and developing the hermeneutic process of understanding. Following Stefan Hirschauer and Klaus Amann, this ethnographic approach relies "on a 'soft' concept of method, but a 'hard' concept of empiricism".[35] In other words, methods must be flexible and adapted so that the researcher is best able to explore the phenomenon, rather than prioritising a rigid set of methods even when realising that they are ill-suited to grasp the phenomenon in question.

If the aim is to study the coexistence of wolves and humans, the question arises as to where the anthropologist's 'field' actually is. The usual approach of defining the field in terms of a central location is of limited help here. Nevertheless, I have chosen two geographical areas as the focus of my research, without limiting myself to them. The first, Lusatia in Saxony (and southern Brandenburg), close to the German-Polish border, was the first region in Germany to be colonised by wolves in 2000. Since then, it has become "the largest contiguous area inhabited by wolves in this [Central European] population".[36] In contrast to Lusatia, the Westerwald region of Rhineland-Palatinate only had its first wolf territory at the start of the project. The situation was new for the local communities and the process of learning to live with wolves was just beginning. This constellation of established wolf territory and new wolf territory gave me the opportunity to investigate many different aspects of coexistence.

But my 'field' went far beyond specific locations because my maxim was: follow the wolves! Following the wolves wherever they appeared in my research

---

35   Amann, Klaus/Hirschauer, Stefan: Die Befremdung der eigenen Kultur. Ein Programm, in: Amann, Klaus/Hirschauer, Stefan. (eds.), Die Befremdung der eigenen Kultur: Zur ethnographischen Herausforderung soziologischer Empirie, Frankfurt: Suhrkamp 1997, pp. 7–52, here p. 9.

36   Federal Documentation and Advisory Centre on Wolves (DBBW): Wölfe in Deutschland—Statusbericht 2019/2020, p. 1–34, here p. 2.

areas and where their presence 'made a difference' to people meant expanding my field site into a network of social situations linked by the presence and traces of wolves. In this way, my research became multilocal, a "multi-sited ethnography".[37] I accompanied *Rissgutachter* ('wolf kill assessors') in their work, a dead wolf as it was brought to the Leibniz Institute for Zoo and Wildlife Research for pathological examination, and biologists and *Großkarni-vorenbeauftragte* ('large carnivore commissioners') on monitoring excursions. I also took part in many events: a four-day tourist wolf seminar; many public wolf lectures and discussions; an anti-wolf demonstration of shepherds; wolf exhibitions in Güls, Bonn, Winsen, and Rietschen; an 'open pasture day'; a 'herd protection day'; driven hunts on ungulates in the wolf area; and howling evenings in the Eagle and Wolf Park Kasselburg/Eifel. I observed interactions between visitors and wolves in the Wolf Centre in Dörverden for several days, and I visited and walked through the Westerwald wolf territory on many weekends to familiarise myself with the landscape and fauna favoured by wolves and to engage in conversation with people I met along the way, learning more about what it is like to live with wolves in the neighbourhood.

I also followed the wolves literally. In the credo of etho-ethnological research, I finally had to deal with how I myself (as an anthropologist) could incorporate the life and actions of wolves into my research process.[38] However, I was aware that wolves are one of the most difficult animals to study because they are very mobile, shy and live mostly in dense forests (at least in Germany).

---

37   Marcus, George E.: 'Ethnography in/of the World System: The Emergence of Multi-Sited Ethnography', in: Annual Review of Anthropology 24 (1995), pp. 95–117, https://doi.org/10.1146/annurev.an.24.100195.000523.
38   See Barua, Maan: 'Bio-Geo-Graphy: Landscape, Dwelling, and the Political Ecology of Human-Elephant Relations', in: Environment and Planning D: Society and Space 32.5 (2014), pp. 915–934, https://doi.org/10.1068/d4213; Locke, Piers: 'Elephants as persons, affective apprenticeship, and fieldwork with nonhuman informants in Nepal', in: HAU: Journal of Ethnographic Theory 7.1 (2017), pp. 353–376; O'Mahony, Kieran/ Corradini, Andrea/Gazzola, Andrea: 'Lupine Becomings – Tracking and Assembling Romanian Wolves through Multi-Sensory Fieldwork', in: Society & Animals 26.2 (2018), pp. 107–129, http://dx.doi.org/10.1163/15685306-12341501; Schröder, Verena: 'Learning to Understand Animal Lifeworlds? Perspectives of more-than-human ethnographies', in: Christian Steiner et al. (eds.), More-than-human geographies: key concepts, relationships and methodologies, Stuttgart: Franz Steiner 2022, pp. 317–339; Frank, Elisa: 'Follow the wolves: reflections on ethnographic tracing and tracking', in: Marlis Heyer/ Susanne Hose (eds.), Encounters with Wolves: Dynamics and Futures, Bautzen: Sorbisches Institut 2020, pp. 99–114.

So I had little hope of seeing wolves at all. However, through my research partners in Lusatia, I was able to get to know some places where the chances of seeing wolves were at least not impossible. And so I spent a total of ninety-eight days on the lookout (about three hours a day at dawn or dusk) and was actually able to observe wolves fifteen times. These disjointed few (and mostly short) observations over more than two years could hardly be called a 'behavioural study'. But as I explain in the next chapter, even single episodes can be worth telling and provide valuable insights into the lives of wolves.

I kept abreast of developments and news (from local to international) using Google Alerts, the local/regional press, Facebook groups that I followed regularly, and the official websites of wolf organisations, associations (e.g. hunting or shepherds' associations), ministries and the DBBW (Documentation and Advisory Centre for the Wolf). The latter provides official news and facts on wolf management and monitoring.

I conducted informal conversations and more than forty semi-structured interviews with hunters and foresters, (wolf) biologists, official state wolf managers, NABU wolf ambassadors, wolf kill assessors, wolf friends, vets, shepherds and other livestock keepers, mayors and people who happened to live in a wolf area.

I also collected and familiarised myself with a range of popular science, journalistic and scientific books (and films) on wolves, focusing on (but not limited to) literature recommended by research participants and typically found on the bookshelves of wolf critics or supporters.

The whole research process unfortunately had to adapt spontaneously to the effects of the coronavirus pandemic. After the first six months of research went according to plan, public life was put on hold for two months in March 2020, so that neither participant observation of events and practices nor face-to-face interviews were possible, and meetings had to be postponed or switched to telephone interviews. The same was true for the long lockdown from November 2020 to spring 2021. Fortunately, I was still able to use the summer of 2020 for research visits to Saxony, where the incidence of coronavirus was low at the time and public life was still largely intact. Nevertheless, I extended the research process until 2022 to compensate for cancelled events and meetings and to achieve a better dovetailing of research and writing. I reflect on the results I achieved in the next section.

Plan of the book

As this ethnography is the first on the recent return of wolves to Germany, it made sense to write a predominantly descriptive book focusing on the phenomenon (the coexistence of wolves and humans) rather than an overly theoretical, more abstract discussion. To cite Stefan Hirschauer and Klaus Amann again: "If one works out an observational relationship to one's own culture, the cognitive achievement in 'othering' one's own does not lie primarily in explaining or understanding: it lies in explication".[39] Nevertheless, this book is theoretically informed, guided and appropriately structured throughout. Everything described here is selected and guided by the book's key concepts, which revolve around different manifestations of affectivity. These concepts, however, are only indicative and do not replace an examination of the phenomenon itself. Following Clifford Geertz, I have tried to embed these 'big', rather abstract concepts in local, manageable contexts in order to make them more vivid and understandable.[40]

I have chosen a narrative style as the form of engagement. Accordingly, this ethnography consists of an ensemble of stories. The stories are told with the help of (affect) concepts or are at least linked in an interpretive way, and thus become part of a narrative argumentation whose relevance can go beyond what is directly narrated. However, this ethnography of wolf-human coexistence is neither complete nor exhaustive. Rather, what this book offers is what I call, following Tim Ingold, an ethnographic *sketch*. In his call for a graphic anthropology, Ingold notes that many ethnographies seem to be imbued with a painterly aesthetic.[41] With holism as the guiding paradigm, ethnographers – like oil painters – would feel the need (or aspire) to fill in all the blanks to create a complete picture of a phenomenon. To achieve this totality and depth, layers and layers of context are essentially added. This book departs from such ethnographies. As an ethnographic sketch it seeks to capture situations in a few lines but with much expression. Rather than asking what a phenomenon means and offering a context in response, I follow the trajectories of affective impulses in their flows and transformations wherever they erupt within the

---

39   K. Amann/S. Hirschauer: Die Befremdung der eigenen Kultur, p. 13, translated by TG.
40   Geertz, Clifford: The interpretation of cultures. Selected essays, New York: Basic Books 1973, p. 21.
41   T. Ingold: Being Alive, p. 222.

complex shared life of humans and wolves.[42] It is also characteristic of such an ethnographic sketch that it is not made after leaving the field, but during fieldwork. Analogous to sketching as a form of drawing, ethnographic sketching is an example of a mode of description that has not yet detached itself from observation.[43] The writing of this book was constantly inspired and challenged by new events, interviews and observations. Rather than turning away from the field to write and reflect, I have chosen to write and reflect from my position in the field, without losing sight of the wolves.[44] In this sense, this book represents a case of *writing-with-wolves*. The following chapters are structured accordingly and present sketches of the most relevant and meaningful affective structures that shape the coexistence of humans and wolves in Germany today.

In Chapter 2, I introduce the reader to the affective life of wolves and show in detail what it means at a bodily level to affect and be affected. While classical ethological accounts are said to reduce the rich and complex lives of animals to behaviours, which in turn are seen as merely acting out instincts, this chapter proposes a lively style of narrative description that emphasises the agency of animals and the dynamism, ambiguity and openness of encounters. Through descriptions of different situations – a wolf playing with ravens; a wolf hunting wild boar; two wolves encountering two hunters – I show how wolves are sensitive and responsive to other bodies in encounters, even across species boundaries. This form of ethno-ethological storytelling offers a new perspective on what it might mean to coexist with wolves at the most basic level.

Chapter 3 places wolf agency in a broader context: it shows how wolves, as affective agents, trigger social processes in a shared, hybrid, multi-species lifeworld. It traces the recent arrival of wolves in the Westerwald, describing how a region has been transformed into a new wolf territory for the first time since wolves were extirpated more than a hundred years ago. I follow the actions, presence and traces of the wolves (in combination with those of other wolves in other parts of Rhineland-Palatinate and in other parts of Germany), as well as the human responses at local and regional levels, ranging from news on social media, to public events and discussions among hunters, to changes

---

42   See Ogden, Laura: Swamplife. People, gators, and mangroves entangled in the Everglades, Minneapolis: University of Minnesota Press 2011.

43   T. Ingold: Being Alive, p. 224.

44   See C. Geertz: The interpretation of cultures; T. Ingold: Being Alive, p. 223.

in ministerial wolf management. Rather than looking for linear chains of causation, this chapter shows how wolf actions provide multidirectional affective impulses that entangle a variety of human and non-human actors in complex affective arrangements.

Knowing that wolves are complex and active affective agents that can affect a region by their very presence, Chapter 4 zooms into the middle of a wolf territory to examine the coexistence of local residents with a wolf pack. Based on a central idea from the behavioural ecology of predators, namely that wolves create landscapes of fear in relation to their prey, I try to understand the lifeworld of the residents of Rosenthal in Lusatia who feel threatened and frightened by the presence of wolves. In a double step, I conceptualise Rosenthal as a landscape of fear and the landscape of fear as an animal atmosphere. What contributes to the creation of such an atmosphere in the eyes of the locals and how do wolves play a role in its dynamic development? Is fear enough to characterise this atmosphere, or is it also shaped by other emotions? And besides the wolves and the locals, who else might be involved? Ultimately, wolf atmospheres turn out to be processes of affective intensities generated by more-than-human entanglements.

While the fourth chapter deals with wolf atmospheres, spatially extended feelings that fill a landscape, chapter 5 turns to three categories of people who are particularly affected by wolves in one way or another: shepherds, hunters and wolf friends. Rather than trying to understand their attitudes towards wolves, their opinions and knowledge, I look at the affective dimensions of their relationships with wolves. How exactly are they affected by wolves? What feelings and sentiments shape their relationships? And how do these relate to more enduring affective structures that result from what it means to live the life of a shepherd, hunter or wolf friend today?

With these insights into different dimensions of human-wolf affect, Chapter 6 continues with an examination of wolf management regimes as a form of affect management. While it has often been emphasised how wolf management can be understood as a disciplinary regime of power that establishes and seeks to maintain a (semiotic) cultural order of meaning, here I focus on wolf management as a way of disciplining, regulating and mobilising both human and wolf affects. Fundamental to the disciplining of affects is the guiding principle of 'rationality' used by all actors involved. On the part of official wolf management and politicians, this is complemented (if not counteracted) by the affective practice of taking worries and concerns seriously. Other actors rely more on the practice of creating or stirring up moods, which in turn is countered by spaces for letting off steam. In the following excursus, I examine the so-called problem wolves to see how management regimes, based on classical-ethological ideas of habituation and conditioning, attempt to extend a human, cultural order to the lives of wolves. In doing so, the 'natural' or 'unnatural' affects of wolves must be made controllable in the sense of being conducive to successful coexistence.

The threads of the previous chapters are brought together for the epilogue in Chapter 7 and reconsidered one last time. My method of following affective traces inevitably focused the book on the conflictual situations of living with wolves. Moreover, the fragmented geographical and temporal distribution of the return of wolves to different regions leads to a constant affective fire that can easily be misinterpreted as the normal state of coexistence. Therefore, in the epilogue, I use a final ethnographic example from Lusatia to trace the resting pulse of coexistence resulting from years of living with wolves. I conclude with a plea for an affect-guided way of thinking about the human-wolf relationship, a 'thinking-with-affect' that offers a reflective alternative to the affect-denying call for objectivity and rationality on the one hand, and the therapeutic approach of taking affects seriously on the other.

2. Wolf Affects

Affective wolf bodies

At birth, wolf pup behaviour is little more than a simple series of reflexes (e.g. seeking warmth, cuddling, sucking, excreting in response to mother's licking, crying when injured, whimpering when cold, hungry or isolated).[1]

Wolves are born, after a gestation period of 61–63 days, in a den dug by the mother: about four to seven pups per litter. At birth they are blind and deaf. They can move slowly by crawling. The belly is exposed and the head swings back and forth. If they touch something warm with their head, they move in that direction. This is how they find the mother and the teats to drink from, and when the mother is away, this is how the pups find each other. For the benefit of heat regulation, they lie huddled together in a small pile, their heads hidden in the tangle as much as possible. When the mother returns to the den, the pile comes to life. Presumably the pups notice this by movement, by the shaking of the earth, because they do not react to loud and sudden noises until much later, around the age of fourteen days.[2]

Wolves—like all animals, human and non-human—are born into their environment as open and vulnerable organisms. Rather than seeing them as simple bodies endowed with a simple series of reflexes to external stimuli (as in the first quote above), I consider them as sentient, sensitive bodies, receptive and responsive to their environment (as indicated in the second quote). At the earliest stage of development, they *are* their bodies; their intentions *are* bodily

---

1   Packard, Jane M.: Wolf behaviour: reproductive, social and intelligent, in: D. Mech/L. Boitani (eds.), Wolves, pp. 35–65, here p. 47.

2   Zimen, Erik: Wölfe (= Was ist was, Band 104), Nuremberg: Tessloff 2010, p. 21, translated by TG.

intentions. They learn about the world, their mother, their brothers and sisters, the den, the milk with and through their sentient bodies. Over the next few weeks, these bodies become more and more sentient as more senses open up to the world.

This 'being-towards-the-world'[3], the open and outwardly directed bodily existence of wolves, ensures that they are actively exploring and learning creatures from the very beginning. In the words of the philosopher Jean-Luc Nancy:

> The living are above all excited, called upon to respond to an outside. As a result, the living being is always already responding to this call, always already excited, affected by an outside. Indeed, it is being affected by an outside that brings anything to life, whether we are talking about a plant or a human animal.[4]

Unfortunately, there has been and continues to be a strong tendency in wolf biology and ecology to over-emphasise reflexes, instincts and (genetically determined and ecologically adapted) behavioural mechanisms, thus turning wolves into passive creatures, unable to escape a behaviourally impoverished world predetermined by their species body. Classical ethology, in particular, often reproduces behaviourist models of stimulus-response causality that usually fail to understand the complexity of human and non-human animal behaviour.

This becomes clearer when we look at the methods of classical wolf ethological research. A typical ethological research design would involve observing and recording behaviour in an experimental setting. The observed behaviour would then be matched to behavioural categories defined in an ethogram. This coding of behaviour is then used for statistical analysis, which quantifies behaviour to identify reliable patterns of behaviour. Since the goal of such research designs is to quantify behaviour, and thus less attention is paid to the qualities of the

---

3   Merleau-Ponty, Maurice: Phenomenology of Perception, London: Routledge 2004; In German editions of Merlau-Ponty's works, the phenomenological phrase 'being-in-the-world' is usually translated as 'Zur-Welt-Sein', whereby the directionality of the word Zur indicates that being is always already directed and engaged with the world. This is a particular apt description of how affective bodies operate; see also Despret, Vinciane: 'Responding Bodies and Partial Affinities in Human-Animal Worlds', in: Theory, Culture and Society 30.7/8 (2013), pp. 51–76, https://doi.org/10.1177/0263276413496852.

4   Nancy, Jean-Luc: Corpus II: Writings on sexuality, New York: Fordham University Press 2013, p. 94.

details of behaviour, the subtleties of the affective dynamics of an encounter are difficult to capture in such a framework.

Another problem with this classical ethological wolf research is the role intelligence plays in it. Indeed, much of the behavioural research on wolves attempts to determine the extent of the animals' intelligence (e.g. in comparison to dogs or in hunting behaviour). In explaining intelligence, wolf researchers use approaches from the social sciences that seem congruent with those of the natural sciences. David Mech and Rolf Peterson, for example, allude to the rational choice theory that dominates quantitative economics:

> While elements of learning, tradition, and actual preference may be involved in apparent prey species preferences, the most likely explanation for these patterns involves a combination of capture efficiency and profitability relative to risk, which boils down to prey vulnerability.[5]

In this view, the question is how wolves can calculate the cost-benefit ratio of different hunting strategies—a question posed by the framework of evolutionary theory, which states that any behaviour should be efficient to ensure the survival of the animal (species). Alternatively, cognitivist perspectives from psychology are often used to explain intelligence by using machine or computer metaphors, such as when Mech, Douglas Smith, and Daniel MacNulty metaphorically describe wolves as "programmed to kill and eat whenever they can",[6] or when they seek to explain wolf hunting strategies by comparing them to robot experiments.

But wolves are not a variant of *homo economicus*, nor are they computers or robots. Describing and trying to understand wolves in this way may be coherent within the framework of evolutionary theory, but it misses the empirical reality. In Mech, Smith, and McNulty's latest book, *Wolves on the Hunt*, the researchers have painstakingly compiled decades of combined observations of wolf behaviour, showing in hundreds of examples how varied and creative wolf hunting behaviour is. Nevertheless, they apologise for not having more examples available to show the behavioural patterns in the apparent chaos of individual differences through regular statistical analysis. One wonders if it is im-

---

5   Mech, David/Peterson, R.: Wolf-prey relations, in: D. Mech/L. Boitani (eds.), Wolves, pp. 131–157, here p. 140.
6   Mech, David/Smith, Douglas W./MacNulty, Daniel R.: Wolves on the Hunt, Chicago/ London: University of Chicago Press 2015, p. 162.

possible that wolves could develop 'traditions' or even 'wolf cultures' that are not programmed into the DNA of the species.[7] The problem with their analyses, I argue, is that—in their zeal to reconcile empirical reality with theory—they overemphasise the role of the mind and intelligence, which makes wolves primarily thinking, rather than affective, bodily creatures.

For this dilemma, I offer an attempt at description that follows an etho-ethnological approach. This approach is inspired by qualitative, ethnographic, and (new) ethological descriptions of human and non-human behaviour. It takes as its starting point what humans and animals have in common—namely, their corporeality and the corporeal reality that it produces,[8] a lifeworld in which they "live and die together, the one with the other, the one like the other, they coexist, they sympathise, they are con-vival, they co-habit the world that is the same".[9]

In this shared lifeworld, their sentient bodies are oriented towards others and the environment as a potential behavioural setting. The environment attracts, invites, repels and mobilises an affected body to act, and is not simply there (physically), independent of a perceiving subject. Both subject and environment are intertwined in what I have called an affective arrangement. When wolves encounter other animals, they become entangled in such an affective arrangement, and affective forces begin to act upon them, mutually animating their bodies.

Every movement, every look, every sound, every gesture, every change in facial expression or posture alters the dynamics of the arrangement, creating ever new situational meanings that help the participants to intuitively grasp

---

7   See Lorimer, Haydon: 'Forces of Nature, Forms of Life: Calibrating Ethology and Phenomenology', in: Ben Anderson/Paul Harrison (eds.), Taking-Place: non-representational theories in geography, Farnham: Ashgate 2010, pp. 55–77. Hayden Lorimer finds a similar paradoxical logic here in the work of Konrad Lorenz, who was able to describe affective encounters with animals vividly, but always returns to explaining animal behaviour with simplistic mechanisms of instincts and drives. John Hartigan expresses a similar view, conceding that ethologists have a great deal of descriptive competence, but that their attempts to explain behaviour in terms of evolutionary theory are often problematic. (See Hartigan Jr., John: Shaving the Beasts: Wild Horses and Ritual in Spain, Minneapolis/London: Minnesota University Press 2020).

8   D. Lestel/ L. Brunois/L. Gaunet: Ethno-ethology and etho-ethnology.

9   Derrida, Jacques: The Beast and the Sovereign, Vol. 2, Chicago: Chicago University Press 2011, p. 264.

what the encounter is about. Ideally, each change adds something to transform an (initially) indeterminate and ambiguous situation into something
more definite. What has to happen for an encounter to be understood by
the participants as a hunting or fighting situation, as a meeting of possible
partners or as an opportunity to play? A thick description of encounters must
carefully trace the lines of these affective forces and what they are built upon.

Classical, cognitivist-oriented ethological research into wolf intelligence
typically looks for evidence of intentional, strategic behaviour. In this approach, intelligent behaviour is exhibited when a wolf can solve a problem by
formulating a plan of action (in its mind) and executing it. Behaviour is thus
defined as anticipatory intention followed by mind-led, physical execution.
An etho-ethnological, affect-based approach, on the other hand, does not try
to explain behaviour as always strategic and guided by the mind, but stays
close to what happens at the bodily level.[10] Like practice-based social theories,
it recognises an embodied motor intentionality (or movement intentionality),
an intentionality of the body in routine actions that is not necessarily informed by rational thought and pre-planning. Bodies here have their own *tacit
knowledge*, acquired through the habitual experience of affecting and being
affected by other bodies, through receptive multisensory attention coupled
with responsive movement.

Such a form of etho-ethnological description is more akin to *storytelling*
than an observation protocol or an ethogram.[11] Both observation and storytelling should focus on how an indeterminate, ambivalent encounter becomes
a tangibly meaningful one. This approach may produce data that is less clear
and quantifiable, but it helps us to better understand the nuances and com-
plexities of behaviour and its dynamics by paying more attention to details and
the flow of processes. Rather than looking for patterns of behaviour out of context, we are broadening our understanding of wolf behaviour by showing the
range and diversity of what is possible and becomes evident in unique events.

---

10   Sinha, Anindya/Chowdhury, Anmol/Anchan, Nitesh/Barua, Maan: 'Affective ethnogra-
      phies of animal lives', in: Hovorka, Alice/McCubbin, Sandra/Van patter, Lauren (eds.). A
      Research Agenda for Animal Geographies, Cheltenham: Elgar (2021), pp. 129–146, here
      p. 135.
11   Interestingly, one of the first field studies on wolves is also qualitative-descriptive in
      this sense: Murie, Adolph: The Wolves of Mount McKinley, Seattle: University of Wash-
      ington Press 1985. In follow-up studies at the same location, however, observational
      descriptions are only sparsely incorporated into the text, see Mech, David et al.: The
      Wolves of Denali, Minneapolis: University of Minnesota Press 1998.

As Ingold puts it, "In such a world, we can understand the nature of things only by attending to their relations, or in other words, by telling their stories".[12] The result of such descriptions is what van Dooren and Rose called "lively ethography".[13] It's the prerequisite for seeing wolves not just as typical representatives of a species, but as true individuals. Ultimately, this will help us to understand wolves better and develop more realistic expectations of their behaviour in potentially problematic encounters.[14]

In what follows, I attempt to understand and describe wolves as active and living beings who affect and are affected by others in a shared world of coexistence. In doing so, I try to open up our 'zoological imagination' and counter the double reduction of classical ethology, which reduces animal life to behaviour and behaviour to causal mechanisms.[15] The focus is on stories of encounters between wolves and other species—ravens, wild boars and humans—and the question of what kind of interspecies sociality is revealed in them. The stories are based on my own field observations of free-ranging wolves in Saxony (the Knappenrode/Seenland Pack) as well as on video recordings of an encounter available in the LUPUS Institute archive. To be able to be present when humans and wolves meet is almost impossible and therefore requires the viewing of video footage, provided that the encounter has been recorded by those involved.[16] However, I will point out the problems of such documentation later in the chapter.

---

12   T. Ingold: Being Alive, p. 160.

13   van Dooren, Thom/Rose, Deborah B.: 'Lively Ethography', in: Environmental Humanities 8.1 (2016), pp. 77–94, https://doi.org/10.1215/22011919-3527731.

14   See Van Patter, Lauren: 'Individual animal geographies for the more-than-human city: Storying synanthropy and cynanthropy with urban coyotes', in: EPE: Nature and Space 5 (2022), pp. 2216–2239, https://doi.org/10.1177/25148486211049441.

15   D. Lestel/J. Bussolini/M. Chrulew: The Phenomenology of Animal Life, p. 127.

16   I describe and analyse more human-wolf encounters elsewhere: Gieser, Thorsten: Wolfsbegegnungen – eine Annäherung des Fremden. in: Uzarewicz, Charlotte/ Gugutzer, Robert/Uzarewicz, Michael/Latka, Thomas. (eds.) Berühren und berührt werden – Zur Phänomenologie der Nähe (Neue Phänomenologie 35). Baden-Baden: Verlag Karl Alber, pp. 309–332.

Figure 2: A wolf cautiously approaches a raven.

Source: Author

Figure 3: The wolf slowly walks towards the raven on the right while the raven on the left watches him. The raven on the right is already spreading its wings restlessly and is about to take off.

Source: Author

Figure 4: The raven (from Figure 3, on the right) has flown to the other end of the sand dune, the wolf slowly following it. In doing so, he comes too close to the other observing raven, which is already in a crouching position—ready to take off.

Source: Author

Figure 5: The wolf seems to be inviting the raven on the right to play.

Source: Author

Encounter I: playful affects

> Animals play just like humans. We need only observe young dogs to see that
> all the essential features of human play are present in their joyful activity.
> They invite each other to play by a certain ceremony of posture and gesture.
> They abide by the rule that one does not bite one's brother's ear, or bite hard.
> They pretend to be terribly annoyed. And—most importantly—they clearly
> experience tremendous fun and joy in doing all this.[17]

One late afternoon in September, I am watching a young wolf wander aimlessly
across the plain, away from the rest of the pack, as if looking for something to
do. Eventually he notices two ravens standing on a sand dune a little further up
and goes over to them.

As he slowly climbs the dune, first one and then the other raven flies away,
cawing, and both settle down on the next dune. The wolf follows them down
the first dune and up the other, and the ravens fly away again, squawking, one
of them to the first dune, the other to the slope of the same. The wolf then trots
to the edge of the dune he is on, lies down with his paws neatly parallel to the
edge, and watches the ravens carefully.

Suddenly he stands up again, wags his tail loosely and runs—with a little
jump—down the slope, while the raven, cawing, flies off to join the other one
on the next dune, who is watching him. They both caw as the wolf climbs up
the slope and when he is almost at the top, the ravens fly off to the other end of
the slope.

The wolf now trots slowly towards the raven sitting further away, his tail
wagging in a relaxed manner. As he approaches, the raven takes off again,
squawking, and the wolf turns to the other raven that has been watching him
all along. This raven also takes off squawking when the wolf gets too close and
lands a few metres away. The wolf begins to sniff intensely at the spot where
the raven was standing a moment ago and bites into a stone or piece of wood
that is lying there, his tail still wagging loosely. Then he turns back to the raven
and makes a small leap towards it, causing the raven to screech and fly even
further away.

The wolf then looks at the two ravens for a moment, trots over to the place
where the raven had been standing, sniffs again, bites into some objects lying

---

17   Huizinga, Johan: Homo Ludens. Vom Ursprung der Kultur im Spiel, Hamburg: Rowohlt
      1981, p. 1, translated by TG.

around, and finally drops to the ground. Still keeping an eye on the ravens, he gets up a moment later and slowly trots towards them, tail held high and wagging, while the ravens walk around nervously, watching him, and one of them caws and flies off to the top of the dune.

The wolf turns around and follows the other raven, but it jumps further and catches up with the first raven. The wolf follows them both, but the closer he gets to them, the further they hop away from him, until one finally flies off to the other dune, cawing. The wolf looks after it for a moment, then turns around, sniffs where the raven was standing and goes towards the other raven, which first hops away five times before flying to the outer edge of the dune, squawking.

The wolf turns back to the raven and begins to stretch out, head flat over its paws, rump and tail raised, looking first at one, then at the other raven, who continue to watch him. Then the wolf gets up again and walks slowly towards the raven on the edge, sniffing the ground all the way. As he gets closer, the raven flies away, cawing, and joins the other raven on the other dune. The wolf turns to them, pauses for a moment and looks over ...

I introduced this story by calling it a play situation, but that is only partly true, as should be clear by now. The wolf seemed to be in a playful mood, but the ravens were clearly not interested in playing along and seemed rather annoyed by the wolf's attempts to involve them in the play. Were the wolf's movements really indicative of play, or were they attacks? One indication of how the ravens experienced the situation (and that they were aware of the wolf's intentions) might be that they only retreated a little at a time, rather than flying away altogether. So we need to understand the 'shared complexity' of any encounter, "in the sense that the *same* complex situation is complex in *different* ways for the different actors involved".[18]

I have told this first story to introduce the affective dynamics that develop during encounters—a form of "interanimality".[19] As we follow the story, several features reveal how the wolf and the ravens affect and are affected by each other. When the wolf first noticed the ravens (and the ravens in turn noticed the wolf), all three were drawn into a shared situation and affective forces be-

---

18   D. Lestel/F. Brunois/F. Gaunet: Etho-etnology and ethno-ethology, p. 160.

19   Merleau-Ponty, Maurice: Nature. Course Notes from the College de France, Evanston/ Illinois: Northwestern University Press 2003, p. 169.

gan to build a web of tension between them—initially maintained merely by an exchange of glances.[20]

This affective tension then developed along the lines of movement, a play of approaching and distancing, of slow and fast, of continuous and abrupt movements. What is negotiated in this "push and pull of intimacy and distance"[21] is the animals' "personal space", as the anthropologist E. T. Hall called it.[22] As a felt extension of the self into the surrounding space, personal space structures the experience of space in encounters according to the social relationship of the participants. The closer and more intimate the relationship, the closer we allow the other to be to us spatially. The less we like someone, the greater the distance we want to keep between us and them.

The wolf and the ravens were constantly negotiating their personal space in this situation. If personal space denotes *what* is negotiated in these affective encounters, kinaesthesia or "the qualitatively felt kinetic flow"[23] unravels *how* these encounters are negotiated. The phenomenologist of movement, Maxine Sheets-Johnstone, distinguishes four qualitative dimensions of movement that help to analyse encounters in a much more nuanced way:

1) Speed or the projectional quality (how fast or slow is the movement and what is the melody of the movement – abrupt, sustained or ballistic)
2) Force or the tensional quality (the felt intensity of the effort of the movement)
3) Range or the areal quality (how constricted or expansive is the body itself and as it moves through space)
4) Direction or the linear quality (the lines of movement through space and of the body as a whole and of body parts)[24]

---

20 I would even argue here that the wolf's gaze is crucial in maintaining the tension, since the eyes of this predator are directed forward, whereas ravens—with their eyes on the sides of their heads—cannot stare. Again and again, the ravens react to the wolf's clear line of sight and direction of movement. The ravens' behaviour is less clearly directed.

21 Probyn, Elspeth: Eating the Ocean. Durham: Duke University Press 2016, p. 50.

22 Hall, Edward T.: The Hidden Dimension. Garden City, N.Y.: Doubleday 1966.

23 Sheets-Johnstone, Maxine: Body and Movement: Basic dynamic principles, in: Schmicking, Daniel/Gallagher, Shaun (eds.) Handbook of Phenomenology and Cognitive Science, Dordrecht: Springer 2010, pp. 217–234, here p. 218.

24 Ibid; see also Sheets-Johnstone, Maxine: The Primacy of Movement, Amsterdam: John Benjamins 2011.

Let us take a closer look at how these qualities play out in the encounter and how they help us to make sense of what is happening. While the wolf wanted to come into playful contact with the ravens (as wolves do when they play with each other), the ravens did not allow the wolf to cross the boundaries of what they probably saw as the wolf's 'striking distance'. They were constantly alert and attentive to any movement and responded (tensional/projectional) either timidly (when the wolf moved slowly and steadily, with little purpose and at some distance (projectional)) or energetically by opening up, spreading their wings (areal and tensional), flying off to the next dune (linear) (when the wolf moved quickly or abruptly, or came too close (projectional)). The affective tension between them rose or fell accordingly.

But the wolf always let the ravens know what he was up to, even when he jumped at them three times. From the beginning and throughout the encounter, he moved mostly slowly and carefully (projectional), not too forced, but relaxed (tensional) and wagging his tail (linear). The wolf's general attitude was also evident in his playful jumps, which were always somewhat half-hearted (tensional), as he quickly realised that the ravens were repulsed by his approach and tried to get out of the immediate situation.

The affective kinaesthetic dynamic described here is more than a series of changes in spatial position or the sequence of clearly defined and causally linked actions and reactions that add up to something like an interaction and that we know from ethological observation protocols. Tim Ingold has pointed out that "[t]he implication of the prefix *inter-*, in 'interaction', is that the interacting parties are closed to one another, as if they could only be connected through some kind of bridging operation".[25] To break behaviour down into individual parts, to classify and code it, would be to lose sight of what makes sense in the dynamics of the encounter.

Instead, the encounter between the wolf and the ravens shows that actions are always in the process of becoming: they are continuous, incomplete, ambivalently merging into one another and thus in ongoing transformation. When the actions of different actors relate to each other, then the 'becoming' of the actions accordingly must be seen as a 'becoming-with'. During the phases of movement, the animals observe each other attentively and adapt themselves continuously, often not even waiting for the complete execution

---

25   Ingold, Tim: Making. Anthropology, archaeology, art and architecture, London/New York: Routledge 2013, p. 107 (emphasis added).

of a movement. In this "dance of animacy",[26] the actions are not so much intentional, mentally planned in advance and executed as planned, but 'attentional', a lively attentiveness and responsiveness of the sensitive bodies in co-responding movements.[27]

As the wolf approaches, the raven becomes more and more nervous-turning away-taking a few steps-jumping a few times-crouching down-croaking-spreading its wings-flying away – one unfolding movement in response to the unfolding movement of the wolf.

Figure 6: A wild boar positions itself on the left, while another sow is close on the wolf's heels on the right edge of the picture.

Source: Author

---

26   T. Ingold: Making, pp. 100–102.

27   Ingold, T.: Anthropology and/as education, London: Routledge 2018, pp. 24–27.

Figure 7: The wolf circles back, the sow now very close to him.

Source: Author

Figure 8: The wolf accelerates and breaks away from its pursuer. Two other sows position themselves by the birch trees in the middle where the piglet is hiding.

Source: Author

Figure 9: The wolf has outmanoeuvred the sows and runs towards the birch trees, where the piglet is now hiding unprotected.

Source: Author

Encounter II: dangerous affects

On a late June evening – the sun has already sunk below the horizon and it is getting harder and harder to see anything in the growing darkness – a group of wild boars come out of the woods into a clearing at the edge of a bare plain that stretches out in front of me. Four large shadows and, by the looks of it, one smaller shadow, four sows and at least one piglet are moving through the tall grass in search of food. After a few minutes they disappear, one shadow after another, back into the forest.

Not long after they have gone, a lone wolf comes trotting across the plain. He passes the clearing and pauses, then turns and trots off towards the forest, disappearing into it.

Suddenly a thunderous grunt echoes from the woods and seconds later the wolf comes running out onto the plain – its tail sticking out stiffly – followed by four sows who are chasing it at full gallop. As the wolf runs off, he keeps turning his head back to see where the sows are, then he slows down a little and circles back in a wide arc. Three of the sows have previously stopped their pursuit at different points, as if to keep watch, while the fastest sow continues to chase the wolf. The sow and the wolf are now almost touching as they run in an arc, but the wolf seems to be a little more agile, a little faster, and manages to keep his distance from the sow who is following him. The wolf looks back at a small stand of birch trees where one of the sows is standing, with the sow still hot on his heels.

He picks up the pace again (the sow standing by the birch trees also turns and gallops towards the wolf for a few metres before stopping), the chasing sow behind him, kicking up clouds of dust that envelop the whole scene. Then, after about 100 metres, the wolf suddenly turns left, the sow right. The wolf quickly turns back towards the stand of birch trees, past another sow moving hesitantly on the spot, and past the sow standing by the trees. He rushes between the trees, grabs something and rushes out into the open, now followed by three sows. But soon the three sows slow down, stop abruptly in their cloud of dust and look over at the wolf.

A lifeless piglet dangles loosely from the wolf's snout, who now also stops to watch the sows. As if on command, they suddenly turn and run back into the forest at full gallop, while the wolf drops the piglet to the ground and continues to look in the direction where the sows have disappeared. A few seconds later, he shakes himself, looks around and grabs the piglet again. With his tail relaxed, he trots across the plain with his prey, disappearing like the sows into the darkness of the night.

Who is hunting whom? The roles in such a hunt are not always clear. On the one hand, it is clear which species is hunting, killing and eating the other. On the other hand, the course of the hunt shows that the division into 'hunter' and 'prey' does not automatically indicate who is stronger, or even who is attacking whom. The interesting thing about the above example is that, strangely enough, it is the wolf that is being chased by the boar for most of the chase, and not the other way around! It is only in the final seconds of the chase that it becomes clear who the real hunter is.

The main question for wolf biologists watching such a scene is whether the course of events is random or follows a plan. If the wolf is to be understood primarily as an instinctive creature, its hunting technique would follow a genetically determined behavioural protocol, like an automatism; if it is driven by uncontrolled instinct, it would show no behavioural pattern at all. If, on the other hand, the wolf is an animal endowed with intelligence and consciousness, its behaviour should reveal a goal-directed strategy: a strategy developed in advance with planning and foresight, and then implemented during the hunt. In broad outline, wolf biologists imagine such a hunting strategy in wolves as follows: Wolves actively search for prey (search); wolves approach the prey within sight (approach); wolves watch the prey (watch); wolves attack the prey group as a whole (attack-group); wolves select an individual from this group and attack it specifically (attack-individual); wolves capture and kill the animal (capture).[28]

But the example above shows that it is not so easy to identify a pattern of behaviour, or even a strategy. One of the greatest challenges in wolf research is to be able to observe the entire course of a hunt from beginning to end. This was the case in my example. I was able to watch the wolf during the initial search, picking up the scent and running after the boars. I could not see the approach, the observation and the initial attack (if there was one) – I could only hear the loud grunt, which was probably the start to the hunt in the narrower sense.

But even if one has to guess at the missing parts of the sequence of events, it seems clear that the hunt did not seem to proceed 'according to plan', on the basis of a strategy. A constant back and forth, with changes in direction and speed, characterised the events, and the wolf hardly seemed to be 'in control' and directing the events. Or perhaps he was? If a strategy is understood as a planned, anticipated sequence of actions and reactions by hunter and prey leading to the capture of the prey, then it seems unlikely that we are dealing with a strategy here. In any case, I do not see any dynamics here that are characterised by mere chance or that follow simple automatisms.

So how can we understand this hunt if we understand the animals involved as living, sentient beings and the hunt as an affective dynamic? How do wolves and wild boars affect each other in this hunt? First of all, it is surprising that a single wolf would take on a sounder of wild boars. Wild boars are considered to be very capable of defending themselves; they are dangerous and could seriously injure or even kill wolves in a fight. It is therefore not surprising that wolf biologists generally argue that "the central problem for wolves on the hunt is to kill without being killed".[29] So the single wolf in our example is therefore either desperate and hungry or he was very experienced and knew exactly what he was doing. In the following, I would like to explain why I think the latter is more likely the case and how we can understand such wolfish experiential knowledge.

What and how does the wolf know about hunting wild boar? When I speak of experiential knowledge in this context, I mean that it is not a form of rational, fact-based knowledge that is primarily reflected in thought. Rather, it is

---

28   D. Mech/D. Smith/D. MacNulty: Wolves on the Hunt, pp. 8–9.
29   Ibid, p. 1.

body-based, action-oriented, implicit knowledge that is learned—in the sense of being embodied—through accumulated experience. It is an *affective knowledge, a sense of one's own corporeality and the corporeality of others, a sensitivity to how one affects others or how other bodies affect oneself.* Trained by many encounters, the wolf develops a sense of what his body can do and what a wild boar can do. How strong, how agile, how fast is the boar in relation to the wolf's own body? What weapons does he have, does the boar have? What are the weaknesses, the strengths that can help him to conquer the wild boar? Every time the dynamics of the action suddenly change, the participants have to make decisions and adapt their actions. In the 'heat of the moment', however, there is no time for strategic consideration based on reasoned judgement. Here, the wolf must rely on his well-trained bodily knowledge that has become intuition, on his *skill*[30], which provides him with a *sense of judgement* and allows him to act at lightning speed, picking up on the wild boar's affects and adapting his own *responsiveness* accordingly—always with the overriding goal of seizing the prey.

Rather than a pre-planned strategy, the wolf uses what I would call a *sensitive tactic*. It is less anticipatory than situational, providing only a rough orientation and relying entirely on its own skills for implementation, allowing the wolf to react flexibly to all sorts of circumstances. This tactic is based on the wolf's experience that he may not be the stronger in this situation (certainly not against several boars), but he is the quicker and more agile. How does he know this? There are some documented observations of young wolves encountering an adult boar or red deer. But in these examples, the would-be prey seems rather unimpressed by the wolves' often clumsy attempts at attack. These are 'quasi-hunts', possibly a kind of game for the wolves. There are (mock) attacks and corresponding counter-attacks, a constant balancing, approaching, attacking, evading. In such encounters, young wolves can train their sensitivity and learn how their body responds to the body of the prey. Something similar can be expected when young wolves accompany adult wolves on the hunt.

---

30   Tim Ingold's understanding of skill can be applied to human and as well as to non-human organisms (as he does throughout his book) when he argues that "Skills are not transmitted from generation to generation but are regrown in each, incorporated into the modus operandi of the developing human organism through training and experience in the performance of particular tasks" (in Tim Ingold: Perception of the Environment, p. 5).

It may be a subjective impression, but the wolf in the above example seemed to me to know exactly what he was doing. He also seemed to be in control of the situation overall, even though he was running from the boars all the time. I suspect he knew a lot about wild boars. This would be consistent with the fact that piglet hunting is quite common in this area. One of the most experienced wolf-watchers there told me that he had seen a sow with piglets on several occasions, and each time she had fewer and fewer piglets. The wolves of the Knappenrode-Seenland Pack may have become specialists in hunting piglets.

So, if the wolf was an experienced boar hunter, what might have been its sensitive tactic? Picking up the scent of the boars, the wolf approached its prey and finally made itself known. His presence affected the boars immensely, who – judging by the grunt – were surprised and shaken. *This is the first step in the tactic of letting your presence affect your prey and observing how they are affected. The wolf knows from experience that his presence does indeed affect potential prey, and the more suitable an animal is for prey in its current situation, the more he affects it, and the more unsettling and disturbing his affective power. Disturbance is therefore at the heart of his hunting tactic.* He will know from previous encounters that he will not be able to get to the piglets if the boar can form a defensive formation around them. The wolf will try to prevent this 'fortress formation' by constantly keeping the boars in motion and giving them new impulses by affecting them with sudden changes in speed or direction. Their affects are supposed to run away with them, so to speak. In the affective dynamics of this back and forth, he will look for a gap in space at the right moment to use his superior speed and agility to push through and grab the piglet. In the end, everything seems to work in the wolf's favour: his successfully applied skills and the successfully unsettled (perhaps still inexperienced) 'protecting' boars, who, instead of re-acting decisively and attacking the wolf, appear to be affectively overwhelmed and do not move.

Figure 10: The two wolves, displaying behaviour that is not shy.

Source: Screenshot, https://www.youtube.com/watch?v=hV4LVvLqF1I (Accessed: 30.04.2024)

Figure 11: The wolf stands in the middle only a few metres away.

Source: Screenshot, https://www.youtube.com/watch?v=hV4LVvLqF11 (accessed: 30.04.2024)

Encounter III: playful or dangerous affects?

Near the village of Lohsa, Lusatia. Two hunters in forestry gear, at the edge of the forest, in a field of waist-high herbal vegetation, with brush cutters, a dog waiting in their car.

"That's not normal."

A wolf runs away and hides in the vegetation. The hunter chuckles.

"That's three metres and they're 'shy'. I get it!"

The wolf's head emerges out of the vegetation. He watches the hunter intently for a few seconds and then jumps further back. The other hunter is standing about ten metres away from the first one, his eyes sweeping over the vegetation. There may be more wolves here.

"That's not normal," the other hunter says.

"No, that's not normal," the hunter agrees. He turns around and chuckles again when he sees that the wolf has come back and is now just standing there watching him.

"Look at that! That's about … eight metres!"

The wolf steps a little bit to the left, looks around, returns, sniffs the ground and stands still, facing the hunter, ears pricked. He steps a little to the right, sniffs the ground, looks at the hunter, suddenly jerks back a little and then looks at the hunter again. His body twitches, as if he wants to run back, but then he slowly takes five steps backwards—still watching the hunter. He looks to the right, suddenly turns to the left and then gallops back a few metres, stops again, first looks at the hunter, then looks around.

"Very shy animals!" the hunter comments as his dog sits in the car barking and whimpering. The hunter begins to laugh as the wolf moves forward again, stopping at the same distance from the hunter as before, facing him directly and watching him carefully.

"He's coming towards us."

"Come here!" the other hunter calls, and coming closer to where the hunter is standing.

"Heel!" the hunter shouts, still laughing. Suddenly the wolf turns around and jumps a few metres away. He is now waiting by a tree and looking around.

"This is not normal!" says the other hunter.

"This is not normal!" agrees the hunter.

"Film it, film it, always film it! Here, LUPUS, LUPUS, LUPUS!!!"[31]

---

31   He is referring to the LUPUS- Institute for Wolf Research here. Wolf critics in this region often see the biologists from this private research institute as being in league with 'wolf

Then the other hunter turns around and notices a second wolf ten metres behind them.

"There! Over there by the brushcutter ..."

"Hey, my helmet! He's taking my helmet!" the hunter laughs.

"What's going on?"

"He's taking my helmet. Fetch!" he calls jokingly after the wolf, who quickly
trots off with his helmet.

"Hey, hello!" the hunter calls after him as the other hunter starts to run after
the wolf.

"That is *not* possible."

The wolf quickly lets go of the helmet and runs away, while the other hunter
picks up the helmet and returns to the car—where the dog continues to
bark.

***

'Wolf encounters—what to do

If you are on foot or bicycle in wolf regions, it is rare to encounter a wolf but
it is a possibility. Encounters within 100 m generally only occur if wolves have
not noticed a person's approach, for example due to wind conditions. When
wolves notice people, they generally do not flee in panic, but instead orient
themselves for a moment before retreating. Among all of the documented
wolf sightings in Lusatia, there have been only very few in which wolves approached people despite already being aware of their presence. Usually this
happened in cases involving inexperienced, curious young wolves or when the
wolf's interest in dogs or sheep near the person overrode the impulse to flee.
Generally, in any encounter, it is best to behave calmly and maintain distance.
If the wolf does not withdraw and the situation makes you feel uneasy, speak
loudly or clap your hands to make yourself noticeable. Do not run, as this could
trigger chasing behaviour. Should the wolf approach you, which is unusual,
stay where you are, stand tall and attempt to intimidate the wolf. In this kind
of situation, it is better to take a step towards the animal than to step back.
Like wild boars, wolves are large, powerful wild animals. Show them respect.

---

cuddlers' and as not properly scientific, although they organise Saxony's wolf monitoring program and are internationally respected researchers.

Do not attempt to approach or entice a wolf. Allow the wolf space to retreat. Do not feed wolves under any circumstances and do not leave leftover food in the open. The instinctive caution wolves exhibit towards people can be lost if the animals experience positive stimuli associated with humans. This can foster problematic behaviour in wolves and may lead ultimately to injuries to people.'[32]

What happens when wolves and humans meet face to face? What is brought into the encounter? And how does 'one' (human or wolf) behave in such a new kind of encounter, for which there is no precedent, no routine to follow? These encounters are still rare, but they do happen – as evidenced by the hundreds of sighting reports and videos circulating on social media channels. To sort through all these reports and footage, it helps to first distinguish between encounters and sightings. Looking through the officially reported incidents for Saxony over the last five years, it quickly became clear that most of the reports were related to sightings: Someone had seen a wolf, at a distance of 100 metres or more, for a few seconds, and then the wolf was quickly gone (often without acknowledging the human presence in any way).

If we take an encounter literally as a face-to-face meeting, then these sightings do not qualify as such, as they lack the immediacy and intimacy of an encounter and may be a one-sided affair in which no mutual affective exchange takes place. Encounters in the true sense of the word are what the official documents refer to as 'close encounters', i.e. encounters with wolves that come closer than 30 metres. This is considered an important category for wolf management, as these close encounters could indicate 'abnormal' (and therefore potentially dangerous) behaviour on the part of a wolf that may be habituated to human presence and not showing its 'natural' shyness (expressed in distance from humans), which should therefore be investigated and followed up with the necessary action, according to the Wolf Management Plan. All close encounters are therefore treated as exceptional. As such, they are the rarest, but at the same time the most popular encounters, as they provide the ingredients for captivating media stories, in contrast to the more ordinary sightings.

The close encounter described above is therefore hardly representative or commonplace, but rather unique and exceptional. Nevertheless, an analysis

---

32   Reinhardt, Ilka et al.: How to deal with bold wolves—Recommendations of the DBBW—(= BfN-Skript 577), Bonn: Bundesamt für Naturschutz 2020, p. 45.

can reveal the underlying affective dynamics that help us to understand human-wolf encounters more precisely and generally. Etymologically, the term 'encounter' describes an ambivalent situation. In the words of Alexandra Böhm and Jessica Ullrich: "The contrary aspects of presence, the accidental and unintentional [...], characterise encounters as well as violence, difference and rejection."[33] Unlike discourses in which wolves only appear as off-screen actors and do not actively participate, in encounters wolves become agents that have the power to disrupt discursive meanings and trigger reconceptualisations of how humans understand themselves and their relationship to 'the wild'.[34] This is possible because, in encounters, animals "speak, and indeed communicate, simply by virtue of their presence and activity, through modes of reference that may be indexical or iconic, if not symbolic".[35] Encounters, therefore, are an appropriate starting point for investigating the role of affect in human-wolf relationships.

By contrasting wolf-human encounters with wolf-raven and wolf-boar encounters, I draw attention to the similarities inherent in these variations of interanimality. Wolf-human encounters thus become another type of (human and non-human) animal encounter. But we must also acknowledge the particularity of each encounter—both in terms of the uniqueness of each encounter in a specific here and now, and in terms of the uniqueness of wolf bodies, raven bodies, wild boar bodies, and human bodies and their respective affective capacities.

Part of the specificity of the human-wolf encounter is, of course, the way in which language is used by the human actors. In the example above, we can distinguish three modes of speech: commentary (between the two hunters), performance (to an imaginary audience of the video) and communication (when trying to make contact with the wolves). First, the hunters continually comment on what is happening, repeatedly seeking each other's confirmation of

---

33   Böhm, Alexandra/Ullrich, Jessica: 'Introduction—Animal Encounters: Contact, Interaction and Relationality', in: Alexandra Böhm/Jessica Ullrich. (eds.), Animal Encounters. Contact, Interaction and Relationality, Stuttgart: J.B. Metzler 2019, pp. 1–21, here p. 1.

34   Barua, Maan: 'Encounter', in: Environmental Humanities 7 (2016), pp. 265–270, https://doi.org/10.1215/22011919-3616479; see Poerting, Julia/Verne, Julia/Krieg, Lisa J.: 'Dangerous Encounters. Posthumanist Approaches in the Technological Renegotiation of Human-Wildlife Coexistence', in: Geographische Zeitschrift 108.3 (2020), pp. 153–175, https://doi.org/10.25162/gz-2020-0006.

35   T. Ingold: Making, p. 20.

what they seem to find so unusual. Often their comments are ambiguously directed at the other hunter, at themselves, or even at the imagined audience of
the video. The fact that they imagine an audience for this video at all becomes
clear when one of the hunters directly addresses the intended audience, the
biologists of the LUPUS Institute. At this point it becomes clear that this is
not an 'innocent' encounter between two hunters and two wolves. It quickly
develops into a special kind of encounter, namely a performative one, aimed
at producing (visual) evidence of 'abnormal' wolf behaviour, which is subsequently circulated on social media, for example to refute the scientific statements of the LUPUS Institute. This agenda influenced the whole dynamic of
the encounter. For example, the filming hunter was restricted in his actions
during the encounter, as he had to hold his smartphone and continue filming
and commenting, while only the non-filming hunter was free to run after the
wolf and retrieve the helmet. Videos created through such performative, tech-
nology-mediated encounters are therefore more than mere documentation of
an event. In terms of the affective dynamic between hunters and wolves, filming and addressing the audience distracts the hunters from an immediate and
unmediated interaction with the wolves. Their attention and receptivity to the
wolves' movements is repeatedly interrupted and hindered.

What is interesting, however, is that the hunters are obviously trying to
make contact and communicate with the wolves – albeit in a less than serious
way. And the way they do this is modelled on their knowledge of communicating with dogs. Without the experience and knowledge of how to communicate
with wolves, the filming hunter is using typical dog commands ('heel', 'fetch')
to get in contact with the wolves. The appearance and behaviour of wolves (not
to mention their genetic ancestry) is very similar to that of dogs. As hunters
(with a dog in the car), these men are certainly familiar with dogs and their behaviour, and they may interpret the wolves' behaviour as curious and youthful,
hence the laughter. It is not surprising, however, that communication efforts
similar to those used with dogs do not work with wolves. But in the absence of
alternative means of communication, what else could the hunters have done?

In this encounter, we should not overlook the fact that verbal (one-way)
communication is based on a more fundamental body-affect dynamic. As in
the previous encounters between wolves, boars and ravens, the affective presence is modulated by behaviour, sense of personal space, gesture, movement
and sound/language. Kinesthetically, the wolf interacting with the filming
hunter is initially nervous but curious, constantly moving back and forth,
looking around, then at the hunter, twitching at every gesture, every move-

ment towards him, or at every sound spoken to him. The hunters seem to be less affected by the wolves, but they also respond to them, especially in terms of positioning and maintaining distance. Indeed, the way the hunters move in relation to the wolves is reminiscent of the way hunters and beaters would approach a wild animal (such as a wild boar) on a driven hunt. The very fact that they do not just stand there, but approach the wolves directly and firmly, and do not retreat, shows that they are affecting the wolves more than the wolves are affecting them.

The hunters' confidence may also be related to their expectations and knowledge of wolves as a species and what they consider to be 'normal' behaviour. Their entire conversation during the encounter focuses on one theme: these wolves are not shy, and that is not normal. As mentioned above, shyness is an important distinction between normal and abnormal/dangerous behaviour in the context of wolf management. However, what exactly shyness is remains ambiguous and under-defined. For example, the behaviour of a wolf approaching humans at a distance of less than 30 metres could be interpreted as an abnormal lack of shyness. However, this criterion would not be sufficient to classify the wolf as a problem wolf. The specific details of the encounter would need to be examined. However, when discussing the shyness of wild animals in general (and wolves in particular) in public discourse, the expectation seems to be that the animal should immediately panic, i.e. react clearly and immediately to the presence of humans and flee at high speed. A wolf that cannot decide what to do, that shifts and looks back and forth, that twitches instead of acting clearly, and that jumps away but then turns back to the human – in other words, a wolf that is strongly affected and moved and is carefully trying to find appropriate ways to respond to these affects – is behaving too ambiguously and therefore inappropriately to be considered 'normal'. It is here that we realise that the simplistic stimulus-response theory of behaviour that still dominates our discourse on animal shyness reaches its limits when it comes to the reality of the affective dynamics of encounters.

Every encounter with wolves is necessarily ambivalent, ambiguous and improvised. The unexpected and surprising are part of every encounter, as the affective dynamics of the encounter create new impulses that need to be responsively absorbed and translated into action. But we have also seen that encounters do not necessarily take place in a completely disordered way. Participants never (re)act completely unprepared, their bodies are always already routinised in dealing with affects in general, so that even new affects in never-before-experienced encounters with wolves meet with habitual behaviour and encounter-relevant knowledge (e.g. acquired in dealing with other animal species such as dogs). These forms of prior knowledge can help to correctly assess the wolf's behaviour in some encounters, but can also lead to misjudgments if, for example, you treat a wolf too much like a dog.

Ultimately, all three examples in this chapter show that the course of an encounter depends on an inherent affective dynamic that is primarily given by the corporeality of those involved (sometimes mediated by technology). This corporeality requires constant attention to the affective dynamic and action that is guided and coordinated by attention. Since there are and can be no 'blueprints' for interpreting encounters with wolves, no clear stimulus-response-causality chains by which we can clearly categorise behaviour as, for example, 'harmless play behaviour' or 'threatening aggression', we should begin to study such human-animal encounters in more detail. Rather than prematurely categorising them as a whole, or reducing individual behaviours to ethogram schemes, it seems more useful to acknowledge the inherent ambiguity of any encounter. This creates a space for interpretation that allows for ambiguous behavioural expressions while also tracing the dynamic development over the course of encounters. In this case, I conclude that 'complicating' an encounter in such a way improves our understanding of human-wolf relationships.

***

Germany's biggest tabloid, *Bild*, picked up on the above encounter near Lohsa and turned it into a video article. From the three original videos, they edited a two-minute version entitled "Wolves carry off hunter's helmet – Shy? You must be kidding!".[36] The following written comments were added to the footage:

"Shy wolf? You must be kidding!"

"The hunters Sven Puschel and Sven Schulz are stunned"

"Two wolves sneak up to within a few metres of the car, ...

... while the hunters are cutting a hedge."

"The predators show neither shyness nor respect."

---

36   https://www.youtube.com/watch?v=hV4LVvLqF1I (accessed: 30.04.2024).

"They even carry off a man's work helmet."

"The wolf only lets go of the helmet when owner Schulz runs towards him."

"The hunters retreat into the car for their own safety."

Unlike the original videos, the edited video contained both commentary and an added, slightly eerie spherical background noise. *Bild* framed and narrated the encounter visually and aurally as a threatening and dangerous scenario, despite the occasional laughter of the hunter. They attempted to overwrite the original affective dynamic with another that was congruent with the newspaper's sceptical attitude towards wolves in general.

This "dramaturgy of affect"[37] illustrates how individual, intimate bodily encounters with wolves are recorded, processed, retold, and re-situated within public discursive practices. While the wolves were active agents in an affective multispecies interaction that developed during the encounter, their agency was increasingly replaced by the agency of humans (the filming hunter, the post-processing journalists, the commentators on YouTube) in the subsequent transduction process, whereby the wolves were gradually transformed from living agents into passive symbols and representations that could no longer participate in the now anthropocentric affective dynamics of the media discourse. Their affective traces fade, are superimposed, partially blurred, and become increasingly unrecognisable as the media processing progresses.

---

37   Kappelhoff, Hermann/Lehmann, Hauke: 'The temporal composition of affects in audiovisual media', in: Antje Kahl (ed.), Analyzing affective societies. Methods and methodologies, London/New York: Routledge 2019, pp. 120–139, here p. 121.

Figure 12: This map of wolf attacks shows the approximate territory of the first Wester-
wald pack in Feldkirchener Wald/Neuwied.

© Forschungsanstalt für Waldökologie und Forstwirtschaft | Landesforsten Rheinland-Pfalz
Hintergrundkarte: www.openstreetmap.org

Source: Research Institute of Forest Ecology and Forestry (FAWF)

3. Wolf Agency

Wolf agency and coexistence

What happens when wolves settle in a new region? How does a region become a wolf territory? In this chapter I tell the story of the recent return of wolves to the Westerwald, culminating in the formation of its first-ever pack, the Feldkirchener Wald/Neuwied Pack.[1] This story begins years before my research and becomes a personal narrative from autumn 2019 onwards. It weaves together a variety (and, of course, a selection) of sources into a narrative that unfolds historically through time, but occasionally jumps back and forth, from one perspective to another, from one place to another. Official statements about wolf images, dead wolves, and wolf kills are complemented by local/regional press reports, social media posts, local events, and personal narratives from locals in the near and adjacent area. While the main narrative focuses on the immediate wolf territory, I show how events from outside feed into the local narratives, creating different geographical interconnections.

The purpose of this chapter is twofold. First, *I describe how wolves and humans share a common world in which their lives touch and matter to each other. Second, I explore the role of wolfish 'affective agency' in that process.* In both public debate and scientific discourse, this situation is usually described by the term coexistence, a term that, as Jean-Luc Nancy has noted, "often oscillates in meaning between indifference and resignation, or even between cohabitation and contamination".[2] For wolf advocates, the term conjures up positive images of a community living peacefully together across species boundaries. For those who are sceptical about the wolf, on the other hand, it is an overly positive term,

---

1   The chapter thus concludes in spring 2021. Later developments in 2021 and 2022 and the Leuscheid Pack are briefly discussed in Chapter 6.

2   Nancy, Jean-Luc: Being Singular Plural, Stanford: Stanford University Press 2000, p. 43.

suggesting peace and harmony where they see only conflict and danger. So, the term has its own semiotic baggage that needs to be taken into account. Likewise, we must assume that coexistence is lived in various shades and forms.

As noted in the introduction, the most fundamental form of coexistence is rooted in the shared bodily constitution of human and non-human animal life. Rather than assuming a human exceptionalism that sets us apart from (and above) the rest of the world, it is important to recognise that we all share a common corporeal being (albeit in a variety of forms and capacities) that enables us to affect and be affected by each other in specific ways. In such a perspective, animals do not just exist, they occur and act;[3] that is, animals are (and become for us) affective through what they do.[4] A wolf becomes affective, so to speak, through its *wolfing*.[5] For the return of wolves to the Westerwald, this means that every wolf on its way through the region, with every step, with every urine or scat mark, with every kill, begins to weave itself into the socio-ecological fabric of the region, thus creating the affective ground for a coexistence between wolves, other wildlife, livestock and pets, resident humans, and the landscape.

While this approach may be obvious to readers from environmental anthropology or the interdisciplinary field of human-animal studies, it is certainly less so for readers from the field of Human Dimensions of Wildlife (HDW), a field dominated by (mostly quantitative) sociologists and socio-ecologists working within a social science paradigm of empirical social research. In this field, the actual life of wolves is typically left to the natural sciences to study, while the social sciences deal with the 'human dimensions' of living with wolves, which usually consist of 'opinions', 'attitudes', 'values' etc. about wolves.[6] By reproducing the presumably still dominant Western notion of a dichotomy between nature and culture, along with the accompanying disciplinary division into natural and social science research, they perpetuate a research paradigm that excludes animals from the social world of humans, as if their lives did not influence each other.

---

3   T. Ingold: Being Alive, p. 175.

4   Ibid., S. 170.

5   Ibid., S. 174.

6   In recent years, however, there has been a recognizable trend towards integrating qualitative approaches, and ethnography in particular, into HDW research. Although still marginal, ethnography is now considered not only a legitimate but also a valuable addition to available methodologies, see IUCN: IUCN SSC guidelines on human-wildlife conflict and coexistence. First edition. Gland, Switzerland: IUCN 2023, https://doi.org/10.2305/YGIK2927.

Wolves are thus not considered real agents (i.e social agents) in this field, as the following quote from Ulrich Schraml, a leading German sociologist in this field shows. In an overview chapter titled "Wildlife Management for People", he states: "Colloquially, it is common to speak of a human-wildlife-conflict or human-carnivore-conflict. This perspective assumes that animals also 'go to battle' to assert their interests. From a social science perspective, this is a strange idea". [7] Instead, Schraml argues for a socio-political classification of the conflict that focuses on the 'symbolic content' of the wolf. While other sociologists at least acknowledge that there is a conflict *with* wolves in addition to an internal societal conflict *about* wolves (e.g. between wolf advocates and wolf opponents),[8] Schraml reduces the conflicts to their human-societal dimension and relegates wolves to being passive recipients of human attributions of meaning, whose behaviour has no influence on social processes. In this chapter, as throughout the book, I show that the stories of the conflicts cannot be told without the wolves themselves, and that leaving them out distorts the conflict and hinders understanding of people's problems with wolves. The fact that my argument here are probably another 'strange idea' for Schraml can probably be explained by the fact that most sociologists in the field of HDW do not usually engage with literature from human-animal studies, multispecies ethnography, or more-than-human geography.[9] Furthermore, the concept of culture seems problematic in the field of HDW. It could well be argued that their conceptualisation of culture is a mentalistic and intellectualistic one, focusing too

---

7   Schraml, Ulrich: Wildtiermanagement für Menschen, in: Marco Heurich (ed.), Wolf, Luchs und Bär in der Kulturlandschaft. Konflikte, Chancen, Lösungen im Umgang mit großen Beutegreifern, Stuttgart: Ulmer 2019, pp. 113–148, here p. 113, translated by TG.

8   See Skogen, Ketil/Figari, Helene/Krange, Olve: Wolf Conflicts. A Sociological Study (= Interspecies Encounters, Vol. 1), New York, NY: Berghahn 2017, p. 9. Yet it is noticeable that even in this otherwise very insightful book, wolves as 'real' animals and agents are conspicuously absent.

9   Publication outlets for HDW research focus on a small range of journals such as Human Dimensions of Wildlife, Wildlife Biology, Biological Conservation, Wildlife Society Bulletin, Society and Natural Resources, PLOS Biology, or the European Journal of Wildlife Research. Citations of work outside this scope of journals are not very common. Similarly, though, scholars working on human-animal relations rarely engage with HDW literature and publish in 'their' journals. There is thus a need to start a more serious conversation (for an attempt from anthropology, see e.g. Schroer, Sara Asu: 'The Arts of Coexistence: A View From Anthropology', in: Front. Conserv. Sci. (2021) 2, pp. 711019. doi: 10.3389/fcosc.2021.711019.

narrowly on language, ideas and worldviews, opinions and attitudes.[10] In fact, there is a strong influence of social psychology throughout the field – as evidenced by key social psychological concepts that provide key points of reference for much of the HDW literature, such as beliefs, attitudes, motivation, values, and so on.[11] This may explain why advances in cultural and social theory in recent decades, which see culture as embodied, situated, material, performed, and practised have had little impact on HDW research.[12]

It is therefore my intention to take the underlying ecological approach underlying the HDW literature more seriously by not treating the human social sphere as a *separate* dimension of wildlife and by not reducing wolf conflicts to ones *about* wolves only. Instead, this chapter shows how human-wolf coexistence is fundamentally rooted in the lives and actions of wolves, without which the 'human dimension' is incomplete and difficult to understand. My focus here is therefore on the agency of wolves, their capacity and power to act in ways that might have material effects as well as felt affective consequences. My understanding of animal agency is based on Edward Reed's minimal definition: "This is just what *agency* means: agents make things happen, *they make their way in the world*".[13] Accordingly, the purpose of this chapter is to show how wolves, as affective agents in a shared world of coexistence, repeatedly and consistently provide powerful impulses that trigger individual and social processes, sometimes prompting or even forcing human actors to act. Although wolves can also sometimes become passive objects of discourse (and thus mere representations and symbols), they generally play an active role in shaping the human-wolf relationship.[14] This is not to say that their actions always follow deliberate planning with a preconceived outcome, as might be inferred from a subject-oriented intentional approach to agency. Nor do I want to reduce

---

10   Reckwitz, A. (2017). How the senses organise the social. In M. Jonas & B. Littig (Eds.), *Praxeological political analysis* (pp. 56–66). Routledge.

11   IUCN: IUCN SSC guidelines on human-wildlife conflict and coexistence.

12   Seidman, Steven/Alexander/Jeffrey (eds.) The New Social Theory Reader, London: Routledge 2008; Badmington, Neil/Thomas, Julia (eds.) The Routledge Critical and Cultural Theory Reader, London: Routledge 2008.

13   Reed, Edward: Encountering the world. Toward an Ecological Psychology, Oxford: Oxford University Press 1997, p. 19 (emphasis added).

14   See Lescureux, Nicolas/Garde, Laurent/Meuret, Michel: 'Considering wolves as active agents in understanding stakeholder perceptions and developing management strategies', in: T. Hovardas (ed.), Large Carnivore Conservation and Management, pp. 147–167.

wolves' agency to that of any 'actor' (human or non-human, animate or inanimate), as is the case with some materialist approaches such as Actor-Network Theory.[15] These would be less suited to dealing with questions of a wolf's sentience and affectivity.

Instead, I am interested in the wolfish capacity to affect humans in their own specific ways, from giving us a moment of goosebumps to leaving us stunned with fascination or fear. When it comes to the agency of wolves in relation to humans, I am not suggesting that their actions are necessarily intended to affect us (a scat mark is placed with the intention of affecting other wolves, perhaps other animals, probably not humans). Nor are they agents in the same way that humans are agents. Nevertheless, their actions have the capacity to 'make things happen' or 'set things in motion', and they can act as a catalyst for human responses (wolf officers are contacted, go into the woods to look for the scat, bag it and send it to the Senckenberg Institute for DNA analysis). Moreover, the affective power of wolf agency can have an impact without anything actually having to have happened. In this sense, it refers to both the wolves' *performed actions* and their *virtual capacities* for (inter)action. What do we think wolves are capable of? The mere sighting of a wolf, for example, affects people both through the actual behaviour of the wolf at that moment and through what he might have done or what might have happened.

However, this relational approach to wolf affective agency is necessarily incomplete. While we can trace how wolves affect us humans, it is difficult to work out how they are in turn affected by us. As I show in the following pages, wolves tend to appear suddenly and disappear just as suddenly. For most of their lives they exist unnoticed if not invisible to us. One of the reasons for this may be that wolves have superior hearing and smell, which allows them to hide from us long before we can notice them. This was clearly demonstrated in a recent pilot study of 21 'approach trials' with GPS-collared wolves.[16] The researchers wanted to learn more about how wolves behave when they encounter humans. But in 21 trials not a single wolf was seen by the approaching

15   See Wirth, Sven et al.: Das Handeln der Tiere. Tierliche Agency im Fokus der Human-Animal Studies (= Human-Animal Studies, Vol. 9), Bielefeld: transcript 2016, https://doi.org/10.14361/9783839432266; McFarland, Sarah/Hediger, Ryan (eds.): Animals and Agency: An Interdisciplinary Exploration, Leiden: Brill 2009.

16   Versluijs, Erik/ Eriksen, Ane/ Fuchs, Boris/ Wilkenros, Camilla/ Sand, Hakan/ Wabakken, Petter/Zimmermann, Barbara: 'Wolf Responses to Experimental Human Approaches Using High-Resolution Positioning Data', in: Frontiers in Ecology and Evolution 10 (2022), pp. 792916, https:// doi.org/10.3389/fevo.2022.792916.

researchers. Almost all of them had fled long before. So the story of the return of the wolf is still an anthropocentric one, primarily about how humans are affected by wolves, not the other way around. Although this pilot study at least proves *that* wolves are affected by human presence, the *how* remains largely a mystery outside of experiments.

With this caveat in mind, we can finally turn to the emerging structure of affective wolfish agency, which can be conceived as an ecology of affects or *affective arrangement*. The notion of affective arrangement, which takes a relational approach to affects in their situatedness, allows for "zooming-in on local constellations of elements that give rise to specific relational domains of affecting and being affected".[17] Wolfish affective agency is thus not to be understood here as a simple causal chain between wolfish subjects and human objects, in which wolves as 'first movers' act unilaterally on humans. It expands and transcends any intended goal of action; it always has more than measurable (material) effects. It unfolds through mere corporeal presence as well as in the execution of an action. And it has a lasting effect. Ultimately, it is also about understanding the conditions of coexistence itself as an affective arrangement in which all actors are involved before, during, and after the individual encounters that make up this coexistence.

The term affective arrangement also takes into account the dynamic, unfinished, and unstable nature of affects. Thus, we need to consider the opposing tendencies of affective arrangements to either consolidate into more stable and enduring patterns or to dissolve or transform into something else. Moreover, wolves produce different intensities of affect (a wolf sighting has a different and usually less intense affect than a sheep killed by a wolf). There are also changing thresholds of intensity to consider (as people become accustomed to sightings, the single sighting loses its affective impact). These intensities can also produce polycentric networks of relationships, that is, instead of a uniform wolf territory, we can expect several affective 'hotspots'. Finally, we need to take into account the heterogeneous composition of the affective arrangement, which usually includes a multiplicity of agents who—although increasingly enmeshed in a wolfish arrangement—lead their own lives in a multiplicity of other arrangements.

---

17   Slaby, Jan/Mühlhoff, Rainer/Wüschner, Philipp: Affective Arrangements, p. 5.

How the wolves returned to the Westerwald

The Westerwald was wolf country for centuries before the last wolves were shot in the nineteenth century.[18] After an absence of more than a hundred years, the first unconfirmed sightings of (presumably migrating) wolves occurred in 2010. A year later, another wandering wolf was hit and slightly injured in a traffic accident near Gießen – not far from the Westerwald. DNA testing of the blood on the car revealed that the wolf was from the Alpine population and was therefore named Pierre-Luigi. The injured wolf was seen several times after the accident and appeared to move further into the Westerwald, where it was filmed in the Neuwied district in February 2012 and subsequently became known in the media as the 'Westerwald wolf'.

Then, in April, hikers found a dead wolf near Hartenfels—shot.[19] Pierre-Luigi had been killed illegally, and the National Hunting Association offered a bounty of €1000 (plus a further €3000 from a private individual) to find the poacher. Two days later, an elderly hunter went to the police, admitted the crime and explained that he had mistaken the wolf for a stray German shepherd. A judge imposed a fine of 2500 euros, which the accused hunter refused to pay. As a result, the case went to trial in December – the first time anyone in Germany has been tried for the illegal killing of a wolf. The hunter was fined 3500 euros but appealed. In the second trial, the case was dismissed on the condition that the defendant pay 3500 euros and surrender his hunting

---

18   The retired Westerwald zoologist Dr Frank Wörner has compiled a lot of useful information on the history of wolves in the Westerwald until 2019. I am very grateful for his work and many insightful conversations with him. See Wörner, Frank: Wölfe im Westerwald: Verfolgt bis in die Gegenwart—Ein Plädoyer für Akzeptanz, Tierpark Niederfischbach e.V., Niederfischbach 2013; Wörner, Frank: Rheinland-Pfalz erwartet den Wolf: Ein Management soll das Zusammenleben regeln, Tierpark Niederfischbach e.V., Niederfischbach 2015; Wörner, Frank: Neues vom Wolf im Westerwald: Notizen zu Wolfsnachweisen 2016 bis 2019, Tierpark Niederfischbach e.V., Niederfischbach 2019, Wörner, Frank: 10 Jahre Wölfe im Westerwald: Notizen zu einer umstrittenen Rückkehr—Eine Zwischenbilanz 2011–2021, Tierpark Niederfischbach e.V ., Niederfischbach 2021.

19   Rumours said that the circumstances of the find were considered highly suspicious, as the wolf had died in very difficult terrain and had been found by someone from Cologne and not by a local. This fuelled the rumour that this wolf was not a 'wild' wolf, but one that had been kept in captivity (i.e. marked) and released. After all, it had probably already been seen several times and showed no signs of shyness (interview, district hunting master, 18.02.2020).

licence and weapons (which he accepted). Pierre-Luigi was taxidermised and put on display at the Natural History Museum in the state capital, Mainz.

According to a press release from the State Ministry of Environment, Energy, Food, and Forestry (MUEEF; today: Ministry for Climate Protection, Environment, Energy, and Mobility, MKUEM), the whole incident showed that proper wolf management was needed in Rhineland-Palatinate.[20] The minister at the time, Ulrike Höfken, invited representatives of affected groups (shepherds, hunters, conservationists) to a round table to draw up the state's first wolf management plan. She explained that the wolf could come to Rhineland-Palatinate in the foreseeable future: "This would be an enrichment for our biodiversity. The wolf can live in peaceful coexistence with humans".[21] After two years of debate, the final plan was presented in February 2015. Although not a single wolf had been sighted in the meantime, the ministry felt prepared with the management framework now in place.

And indeed, it did not take long for the wolves to return. From 2016, the wolf presence in the Neuwied district became more dense. On two nights in September, five sheep were killed. A dead deer was found, killed by the same female wolf. A wolf was also photographed in September, and again a year later in November 2017. However, this evidence did not prove a permanent wolf presence in the area. No wolf was yet considered resident, nor was there a pack – as far as was known.

But that was to change in 2018. On 13 May 2018, a local forester photographed a female wolf on the Stegskopf military training area near Daaden in the eastern part of the Westerwald. Wolf GW1072f[22] was photographed several times in the following months, and scat was found and analysed. By this time, wolf traces (both sightings and kills) had accumulated in various areas of the region. In addition to the Stegskopf wolf, there were several wolf kills in the Neuwied district (a fallow deer from a game enclosure, a red deer, a roe deer). The wolves could no longer be ignored, and in May 2018, the ministry officially declared the Westerwald a wolf prevention area, i.e. a potential wolf

---

20   "Ministerin Ulrike Höfken begrüßt Urteil zum Wolfsschützen", https://mkuem.rlp.de/
      de/pressemeldungen/detail/news/News/detail/ministerin-ulrike-hoefken-begruesst
      -urteil-zum-wolfsschuetzen/?no_cache=1&cHash=d31ed411576ce8e28ea2b155842a42
      18 (accessed: 18.06.2022, no longer available, translated by TG).

21   Ibid.

22   Wolves in Germany are named after genetic identification by a consecutive number, together with the abbreviation GW for grey wolf and followed by f (female) or m (male).

territory where herd protection measures are reimbursed. Almost a year later, in April 2019, the Stegskopf finally became the first wolf territory in Rhineland-Palatinate after a urine sample from January was identified as belonging to the same wolf as the scat found in the previous months. After January, however, there were no more traces of this wolf, and people began to wonder about her whereabouts.

Figure 13: The first resident wolf in the Westerwald, the female GW1072f.

Source: Research Institute of Forest Ecology and Forestry (FAWF)

Nevertheless, the ministry organised a regional wolf conference in August 2019 in Hachenburg, in the centre of the Westerwald region, to inform the public and bring together various concerned groups for discussion. Presentations were given by various experts, followed by three workshops to discuss the impact on society, hunting, and livestock farming. [23]

While the Stegskopf wolf had not been seen for more than six months at the time of the conference, the wolf presence in the Neuwied district was becoming more and more established. In May, three sheep were killed by wolves near Dürrholz-Muscheid. In October, six sheep were killed near Rheinbrohl, a week later one sheep near Oberirsen-Rimbach, and two weeks after that two sheep

---

23   I will return to this conference in more detail in Chapter 6.

near Sankt Katherinen. The regional newspaper *Rhein-Zeitung* reported: "Clear wolf traces in the Westerwald"[24] and "Hunters are sure: A wolf pack lives in the municipality".[25] Yet, for the ministry, the only wolf territory in the Westerwald was on the Stegskopf and not in the Neuwied district.

When the public radio station Südwestrundfunk (SWR) hosted a live panel discussion on the wolf in Daaden on 21 November 2019, it became clear that official knowledge and local knowledge differed in their respective assessments of the wolf situation. During the audience discussion, a hunter stood up and remarked:

[HUNTER:] We just had a case down here on the Rhine during a driven hunt. There were nine wolves. It's proven that there were nine. And one of them came within ten metres of a hunter and didn't run away. Only when the hunter waved his arms and shouted did he slowly move away. That is not normal. [...]

[MODERATOR:] Now I have to ask. That just happened?

[HUNTER:] Yes, during the hunt of X.

[MODERATOR:] And you are sure that not [...], that it was not just one and the same animal seen nine times?

[HUNTER:] No, that is absolutely clear [...].

[MODERATOR:] This is sensational news.[26]

What had happened? The following WhatsApp message circulated in the regional hunting community a few days earlier:

Dear colleagues, over the weekend I was told of 9 wolf encounters during the hunts of the Earl of X, Baron Y, Z etc., which were confirmed at the same time in different places. One wolf approached a hunter up to 10m without shyness and could only be frightened away by shouting loudly, but only crept away slowly. X, Y and others have been confirming a full pack for several months through sightings and photos! Despite this, the official authorities believe

---

24   Rhein-Zeitung from 05.11.2019.
25   Rhein-Zeitung from 15.11.2019.
26   SWR panel discussion, Daaden, 21.11.2019, author's minutes.

that there is only one female wolf! We hunters are not doing ourselves any favours by withholding the sightings and photos, which only serves to hide the presence of so many wolves and hence affords no pressure to act! Please, please, please collect scat samples in plastic bags and give them on to the large carnivore officers. Then they won't enter your hunting grounds, if that's your concern! Farmers, shepherds, livestock owners and hunters are now on high alert and we will only achieve the necessary pressure to act when the total number of wolves is officially confirmed! At the moment, whole populations of wild boar are congregating near villages and towns and avoiding the forests. In Bad Hönningen they are already roaming the streets at night, as I was told today! I don't even want to talk about the difficulty of hunting our game. Please convey this to all hunters in your region![27]

The district hunting master of Neuwied started to gather the hunters and asked them to cooperate in the monitoring, arguing that as 'professional experts' they should be involved in the monitoring measures. He organised a hunting contact person for each Large Carnivore Officer (LCO) in order to reduce the 'inhibitions' of hunters to cooperate with wolf management representatives and to increase the 'transparency' of the management processes by involving the hunters.[28] While one LCO welcomed the idea and saw her work made easier by working with the district hunting master, another LCO was more sceptical. He saw it as yet another attempt to influence wolf management in order to incorporate the concerns of hunters. Relations between hunters and LCOs had generally been tense up until then. In the words of one LCO: "We LCOs were frowned upon in hunter circles. This may be due to the fact that two of the three responsible LCOs in the area are also NABU Wolf Ambassadors.[29] The hunters did not like that at all". [30]

---

27   WhatsApp message, received 19.11.2019.

28   Interview, District Hunting Master Neuwied, 18.02.2020.

29   NABU is one of the most established nature conservation organisations in Germany. Its wolf ambassadors are volunteers who do educational outreach work. Wolf sceptics often use 'NABU' as a disparaging acronym for 'wolf friends' in general.

30   Interview, LCO 1, 11.05.2020. Until then, local hunters were quite reluctant to participate in monitoring. There was a general mistrust towards the official wolf management (as too wolf-friendly and in league with conservationists), which was also fed by an earlier incident. A hunter had contacted a LCO because of a suspected wolf attack on a deer. According to his own information, the LCO took a genetic sample, but was also urged by the hunter to take the whole carcass. Although this is not actually the intended approach, he finally agreed, but left the carcass in the forest due to lack of

A meeting was held with the head of large carnivore monitoring, regional LCOs, and local hunters and farmers. When I reconstructed the meeting with one of the participants some time later, he said that people in the area were generally concerned about the presence of wolves. One owner of a riding centre (who is also a hunter) had feared that horse owners would stop renting his stables for fear of riding in wolf territory or turning a horse out to pasture where it might be at risk. This seemed to put his whole financial future on the line. A cattle farmer feared that his animals might escape if they were attacked by wolves. His cattle could be killed or injured by wolves or cause a road accident with cars or motorcycles if driven off their pasture by fear of approaching wolves. He had noticed a sharp increase in such incidents since the wolves had been in the area (whether they were actually caused by wolves or not, he could not say for sure). Sometimes the mere presence of wolves seemed to change the behaviour of his animals, he reflected. When they came back to the barn to feed, he would sometimes see them pacing restlessly, eating a bit and then going back again—as if wolves were somewhere nearby. And the part-time sheep farmer (who had already experienced an attack on his flock once before and is also a hunter) was generally sceptical and unhappy because, in his eyes, the wolves were making animal husbandry impossible.[31]

By the time of this meeting in December, the district hunting master's appeal for cooperation seemed to have been successful. Several photos, videos, and scat samples were suddenly submitted, including a photo of a female wolf with five pups taken in August. After several months of processing and verifying the new evidence, the ministry officially recognised the first pack in Rhineland-Palatinate in February 2020. In addition, the parents of the pack (GW914f and GW1159m) were retrospectively recognised as a resident pair for the previous monitoring year 2018–19.

---

cooling facilities and called the Forest Ecology and Forestry Research Institute (FAFW) to pick it up the next morning. By then, however, another hunter had found the carcass, and since then the story has been doing the rounds that the LCO deliberately wanted to conceal evidence of the presence of wolves. Subsequently, the LCO was repeatedly confronted with this story at public events and the hunters have distrusted it ever since (as well as the entire wolf management). Interview, LCO 2, 08.11.2019.

31   Interview, livestock farmers and hunters, 03.02.2020.

Figure 14: Wolves of the Feldkirchener Wald/Neuwied Pack.

Source: Research Institute of Forest Ecology and Forestry (FAWF)/private source

In other words, the wolves had been living in the area for at least two years without anyone noticing. Not quite, because local residents had known about them for some time. The district hunting master reflected on the last few months before the Neuwied Pack was officially recognised:

[HUNTER:] And then suddenly two (wolves) were seen, and in Mainz they [the ministry] still claimed that there was only one wolf, at the Stegskopf [...]. That's when the hunters got really upset. Not just the hunters, but the whole community here. Even though I talked to people who have nothing to do with hunting. [...] That the state government denied that there were wolves here or only admitted the one in the Westerwald [...].

[INTERVIEWER:] How did people know about the wolves? I suppose they hadn't seen any wolves themselves?

[HUNTER:] At the time it was in the press [...], even when my photo was taken [...], they still claimed [...], even two months ago [...], they still claimed there were only one or two wolves [...]. The people on the ground are saying, the state government, the Greens, the minister, they don't want to admit that we have wolves here [...]. Although we all know it by now, by word of mouth. There are walkers in Rheinbrohl and in Bad Hönningen, they go for walks. There are wives of local councillors who have encountered a wolf in broad daylight [...].

[INTERVIEWER:] Yes?

[HUNTER:] Yes, yes, of course. They were too scared to go into the forest anymore. The mayor of Bad Hönningen told me that there are councillors' wives who don't go for walks in the forest anymore. [...] They are all afraid.[32]

In the same area, a local professional hunter (and several other hunters) had also noticed the presence of wolves for at least two years. Not only did he see wolves every few months when he was hunting from a raised hunting blind, but he also found carcasses of game animals that had probably been killed by wolves. He noticed that red deer calves were becoming rarer; that red deer were less active during the day; that red deer were moving right up to the outskirts of the village; that red deer herds had become larger, as had the wild boar sounders; that wild boar had become more aggressive towards hunting dogs, resulting in more dogs being injured during the big driven hunts; that the roe deer had become very cautious, almost invisible. By now he had learned to read the signs of when wolves were moving through (and when they were leaving) his hunting district by observing the changing behaviour of his game.[33]

Then the COVID epidemic started and suddenly wolves became less of an issue for most people. For example, a local mayor (of Hammerstein) in the wolf territory told me: "No, I haven't noticed that people here are worried about the presence of wolves. And frankly, we have other things [the epidemic] to worry about now." But he had heard about one wolf encounter from the wife of the local councillor in Rheinbrohl. His godmother, who knew an acquaintance of this woman, passed on a message about it through social media channels.[34]

As public activities were severely restricted during the lockdown in the spring of 2020, many people went for walks in the local woods. Older people were out and about, alone or in pairs, with and without dogs, and there were riders on horses, mountain bikers, young families with prams. The woods

---

32   Interview, District Hunting Master Neuwied, 18.02.2020.
33   Interview, professional hunter, 27.04.2020.
34   Interview, Mayor of Hammerstein. 08.06.2020.

seemed to be full of people, especially on sunny weekends. The mayor of Hammerstein was happy to see so many people out walking all year round, and he could not see that the wolves had either reduced or increased the number of hikers. Everyone I met on my regular walks through the wolf area was aware that they were in a wolf area, but none had ever seen or otherwise noticed a wolf. Yes, some had seen photos or videos circulating on Facebook or WhatsApp groups. No, the dog walkers were not worried about their dogs. After all, they weren't moving far from them, I was told more than once.

One day a group of three elderly people sitting on a bench right in the heart of the wolf territory noticed me searching the ground on the path. After I told them I was looking for wolf scat, as a lot had been found in the area, we started talking about wolves. They told me that they were local people who regularly walked in this part of the forest. One of the men said it didn't bother him at all that there were wolves here; he went into the forest anyway. "But didn't you stop walking for a while when it came out?" the lady sitting next to him interjected. "Well, yes, but only for a short while", he replied apologetically, slightly embarrassed. He had simply not been sure whether wolves were dangerous at the time, so he had done his research first and only returned to the forest when he was sure that wolves were not dangerous.

When I returned from another field trip to Lusatia in June, my first impression was that things had become a little quieter in the Westerwald. I remembered that I had not yet introduced myself to the new conservation officer at the ministry and decided to give her a call. I told her about my research and mentioned the exciting developments in the Westerwald with the new pack. But her response was hesitant. We couldn't be sure that there was still a pack, she told me. There had been stories circulating recently about possible illegal wolf kills in the area. And no one had reported any signs of wolves in recent months. "What kind of stories?" I said. I hadn't heard anything like that. Everything had seemed fine before I went to Lusatia. I had regularly found wolf scat and no evidence that anything was wrong. I wanted to investigate.

A few phone calls to my various informants later, the situation became clearer. Someone had contacted NABU on the evening of 10 April 2020 because he had noticed a disturbance in a flock of sheep near Neuwied (close to where a wolf had been filmed by a hiker two weeks earlier). Shortly afterwards, two or three shots were fired. When I later asked the shepherd later what had happened, he told me that a hunter had indeed seen a wolf. But he could not say whether the shots were related to the sighting, he could not say. Since NABU was not responsible for further investigations, they first forwarded the email to the Nature and Environment Foundation (SNU). As they were not responsible either, they forwarded the email to the Research Institute for Forest Ecology and Forestry (FAFW). From there, a local LCO was informed.[35] But nothing could be found out. There was no evidence and no clear indication that an illegal killing had taken place, he told me. Due to a sports injury, he had not been actively searching for wolf tracks, which explained why no evidence of wolf presence had been found recently. At the end of June, another informant sent me a photograph of what appeared to be a wolf pup from the core area of the wolf territory. As I was not sure whether this photo was private or had been passed on to the official monitoring agency, I was not allowed to pass it on. Yet I took it as a sign that the pack was still there and had even reproduced.

On the other side of the Rhine, in the Hunsrück region, a wolf killed a sheep on the night of 1 May 2020. The next day, a shepherd in nearby Boppard-Uden-hausen decided to replace the fence for her seven sheep with a wolf-proof bar-rier. The sheep that was killed was less than 20 kilometres away, so her sheep were within range of this wolf. It did not bother her that there was a whole pack of wolves 50 kilometres away near Neuwied, because the Rhine was considered a border that the wolves were unlikely to cross. But now there was a wolf in her area. Moreover, her neighbour (who later joined our conversation) claimed to have recently heard a wolf howling in the nearby village of Hünenfeld. Then there was a video of a wolf recorded by a hunter near Halsenbach, less than ten kilometres away. And when we met in mid-June, the shepherdess told me that a dead deer, possibly killed by a wolf, had been found a few days earlier near the next village, Buchholz. I mentioned that a local forester had told me the day before that the first month of the roe deer season had been exceptionally diffi-cult. Compared to previous years, far fewer roe deer had been shot and hardly any had been seen. This was highly unusual. When I mentioned this, the shep-herdess's sister remarked that, strangely enough, she too had also seen very few roe deer over the past month or two on her daily walk around the village with her dog. Normally she saw them regularly.[36]

---

35   This information comes from several emails from 16.04.2020 to 24.04.2020. The report of the alleged illegal killing of a wolf never went public (presumably because there was no evidence) but was subsequently discussed internally among the LCOs as events unfolded over the coming months.

36   Interview, shepherdess and sister, 18.06.2020.

So, while it was clear that a lot was happening at the time, it was uncertain what exactly was going on.[37] At the end of June, however, a new hotspot emerged in the Hunsrück, temporarily diverting attention from the Westerwald pack. After a series of alleged wolf attacks near Emmelshausen, local livestock farmers had organised themselves in a WhatsApp group to exchange information about wolves in the region and to find out "how we can continue to keep our animals on pasture without living in constant fear of the wolf".[38] They were planning a public lecture in the village of Niedert, with a shepherd known as a radical wolf opponent billed as the evening's 'wolf expert', followed by a bonfire (and a barbecue). According to a member of the official wolf management agency, no wolf management representative wanted to go because it was considered 'counterproductive' to appear at a time of high emotion. Wolf advocates disagreed, as evidenced by an email I received shortly before the event:

> Next Saturday X, you know him, is going to give a lecture [...] in Niedert (near Emmelshausen/Hunsrück). Mr X is rhetorically gifted, but he is a self-confessed wolf hater and he knows how to twist facts and present them in such a way that someone who is not familiar with the subject will fall for his abstruse representations. When facts are lacking, he is quick to make them up. When he speaks uninhibitedly in front of what is a probably a rather uniform audience, his ideas are extremely dangerous for the cause of the wolves. I would have loved to go, but for family reasons I cannot. It would be nice if some of you (especially GzSdW members[39]) could go there and bring some objectivity and above all FACTS to what is sure to be a heated discussion.[40]

More than eighty farmers and a few hunters were present that evening (and no GzSdW members). It was not the mixed crowd one usually finds at such events. At the entrance I mentioned that I was also a hunter, and this was well noted: "Ah, then you are practically in the same boat as us. You are also affected by the wolf." The mood that evening was subdued and uneasy, perhaps a little angry, but not defiant. The speaker lived up to his reputation and gave a rousing speech (see Chapter 6), but the reaction of the audience was more sober.

---

37   "Noch kein Beleg für die Rückkehr des Wolfs", in: Rhein-Zeitung from 03.07.2020.
38   Press information of the organisers, n.d.
39   Society for the Protection of Wolves (GzSdW), one of the oldest and largest wolf protection organisations in Germany.
40   Email from a local GzSdW member, 30.06.2020.

"Couldn't the Farmers' Union do something?" was the first comment after a period of awkward silence when the speaker had ended his talk with a call to arms. And the planned bonfire and barbecue turned out to be just a barbecue.

Eventually, all the alleged wolf kills near Emmelshausen that had led to this meeting turned out not to be caused by wolves, and the situation calmed down (but, doubts remained: hadn't the wolf expert explained that evening that the official DNA tests could not be trusted because there was a monopoly of a single laboratory that was in league with the wolf management?).[41] Two months later, however, a wolf (later identified as GW1554m) attacked livestock in the Bitburg-Prüm district of the Eifel region (north of the Hunsrück and west of the Westerwald). One calf and three sheep were killed in four attacks within ten days. Again, a public meeting was organised, but this time by wolf management officials and with the participation of various experts, from shepherds to conservationists to politicians, "mainly to give the local people an opportunity to voice their fears, concerns, and needs". Despite this, FDP member of state parliament Marco Weber and farmer president Michael Horper publicly called for the 'removal' (the killing) of 'Billy' (the new name for this wolf).[42]

But back to the Westerwald: After the unofficial photo of a pup in the territory of the Neuwied pack, there was no further news. But since March there had been regular indications in the form of scat and photos of a wolf (or several?) in the Altenkirchen district of the Westerwald, not too far from the Neuwied pack's territory. As it turned out, one of these photos, taken in June, even showed a female wolf with swollen teats (GW1415f), which the ministry took as evidence of reproduction. In other words, there was now a second pack in the Westerwald! There was also a photo of a wolf (the same one?) with two pups, so the pack was officially recognised in July.

Curiously, signs of the adult male wolf from the Neuwied Pack were found in the new pack's territory from June onwards. He even killed two sheep there in mid-July.[43] What was he doing there? Could he be the father of the new pack's pups? Had something happened to his mate from his pack? Had she perhaps been killed in the April incident after all? One LCO began to speculate, but the situation was unclear.

---

41   "DNA-Analyse zeigt: Kälber im Hunsrück wurden nicht vom Wolf gerissen", in: Rhein-Zeitung of 15.07.2020.

42   "Naturschützer fordern: Kein Bumm für Wolf Billy", in: Rhein-Zeitung of 12/09/2020.

43   "Wolf aus Kreis Neuwied hat Schafe gerissen", in: Rhein-Zeitung of 10.08.2020.

A local resident expressed his displeasure with the wolf situation in a letter to the *Rhein-Zeitung*:

> How many wolves can our region take? Once packs have formed and are roaming through our forests, who can be safe? Neither animals nor humans? Or do we have to wait until a pack of wolves, starved for days, attack a human being? [...] What benefit and what enrichment is there in this enormous potential danger for us and our native environment?[44]

Even a local Westerwald member of parliament from the conservative CDU party (who had already been recommended to me by hunters and livestock farmers as someone with 'reasonable views' on wolves), called for a change in wolf policy. Presumably summarising all the incidents from the Westerwald, Eifel, and Hunsrück, Erwin Rüddel issued a press release calling for action in the face of increasing problems with wolves in the region:

> Hardly a day goes by without a report in the local press about wolves and wolf attacks on livestock in the Neuwied and Altenkirchen districts. The wolf population is growing by 30 per cent a year, the packs are getting bigger, and there are more and more wolves and packs also in our region. Therefore, it is time for rational politics instead of wolf romanticism.

He saw not only a problem for farm animals; it was 'only a matter of time' before people themselves feel threatened and wolves are seen near or even inside settlements. Rüddel finally proposed a rigorous management regime, including the killing of problem wolves and even the establishment of wolf-free zones.[45]

In the neighbouring Siebengebirge region of North Rhine-Westphalia (to the north of the Neuwied Pack's territory and to the west of the Leuscheider Wald Pack's territory), livestock owners applauded Rüddel's proposals at an 'Open Pasture Day' in September.[46] He and some politicians from the liberal FDP party had understood the threat posed by wolves. The invitation to the event mentioned the wolf as one of several problems facing livestock farmers today: the radical decline of both sheep and shepherds over the last twenty

---

44 "Enormes Gefährdungspotential" (letter to the editor), in: Rhein-Zeitung of 24.07.2020.

45 "Immer mehr Wölfe—und trotzdem 'weiter so'?", in: Blick Aktuell from 17.08.2020.

46 "Lammflüsterer zwischen Idylle und Existenzsorgen", in: Rhein-Zeitung from 10.09.2020.

to thirty years, the near extinction of old regional sheep breeds, the costs of animal health and welfare, and the economic challenges (prices for animal products, fencing, etc.). But on the day itself, the wolf dominated many of the conversations. Local politicians and journalists were listening. A representative of the Society for the Protection of Wolves was present (which was welcomed by the shepherds, although it did not dispel their doubts about the wolf). But not a single person from the official wolf management agency "dared to show up", said one livestock farmer, adding, "as was to be expected". Farmers were becoming increasingly concerned about the two packs in the area and the disturbing images of the 'Schermbeck incident' further north. A video circulating on social media channels, filmed through the window of a house, showed two wolves chasing and attacking a deer in a field just beyond the garden fence.[47] This video was used as further evidence of the scale of the threat posed by wolves.

In Rhineland-Palatinate, a tenth Round Table was organised by the ministry in October.[48] Due to the incidents caused by wolf Billy, the Eifel was declared a new wolf prevention area. It was also agreed that the regulations for dealing with problem wolves would have to be revised.[49] The latest press release from the ministry (October 2020) reported that the first pack in the Westerwald, the Neuwied Pack, had disbanded for unknown reasons. Only the adult male wolf, GW1159m, appeared to remain, but he was now officially recognised as the lead wolf of the Leuscheider Wald Pack—now the only pack in Rhineland-Palatinate.[50]

---

47   "Experten bestätigen Video: Wölfe haben Hirsch in Hünxe angegriffen", in: Dorstener Zeitung from 15.04.2020.

48   I had actually asked to be allowed to participate in this event. However, I was told that no 'outsiders' were wanted, especially in view of the elections coming up next year. Not for the first time during my fieldwork, I had the impression that I encountered reservations about my research because I was someone who 'made things public'. I learnt from one of my research participants that my name had recently come up at another management meeting where someone asked how much I could be told, as I was not part of wolf management.

49   "Griese: Wolf-Präventionsgebiet 'Eifel-West' kommt", MUEEF press release, 06.10. 2020, https://mueef.rlp.de/de/pressemeldungen/detail/news/News/detail/griese-wo lf-praeventionsgebiet-eifel-west-kommt/?no_cache=1&cHash=88065029cd9fbcd528 772ef668e7c7c1 (accessed: 18.06.2022, no longer available).

50   "Umweltministerium informiert: Totes Tier an B8 bei Rettersen vermutlich Wolfswelpe", 23.10.2020, https://mueef.rlp.de/de/pressemeldungen/detail/news/News/detail /umweltministerium-informiert-totes-tier-an-b8-bei-rettersen-vermutlich-wolfswel

Wolf agency in affective arrangements

Let's leave the story of the wolves' return to the Westerwald at this point and see what it tells us about wolfish affect and agency. So what did the wolves do to make the Westerwald a wolf territory? They wandered around the Wester-wald and neighbouring regions; some of them decided to stay and 'settle down'; some of them got together and became a pair; two pairs (albeit perhaps with the same male wolf?) bred and became a pack/family; one of these packs prob-ably ceased to exist, as something may have happened to the female wolf; they marked their territory with their scat; they killed wild animals, such as deer; they killed livestock, such as sheep, a calf and fallow deer.

How did people respond to these wolves and their actions? How were they affected? They carried out monitoring activities, looked for scat, took genetic samples and set up camera traps; they started political processes of wolf man-agement, including round tables, conferences and public lectures; shepherds started to increase the protection of their animals, building new fences or im-proving old ones, integrating dogs into herds; Some people stopped going into the forest, some started going again; pictures and videos circulated on social media channels; someone may have killed a wolf; some people had encounters with wolves, most did not; (some) hunters actively participated in the monitor-ing regime and tried to increase their influence on wolf management.

Summarised in this way, the story of the return of wolves to the Wester-wald is a typical one, as it contains all the elements of the return of wolves any-where in Germany (or indeed in any other country). A wolf biologist who has followed developments over the last twenty years commented that there is a certain tragedy in the eternal stories of conflict that play out year after year in each new wolf region. In this sense, I believe that the story of the Westerwald wolves has significance beyond the regional specifics.

One of the most important lessons of this story is that very little happens without the wolves doing something first. This is the quintessence of wolfish agency. It was not enough for the wolves to return to Germany. The wolves had to enter the territory of Rhineland-Palatinate for the agency to become active. If a wolf has decided to settle, a regional wolf conference is organised to inform local people and listen to their concerns and fears. If a wolf kills livestock, pub-lic events are organised to counteract the negative public outcry and shepherds

pe/?no_cache=1&cHash=12d3d7305504e4d6969fd161d5ca5338 (accessed: 18.06.2022, no longer available).

suddenly feel compelled to build a fence. If a wolf attacks livestock too often, politicians are forced to react and call for the wolf's removal and stricter management. When several wolves suddenly appear during a big hunt, hunters feel compelled to take action. This list could go on and on. What would be left of the story if we wrote it without individual wolves and their actions?

Wolf activity and agency is everywhere. Sometimes it is just one wolf that touches us, moves us, shakes us. A migrating wolf also has a different kind of affective impact than a resident wolf (though not necessarily a less intense one, as the kills of Billy the Eifel wolf have shown us). But migratory wolves come and go; resident wolves are here to stay, and people expect to be affected by them all the time (though even that may not always be the case, as the Stegskopf wolf showed; she disappeared shortly after being officially recognised as resident). Packs, on the other hand, have a different kind of agency. They multiply, and with them the wolf's presence and agency in the region multiplies. Shepherds suddenly find themselves surrounded by packs of wolves. But the presence of a large river might be enough to prevent wolves, even whole packs, from affecting you. Wolves in another region will affect you differently than those on your doorstep. But sometimes wolves from several regions combine in their affective impact, so that a politician feels a condensed wolf presence around him, with wolf kills every day, and decides that enough is enough. Finally, the agency of wolves as a species manifests itself in the form of expectations about the capabilities attributed to them. A man stops walking in the forest when he hears for the first time that wolves live there. He is a little afraid because he does not know what to expect and whether he is in danger. After all, you hear stories ... hunters believe that it is 'only a matter of time before something happens'.

Another lesson from this story is the variation in the intensities of wolfish affect. A wolf on the move, captured in a blurry image from a camera trap (and subsequently not classified as C1,[51] not officially recognised, and not published in the press), does not produce the same affect as a verified C1 image. An image, as a testimony of an encounter, perhaps shared through social media channels,

---

51   In scientific monitoring, wolf signs are classified according to the so-called SCALP criteria (Status and Conservation of the Alpine Lynx Population) into C1: clear evidence (e.g. dead wolf, genetic evidence, photo), C2: confirmed evidence (e.g. tracks or wolf kill), C3: unconfirmed evidence (e.g. visual observations without photo evidence), plus non-evaluable evidence and false observations. See Reinhardt, Ilka et al.: Standards for the monitoring of the Central European wolf population in Germany and Poland (= BfN-Skript 398), Bonn: Bundesamt für Naturschutz 2015.

accompanied by a personal narrative of the experience, may have more impact. If the image captures a close encounter with a wolf, for example by hunters out on a hunt, the affective impact may be even greater (with questions of 'proper', 'natural' behaviour and shyness immediately raised). The intensity of sightings or encounters is again different from the intensity of wolf kills. While the killing of wild animals mainly concerns hunters, the killing of livestock seems to concern not only the owners but also the local community. Indeed, livestock kills seem to be the driving affective force behind concern about the return of wolves to the Westerwald. But the example of the Schermbeck incident shows that the killing of wild animals on one's own doorstep is likely to be experienced no less intensely.

The videotaped incident in Schermbeck, which so upset visitors to the North Rhine-Westphalian 'Open Day', also shows us what I have previously called the polycentric web of relationships. The livestock farmer I spoke to that day felt affected by the presence of the Westerwald wolves, but also by other wolves living further away, but in the same federal state. The shepherdess in the Hunsrück did not feel affected by the Westerwald wolves, but by those in her Hunsrück region. The minister, on the other hand, was affected by everything that happened in her federal state. As we can see from these examples, the affective arrangement traced in the story of the return of the wolves to the Westerwald develops from different centres and forms ever new smaller arrangements, which – depending on the actions of the wolves and their affective intensities in the region – can solidify or fade away. These affective centres come and go with the movements of individual wolves, and consolidate as wolves become established in a region.

Taken together, these findings suggest that the affective arrangements of human-wolf coexistence in an emerging wolf region are highly precarious, dynamic and thus open. Even the establishment of a wolf territory does not seem to guarantee the consolidation of these arrangements, as the Stegskopf wolf soon disappeared, the Neuwied Pack (presumably) disappeared, and the adult wolf of the Neuwied Pack changed territory and probably established a new pack elsewhere. As we can see, even two years after the return of wolves to the Westerwald, the region is still an emerging (or even declining?) wolf territory whose development is far from complete. What has stabilised are the efforts of the wolf management regime to produce a wolf management plan, to establish a monitoring regime (now with the support of the hunters?), to formalise the designation of new wolf prevention areas, and to plan the concentration of the regime in a new wolf competence centre.[52] Many shepherds have stabilised their responses to wolf presences by investing in new fences and, in at least one case, in livestock guardian dogs. Hunters—as far as I can tell—have not changed their hunting practices. Nor have the local people made any significant changes to their daily practices in response to the wolves' presence.

The dynamic instability of the affective arrangement here goes hand in hand with a sense of uncertainty related to a lack of knowledge about the past, present, and possible future of one's region as wolf territory. What the American nature writer Barry Lopez wrote in the introduction to his classic book *Of Wolves and Men* still holds true today: "The truth is we know little about the wolf. What we know a good deal more about is what we imagine the wolf to be".[53] Even with wolf research projects and wolf monitoring regimes, wolves in Germany remain largely phantoms, 'haunting' their territories and only occasionally touching human lifeworlds, becoming visible and thus allowing their affective power to be felt, causing ripples through the affective arrangement.

The question is: Does this precarious state of affective arrangement ever stabilise? Will the feeling of insecurity ever fade? Will we ever know more about the lives of wolves once they have established themselves as long-term neighbours? And does their affective presence eventually give their territory an affective tone, something we might call a wolf atmosphere?

---

52   The new *Koordinationszentrum Luchs und Wolf*, founded in 2021.
53   Lopez, Barry H.: Of Wolves and Men, New York: Simon & Schuster 1995, p. 3.

Figure 15: *Wolf territories in Saxony in the monitoring year 2020–21, including the protagonists of Chapter 4, the Rosenthal pack (RT).*

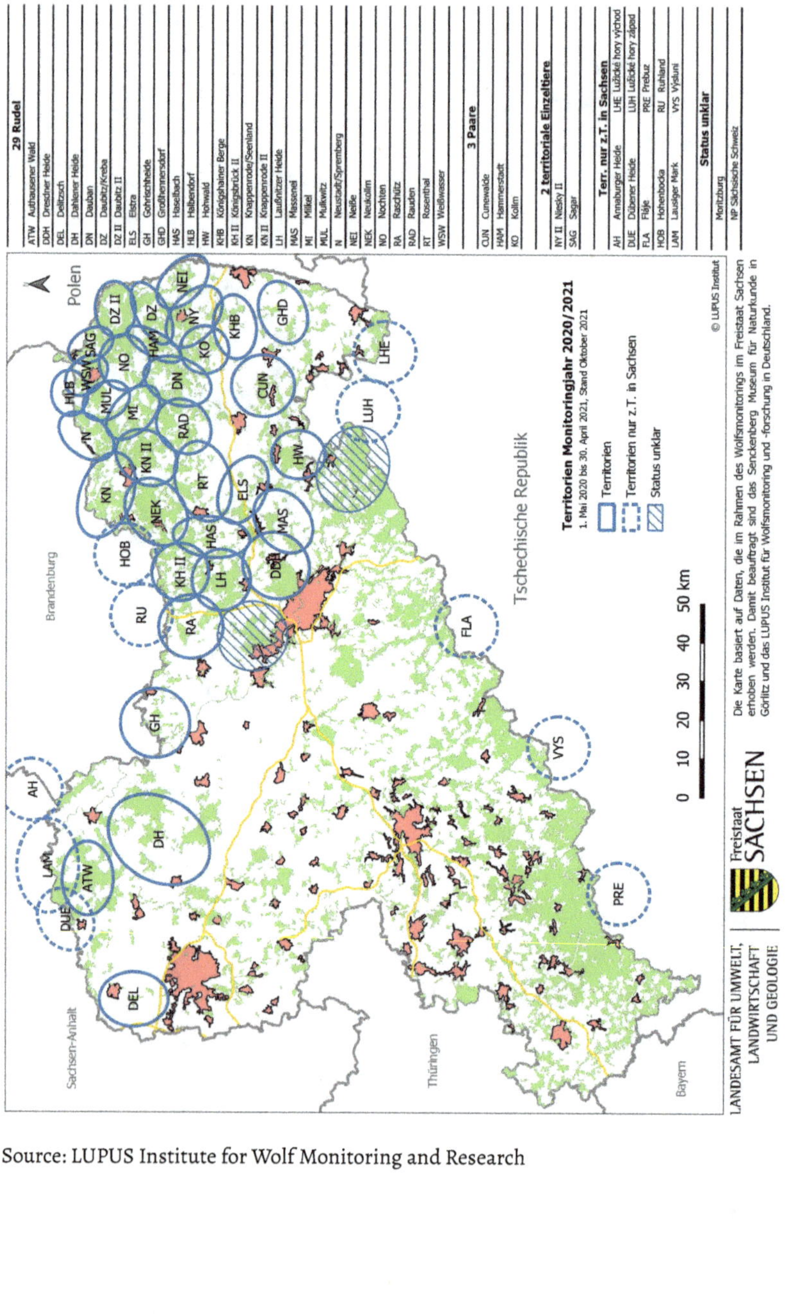

Source: LUPUS Institute for Wolf Monitoring and Research

4. Wolf Atmospheres

Wolf atmospheres and the ecology of fear

In the last chapter, I told the story of the wolves' return to the Westerwald in order to show how the coexistence of wolves and humans entangles both in affective arrangements. In particular, I was interested in tracing how wolves 'make things happen', both in terms of affects (presences and traces) and effects (material), and thus become visible as affective actors in the web of these arrangements. In doing so, I have drawn on the most basic definition of affect as a vital force that sets things in motion. We have also seen how these vital forces condense into ever denser presences, or fade away again, to eventually pass away. In this chapter, I further explore how certain affective dynamics can condense into a particular affective arrangement, which I call *wolf atmosphere*.[1]

Whereas my previous remarks on wolf agency were primarily concerned with wolfish actions and how they affect humans, the focus on atmospheres attempts to clarify the *felt* affective forces of wolves on their human and non-human co-inhabitants. An atmosphere is understood here as a precarious, dynamic, affectively charged structure that emanates from wolves, envelops their territory and thereby also emotionally colours the lives of the people who live there. But wolves are not the sole producers of atmospheres. Rather, their affective lives assemble a variety of elements (each with its own affective power) in an arrangement that includes other beings, materials, and material objects, as

1   See Lorimer, Jamie/Hodgetts, Timothy/Barua, Maan: 'Animals' atmospheres', in: Progress in Human Geography 43.1 (2019), pp. 26–45, https://doi.org/10.1177/0309132 517731254; Keil, Paul: 'Rank Atmospheres: The more-than-human scentspace and aesthetic of a pigdogging hunt', in: Australian Journal of Anthropology (2021), pp. 1–18, h ttps://doi.org/10.1111/taja.12382.

well as landscapes. As an "indeterminate, spatially effused quality of feeling",[2] atmospheres offer a way of thinking about how subjective emotional experiences emerge from larger intersubjective affective structures.

It is wolf atmospheres that wolf friends allude to when they talk about the thrill of being in a wolf territory and having the chance to meet wolves 'for real'; when wives of local councillors talk about being too scared to go into a wolf territory; when shepherds describe the distressed feeling of their flock after a wolf attack; when hunters try to find words for the queasy feeling they have when walking through a wolf territory with a freshly killed deer; when they talk about wild boars gathering in ever larger sounders out of fear; when they claim that it is only a matter of time before something happens; or, on the most general level, when people in the countryside talk about how they now have to live in fear now and how their whole lives have been changed by the mere presence of wolves.

Studying the lives of animals through their atmospheres may at first seem unusual. The field of human-animal studies became aware of this in the course of the affective turn in the humanities and social sciences. But natural scientists have also been concerned with the affective forces of animals, albeit not under the heading of 'atmosphere'. In behavioural ecology, researchers began to distinguish between 'lethal' and 'non-lethal' effects of predators on prey.[3] For decades, ecologists have studied the role of predators in regulating ecological systems. Predators are said to have 'density-mediating effects', meaning that they influence the mortality rate and thus the population size of the prey species. Ecosystems are thought to be regulated *top-down* by trophic levels. However, another approach argues that primary production and its effects on herbivores regulate ecosystems *bottom-up*, with predators having no significant influence. Recent studies further complicate ecological modelling by suggesting that top-down and bottom-up regulatory systems are intertwined and may overlap. So, the role of predators in the ecosystem is still a mystery.[4]

To complicate matters further, ecologists now also recognise non-lethal (behavioural) effects of prey predators on prey. The (not uncontroversial) hy-

---

2   Böhme, Gernot: Atmosphären. Essays zur neuen Ästhetik, Frankfurt a.M.: Suhrkamp 2013, p. 27, translated by TG.

3   For overviews of wolf-prey relations in general, see Mech, David/Peterson, R.: Wolf-prey relations, ; D. Mech/D. Smith/D. MacNulty: Wolves on the Hunt.

4   See Heurich, Marco: Die Rolle der großen Beutegreifer im Ökosystem, in: Ders. (ed.), Wolf, Luchs und Bär in der Kulturlandschaft, pp. 71–94.

pothesis here is that the mere presence of a prey predator has an effect (in the terminology of this book: affect) on prey animals in the environment. They live in an 'ecology of fear'.[5] Prey animals are thought to live a life in constant fear of becoming prey, to be constantly alert and on the lookout for predators, to avoid areas of high risk or spend little time there, to seek out areas of low risk or congregate in larger groups. In this model, fear is an existential emotion that keeps them alert and therefore alive. It permeates their environment and transforms it into 'landscapes of fear'. [6]

Interestingly, this behavioural ecology of the predator-prey relationships has been studied primarily in wolves. Several studies using wolves of Yellowstone National Park in the United States have investigated how prey species such as wapiti deer respond to the presence of wolves.[7] However, the results seem inconclusive in terms of clear top-down effects. Wolves and their prey do not appear to follow a standard behavioural protocol, but instead exhibit a variety of responses and behaviours. Studies of wolves in central Europe are sparse and similarly inconclusive.[8] There is also evidence that fear of humans overshadows fear of wolves in prey animals.[9] Finally, a study in Germany found

---

5   Brown, Joel S./Laundré, John W./Gurung, Mahesh: 'The ecology of fear: optimal foraging, game theory, and trophic interactions', in: Journal of Mammalogy 80.2 (1999), pp. 385–399, https://doi.org/10.2307/1383287.

6   Laundré, John W./Hernández, Lucina/Altendorf, Kelly B.: 'Wolves, elk, and bison: re-establishing the 'landscape of fear' in Yellowstone National Park, U.S.A', in: Canadian Journal of Zoology 79.8 (2001), pp. 1401–1409, https://doi.org/10.1139/z01-094.

7   Ibid; Creel, Scott et al.: 'Elk Alter Habitat Selection as an Antipredator Response to Wolves', in: Ecology 86.12 (2005), pp. 3387–3397, https://doi.org/10.1890/05-0032; White, P. J./Proffitt, Kelly M./Lemke, Thomas O.: 'Changes in Elk Distribution and Group Sizes after Wolf Restoration', in: The American Midland Naturalist 167.1 (2012), pp. 174–187, https://doi.org/10.1674/0003-0031-167.1.174.

8   Kuijper, Dries P. et al.: 'Landscape of fear in Europe: Wolves affect spatial patterns of ungulate browsing in Białowieża Primeval Forest, Poland', in: Ecography 36.12 (2013), pp. 1263–1275, https://doi.org/10.1111/j.1600-0587.2013.00266.x; Kuijper, Dries P. et al.: 'Context dependence of risk effects: Wolves and tree logs create patches of fear in an old-growth forest', in: Behavioral Ecology 26.6 (2015), pp. 1558–1568, https://doi.org/10.1093/beheco/arv107; Theuerkauf, Jörn/Rouys, Sophie: 'Habitat selection by ungulates in relation to predation risk by wolves and humans in the Białowieża Forest, Poland', in: Forest Ecology and Management 256.6 (2008), pp. 1325–1332, https://doi.org/10.1016/j.foreco.2008.06.030.

9   Zbyryt Adam et al.: 'Do wild ungulates experience higher stress with humans than with large carnivores?', in: Behavioral Ecology 29.1 (2018), pp. 19–30, https://doi.org/10.1093/beheco/arx142.

that wolves themselves show signs of fear of humans, as they seem to avoid roads and other anthropogenic structures in the landscape.[10]

As we can see, a broader view of an ecology of fear can operate in several dimensions: from animal predator to animal prey, from human predator to animal prey-predator (wolves), from human predator to animal prey (deer) and perhaps even from animal predator (wolves) to human prey.[11] This last dimension in particular is often used by those who are sceptical about wolves (see Chapter 5). Although there has not been a single incident of human harm in Germany since the return of wolves, some people seem to be alarmed or at least unsettled by the sheer possibility.[12] And wherever wolves appear, wolf sceptics claim that they turn the place into what could be called a landscape of fear.

In this chapter, I examine in detail one of the most prominent examples of such a landscape of fear, using the concept of animal atmosphere to unravel the complexity of the socio-ecological relationships involved. How can the wolf atmosphere be described? What emotions are involved? What or who contributes to the atmosphere? Is it stable or dynamic? If it is dynamic, what influences its transformations and intensities?

We are investigating these questions in the municipality of Ralbitz-Rosenthal in Saxony, home to the Rosenthal Pack,[13] which is led by a female named Marie. Ralbitz-Rosenthal consists of ten villages with about 1750 inhabitants in rural Lusatia. The majority of the inhabitants are Germans with a (Catholic)

---

10   Reinhardt, Ilka/Kluth, Gesa: Untersuchungen zum Raum-Zeitverhalten und zur Abwanderung von Wölfen in Sachsen. Final report project 'Wanderwolf' (2012–2014), commissioned by the Saxon State Ministry for the Environment and Agriculture (SMUL), 2015.

11   J. Soentgen: Ökologie der Angst.

12   See the classic review of wolf attacks on humans compiled by Linnell, John et al: The fear of wolves: A review of wolf attacks on humans, NINA Oppdragsmelding 731, Trondheim: Norsk institutt for naturforskning 2002, https://www.nina.no/archive/nina/pp pbasepdf/oppdragsmelding/731. pdf (accessed 30.04.2024) or the new edition Linnell, John D./Kovtun, Ekaterina/Rouart, Ive: Wolf attacks on humans: an update for 2002–2020.pdf (accessed: 30.04.2024) or the new edition Linnell, John D./Kovtun, Ekaterina/Rouart, Ive: Wolf attacks on humans: an update for 2002–2020. NINA Report 1944. Trondheim: Norwegian Institute for Nature Research 2021, https://brage.nina.n o/nina-xmlui/handle/11250/2729772 (accessed: 30.04.2024).

13   The "exceptional wolves of Rosenthal", as one of the most popular German hunting magazines, Jäger (25.09.2015), called them, https://www.jaegermagazin.de/jagd-a ktuell/woelfe-in-deutschland/die-ausnahmewoelfe-von-rosenthal/ (accessed: 30.04. 2024).

Serbian identity (a long-established Slavic minority that has lived in this region for more than a thousand years). Like much of Lusatia, few people work in agriculture these days, instead earning their living in nearby urban centres and the energy industry. In general, however, Rosenthal can be described as a fairly prosperous community with a strong rural identity. It has become known both in the region and throughout Germany as a hotspot of anti-wolf activism and for a wolf pack that has probably killed more sheep than any other pack in Germany. So, it is an extreme and illustrative example, but hardly a typical one. Nevertheless, the Rosenthal case shows us aspects of wolf atmospheres that are regularly found elsewhere, albeit less intensively.

The purpose of this chapter is also to look more closely at wolf sceptics, their arguments and their experiences. Here we immerse ourselves in the lifeworld and worldview of people critical of wolves and try to perceive and understand human-wolf conflicts from their perspective. The story of Rosenthal and the Rosenthal Pack presented here can therefore be read as a particular narrative construction of events and experiences that aims to explore above all the affective dimensions of the conflict. However, this story does not simply repeat the views of the local activists; it also introduces other views that confront, challenge, or contradict their views, thus creating a multi-voiced ethnographic account that pays attention not only to the human-wolf dimension of the conflict, but also to social conflicts. In other words, one could also say that here I consider both conflicts with wolves and conflicts about wolves equally.

However, for the sake of understanding the wolf-critical lifeworld, I also leave out things that are important for a public debate about that very lifeworld. For example, I leave out the question of whether the concerns and fears expressed are in any way 'justified', the dangers 'probable', the proposed solutions 'feasible'. I also leave out the question of whether the views of the wolf critics are representative of 'the people of Rosenthal' or 'the people of Lusatia'. The petition they initiated, which was signed by more than 16,000 people, most of them from Rosenthal and Lusatia in general, suggests that the wolf critics speak for many people in and around Rosenthal. But it is impossible to judge whether those who signed wanted to send a signal against the wolves or in solidarity with the shepherds, who are their neighbours, relatives, and acquaintances. Be that as it may, many questions of representation remain: Who represents whom, for what and with what means?

Figure 16: The female wolf Marie/FT7

Source: André Klingenberger

Figure 17: The Rosenthal Pack

Source: André Klingenberger

Rosenthal, Lusatia: a landscape of fear?

Figure 18: Sheep on a pasture in Rosenthal the day after a wolf attack

Source: Author

As part of a study on space use and movement patterns of wolves,[14] a one-year-old female wolf from the Milkel Pack, hereafter called FT7, GW112f or Marie, was captured in May 2012 and tagged with a GPS transmitting collar. Weighing only 27 kilograms, the researchers described her as small and delicate. Although she was quite mature, Marie preferred to stay with her parent pack during her second year of life, only occasionally venturing out of her territory for a day to explore the world outside. In 2013—aged around 22 months—she was still with her pack and must have become pregnant. But there was no sign of her offspring, so it was thought that her first cubs had not survived.

A short time later, however, Marie appeared to have taken the step of moving away from her family and establishing her own territory, bordering her original territory to the southwest. She had found a partner who came over from Poland (GW294m) and settled in the Rosenthal area. Why there? A resident of Rosenthal commented:

---

14   I. Reinhardt/G. Kluth: Untersuchungen zum Raum-Zeitverhalten und zur Abwanderung von Wölfen in Sachsen.

[ROSENTHAL ACTIVIST:] These are all the meadows of the monastery, all along the Klosterwasser stream, from the village of Panschwitz down, which were leased. This was paradise on earth for the wolves, of course. At that time, in 2013, when the Rosenthal Pack arrived here, there were four large flocks of sheep, really large flocks of sheep [...].

[INTERVIEWER:] So several hundred [sheep]?

[ROSENTHAL ACTIVIST:] Exactly, he [the wolf] didn't need to go to the forest anymore, he had everything here and it was like paradise.[15]

Marie continued to visit her parents until her collar fell off prematurely in November 2013. The following year, Marie gave birth to five pups and the Rosenthal Pack was born. By this time, the wolves were already attracting attention. They attacked local sheep flocks six times in 2013 (officially classified as three C1 and three C3) and seventeen times in 2014 (six C1 and eleven C3).[16] Marie probably knew sheep as prey from her first two years in the Milkel Pack (which was responsible for seven attacks in 2012 and six in 2011 after her birth in May).

For the local shepherds and residents, this was a worrying new situation that soon caused problems:

[ROSENTHAL ACTIVIST:] X [a local shepherd] had previously secured everything with a solid fence, even before the wolves came, and he thought that would work and, well, maybe they learned there, I don't know, they all learned there, the wolves and the shepherds. But then it went blow by blow, which quickly led to a huge resentment. People, it wasn't just the people affected, but the whole population took part [in the resentment] because we had all seen, heard, and read about it, and then it was sold to us as a situation that we had to get used to. This is unacceptable [...].

[ROSENTHAL ACTIVIST:] ... [We were told that] Saxony would manage with five or six packs. That would be possible and then we'll see. But then it

---

15   Interview, Rosenthal activist, 04.08.2020.

16   Marie's first attempts to attack sheep involved breeching a chain-link fence, climbing over it the first time (100 cm) and digging under it the second time. In 2014, she noticed and killed sheep tied with chains six times. In GDR times, it was common for people to keep one or two sheep for meat. These were usually chained to a post next to the house. This practice can still be found sporadically in Lusatia, also in the wolf area.

got really dynamic. Then there were twelve, then eighteen, and when the question was asked, how many packs will we have in Saxony at some point, what is the goal, nobody gave us an answer.[17]

The wolf atmosphere of Rosenthal thus began with a cascade of violent interventions by Marie and her pack into the affective fabric of a local lifeworld—the domestic sphere where everyday life is lived, where routines give shape to a *Heimat* ('home') to which people belong, a place that is known, trusted, and feels familiar, an extension of one's self, family, and relationships. This lifeworld is their *home*, an area that local people have shaped over the centuries into a cultural landscape of their own order and control. It is a species-rich landscape where domesticated farm animals have their place alongside their human owners and wild animals live in the surrounding forests under the stewardship of local hunters. The romantic vein of this German concept of *Heimat* is obvious, as are the idyllic undertones that evoke a certain social aesthetic.[18] In other words, although the concept of *Heimat* can be understood as part of people's worldview, in the context of wolf atmospheres we should better understand it as a certain place-based attitude to life, *a felt quality of existence and a sense of place*. What wolves violate in the eyes of wolf critics is this sense of home, which should be a safe place and should also feel 'homey'.

Marie's intrusion was experienced all the more violently as it went "blow by blow". One resident spoke in this context of the *Schlagzahl* ('stroke count') of the attacks, a term normally used in reference to the rhythm of machines. With each attack, the wolves established themselves step by step and became part of this local lifeworld, which was transformed into a wolf territory—whether the people wanted it or not. The *Heimat* became 'wolfish', as people had to adjust to hitherto unknown and unfamiliar feelings caused by the wolf presence. In contrast to the situation in the Westerwald described in Chapter 3, the people of Rosenthal experienced several years of continuous wolf incidents in their immediate vicinity. As one of the local activists said, they were all in a fix together, not just the shepherds, but all the locals, as both the affective impact and the material consequences were felt by all. As Rosenthal is also a close-knit community, everyone was affected in some way by the wolf attacks and could easily sympathise with the shepherds. Whereas in the Westerwald it was possible to

---

17   Interview, Rosenthal activist and hunter, 04.08.2020.
18   On the concept of social aesthetics, see MacDougall, David: The Corporeal Image. Film, Ethnography, and the Senses, Princeton University Press 2005.

ignore the various wolf presences if one wished to do so, in Rosenthal it was almost impossible to escape from one's lifeworld-turned-wolf territory.

At the centre of this territory were the sheep and their pastures—many of them around the villages. A wolf atmosphere could only develop at this early stage because Rosenthal was a multispecies lifeworld in which sheep formed the nexus for both the human-sheep relationship and the wolf-sheep relationship. And both relationships are ultimately about the death of sheep, as they are primarily a source of food for both humans and wolves. However, there are significant atmospheric differences in the quality of death. The killing of sheep by humans is an orderly affair, it occurs in appropriate places at pre-planned times, it is brought about by professionals, performed using technology, and leads (ideally) to a clean and certain, and thus presumably painless, death.[19] In a way, then, it could be argued that this kind of orderly killing of sheep does not necessarily disrupt the social aesthetics of the home with its familiar sensibilities. But wolf kills are different, as this young woman from Rosenthal told me:

> Well, I haven't actually seen a wolf kill sheep, but a dead sheep, yes, here in Rosenthal [...] well, I know that from Dad, he's a hunter, I know it when an animal is dead. But it's different again if it was from a wolf, when parts are missing, just torn out, that's somehow different [...].[20]

One could argue then that in contrast to human 'virtuous' hunters, wolves are experienced here as 'vicious' hunters: hunting without a moral code, and with cruel results.[21] An animal killed by a wolf is not called a *Riss* ('rip' or 'tear') in German for no reason. The word refers to the wolf's method of hunting, killing and eating, which is characterised not only by a suffocating bite to the throat, but also by tearing open the abdomen and ripping pieces of flesh or a leg from the animal's body. As one shepherd put it, a wolf kill site can look like the scene of a bomb blast, with body parts lying all over the place. Wounded animals with their bellies ripped open, intestines hanging out, or pieces of flesh torn out are also familiar sights to affected shepherds (including in Rosenthal). This is

---

19   Marvin, Garry: 'Wild Killing: Contesting the Animal in Hunting', in: The Animal Studies Group (ed.), Killing Animals, Chicago: University of Illinois Press 2006.

20   Interview, Rosenthal activist, 04.08.2020.

21   This is a distinction made by Plato originally, cited in Scruton, Roger: The Sacred Pursuit: Reflections on the Literature on Hunting, in: Nathan Kowalsky (ed). Hunting Philosophy for Everyone: In Search of the Wild Life, Oxford: Blackwells 2010, pp. 187–197.

what I call the *necroaesthetics* of a wolf kill, a particular multisensory, visceral, material and atmospheric experience of human observers in the presence of death.

All this may be a natural way for a predator to kill. But compared to the social aesthetics of everyday life in Rosenthal, where one can easily ignore the deaths of animals, or at least be sure that everything is going according to a pre-conceived and ethically convincing plan, the necroaesthetics of the *Riss* seems like a shock, *an affective rupture of local sensibilities*. Not only do the wolves make the deaths of animals visible and public, but they do so in places normally re-served for everyday routine activities such as walking, playing, and meeting people. *Risse* also come suddenly and unexpectedly. Since wolves usually hunt at night or at dusk, humans hardly ever have the chance to witness the actual act of killing. It is the *affective traces*, the material and atmospheric results of a kill that can then be found and affect those present. These material remains (sometimes together with what appear to us to be cruelly injured animals) are often anything but the result of a 'proper' killing. *Risse* are *hot kills*, expressions of an *affective wildness* that does not belong to the habitual lifeworld of humans and can be experienced as highly disturbing as they seem 'out of control'.

The affective power of *Risse* and the atmosphere they evoke must there-fore be seen as informed by wider cultural sensibilities and practices around the killing of animals. As Garry Marvin has pointed out, the killing of animals has largely disappeared from view, making it easier to ignore animal suffer-ing, pain, and death, especially as both the keeping and killing of animals has become mechanised and industrialised.[22] Even in the countryside, as in Lusa-tia, but also in other regions of Germany, the death of animals has long since ceased to be part of people's lifeworld. It is not only the average urban popula-tion, which is supposedly alienated from nature (as wolf sceptics often claim), that has hardly any experience with the death of animals. The same is true for most rural people who—apart from hunters and farmers—generally have little to do with the killing of animals. Against this background, the question of the 'naturalness' of a killing becomes an issue and can lead to a necroaesthetic that some find shocking, disturbing, and threatening.

***

---

22   Marvin, Garry: Wild Killing, pp. 10–29.

By the 2013–14 monitoring year, there were ten packs in Saxony, and the first forms of resistance were already being organised. Hunters were the first to protest against the return of the wolves. The Saxon state government tried to appease them by officially declaring the wolf a (huntable) game species in 2011 (albeit with a year-round closed season, as it remained under nature conservation protection). But this change in the law gave hunters—at least in theory—some say in wolf matters, especially to be involved in wolf monitoring and to initiate cooperation between wolf management and hunters. The Saxon State Hunting Association (LJV) appeared to be placated at this point and its protests against wolves dwindled. However, a group of around sixty hunters split from the LJV to form the *Freie Jägerschaft Wittichenau*, which has since taken a more radical stance against wolves. Shortly after the split, the LJV Saxony also stepped up its opposition to the wolf again, and its Wolf Action Group, led by the LJV's Wolf Commissioner, launched a petition, "Our native wildlife asks for your help", which collected around 9,000 signatures.

This petition followed directly on from the first petition organised by shepherds, "Shepherds ask for help", which ran from September 2012 to January 2013 and also gathered almost 9000 signatures. It drew attention to the shepherds' existential fears and their new financial burdens and called for regulated wolf hunting. Although all these previous forms of protest did not seem to have any immediate impact on the wolf management, they did contribute to a steadily heating up debate, which culminated in two applications for the 'lethal removal' of wolves from the Rosenthal Pack by the *Landrat* (district councillor) of Bautzen in 2016. Both applications were rejected.[23] Hunters and anti-wolf activists became increasingly frustrated and refused to cooperate with the wolf management regime.

After another sixteen (eight C1 and eight C3) attacks on livestock by the Rosenthal Pack in 2015 and eleven (nine C1 and two C3) in 2016, the local population became increasingly angry. The district administration organised a wolf symposium in Cunnewitz to address local protests, but the event further escalated the situation. Local activists recall how condescendingly they were treated by the 'wolf managers' that day, and how the event was 'infiltrated' by wolf advocates who tried to stifle any negative comments about wolves and booed anyone who reported the 'facts' of the Rosenthal Pack's attacks. So,

---

23   "Vorerst kein Wolfs-Abschuss", in: Sächsische.de from 18.10.2017, https://www.saechsische.de/vorerst-kein-wolfs-abschuss-3797820.html (accessed: 18.06.2022, no longer available).

a group of local hunters decided to launch a new petition to intensify their protest. This time they collected more than 16,000 signatures and delivered the petition to the Saxon parliament in January 2018.

Previously, in October 2017, after two wolf attacks on sheep flocks near Laske and Cunnewitz and at the official request of the Landrat, the Saxon Ministry for the Environment and Agriculture (SMUL) had finally granted permission to shoot a wolf from the Rosenthal Pack:

> One or more wolves have apparently learnt in recent weeks to overcome the recommended protective measures (electric fence and flutter tape) that are reasonable for the sheep farmers. This means that the conditions are now in place for the wolf to be removed. In order to avert further major economic damage, the removal of the wolves is justified and necessary, despite the strict protection of wolves that still exists in principle, as there are no other alternatives for the protection of livestock that are reasonable for livestock farmers.[24]

Conservationists were furious at the decision. The *Grüne Liga Sachsen* (a coalition of several conservation organisations) and the animal rights activists of *Wolfsschutz Deutschland e.V.* were successful in an urgent appeal against the permit. In addition, activists from *Wolfsschutz Deutschland* came to Rosenthal from all over Germany to check that the fencing was correct and to hold 'night watches' to protect the pack.[25] As one local hunter/activist described it:

> I remember very well when we had all these attacks two years ago, militant wolf protectors came here, I think one came from Frankfurt and others from Hamburg, and then they drove around here in their cars, drove around with torches, lit up the meadows and brought a lot of unrest. Some of them walked through Ralbitz with posters, trying to provoke the residents. But they weren't provoked. [...] It was all very strange. And a great anecdote was that X [a local shepherd] had his sheep up here in a meadow, there was a paddock, and the flock had not been there for two days, and the wolf protectors

---

24   "Staatsministerium für Umwelt und Landwirtschaft erteilt Einvernehmen zur Ausnahmegenehmigung des Landratsamtes Bautzen zur Entnahme eines Wolfes", press release of SMUL/Landkreis Bautzen, 27.10.2017, https://www.medienservice.sachsen.de/medien/news/214194 (accessed: 30.04.2024).

25   "Große Exklusivreportage: Faktencheck und Zaunkontrollen in Sachsen", Wolfsschutz Deutschland e.V., 02.07.2021, https://wolfsschutz-deutschland.de/tag/rosenthaler-rudel/ (accessed: 30.04.2024).

went to these fences, touched them and said that there was no electricity on them, so the wolves could jump in. And they didn't say that the sheep were no longer there, that they were in another paddock. Then they took a nice photo. We all just grinned [...].[26]

But the wolf advocates were certain that the local shepherds had not fenced their pastures properly, and suspected that they were deliberately attracting the wolves to an "unacceptable fast-food offer". And they were not alone in this opinion. I had often heard this suspicion expressed by wolf advocates in the region, that the Rosenthal shepherds were provoking the removal of the pack. Even the SMUL admitted in its press release that the reasons for the wolves' success in killing sheep in Rosenthal was at least partly due to the inadequacy of the fences:

> Why did the wolves in the area of the Rosenthal Pack behave differently? The situation of the Rosenthal Pack differs from other packs in that these wolves were repeatedly able to prey on unprotected sheep (tethered) or on sheep that were not protected as recommended (behind fixed fences). This has resulted in a learning effect which has led to repeated killing of protected animals.[27]

Following the rejection of an application for the lethal removal of a wolf, four regional organisations joined forces and wrote the 'Bautzen Declaration'[28] to the Saxon parliament.[29] The association *Sicherheit und Artenschutz*, the *Initiative Wolfsgeschädigter und besorgte Bürger*, the *Freie Jägerschaft Wittichenau* and the *LJV Sachsen*[30] declared Saxony's wolf management a failure. They demanded,

---

26   Interview, Rosenthal Activist/Hunter, 04.08.2020.

27   "Staatsministerium für Umwelt und Landwirtschaft erteilt Einvernehmen zur Ausnahmegenehmigung des Landratsamtes Bautzen zur Entnahme eines Wolfes", press release of SMUL/Landkreis Bautzen, 27.10.2017, https://www.medienservice.sachsen.de/medien/news/214194 (accessed: 30.04.2024).

28   http://woelfeindeutschland.de/aus-der-gruft-die-bautzener-erklaerung/ (accessed: 30.04.2024).

29   The initiative was mainly due to the four people who head these organisations. All of them are hunters and at least three of them have been actively campaigning against wolves for several years.

30   According to the late wildlife biologist and wolf expert Ulrich Wotschikowsky, the 'Bautzen Declaration' was signed by the LJV President without prior consultation, which (among other reasons) led to the resignation of the President a few weeks af-

among other things, that wolf management be replaced by a more comprehensive wildlife management (led by hunters), that wolves be hunted, and that
wolves only be allowed only in designated wolf areas. And although the statement had received some media attention, there was no reaction from Parliament.

It is clear from these episodes that wolf atmospheres and their dynamics need
to be disentangled, for they are neither monolithic nor stable, but complex,
fragile, ambivalent and constantly evolving. Although I have spoken of a wolf
atmosphere as an atmosphere that develops around wolves, the wolves are
not the only actors contributing to it. We have seen above how the particular
necroaesthetics of wolf kills are central to understanding conflicts with wolves
in Rosenthal. However, we must not forget the many other human actors
involved in social conflicts over wolves. In Rosenthal, an ongoing conflict with
wolves is the driving force. However, I argue that conflicts with wolves have
a tendency to shift to social conflicts about wolves because local people are
limited and regulated in their ability to engage directly with legally protected
wolves. They are allowed to engage indirectly (e.g. through improved fencing)
but not directly (e.g. by chasing or hunting wolves). In terms of the affective
qualities of the wolf atmosphere, this means that the wolf atmosphere is fed
not only by the irritation of people's sense of home through feelings of shock,
horror and threat, but also by a sense of powerlessness among local people –
of being unable to act and react, of not being in control, of lacking self-efficacy
in the face of the wolf.

These feelings are accompanied at the same time by anger at those who
are held responsible for their powerlessness: the wolf management regime as
a whole and its supporters. This shifts the human-wolf conflict into a social
conflict between humans, and thus takes on additional dimensions. To use a
Gestalt metaphor[31], the Rosenthal Pack continues to sting by attacking in the

---

ter the declaration became known. The wolf had caused controversy in the LJV for
years. See Ulrich Wotschikowsky, "Aus der Gruft: die Bautzener Erklärung—aktuali-
siert", Wolfsite. Forum Isegrim, 16.02.2018. http://woelfeindeutschland.de/aus-der-g
ruft-die-bautzener-erklaerung/ (accessed: 30.04.2024).

31   What is meant here is the concept of gestalt from the gestalt-theoretical psychology
of perception, according to which the visual field is divided into a figure (object), a
foreground and a background. The recognition of an object here is not the perception
of an isolated figure, but of an overall context of a figure in front of a background, i.e.
an organised gestalt.

background, while the humans turn their attention to other, human figures in the foreground, engaging in social arenas far removed from the immediacy of their now shared human-wolf lifeworlds at home. Indeed, the engagement of locals in wolf affairs is characterised by a constant shift between foreground and background events and actors, giving the dynamics of the wolf atmosphere an axis around which it can continue to revolve.

This *atmospheric axis* can be further differentiated along two human dimensions, one vertical and one horizontal. The vertical axis refers to conflicts upwards within a social hierarchy. Local people are confronted with the main actors and institutions of wolf management such as the state parliament, ministries, non-governmental institutions such as the Senckenberg Institute (for genetic research), and intermediaries such as regional politicians. The great imbalance of power vis-à-vis these actors fosters the above-mentioned feelings of incapacitation, helplessness, and powerlessness, combined with anger. This constellation of feelings is further confronted by affective interventions from a horizontal axis: other actors within civil society, mainly pro-wolf organisations such as the *Grüne Liga Sachsen* or *Wolfsschutz Deutschland*. These pro-wolf organisations are not officially part of the wolf management regime, but wolf critics consider them to be 'in league' with the regime, as they presumably share the same value of wolf conservation.[32]

The affective qualities of the conflict along the two axes are different. Apart from mediating figures such as the wolf kill assessor, the institutionalised wolf management regime seems far removed from the local lifeworld and faceless; there is no clear target of anger, only a general direction. The pro-wolf organisations, on the other hand, are usually perceived as citizens like themselves; local people become aware of them not only through court cases but also through local events such as the one in Cunnewitz or the activities of *Wolfsschutz Deutschland* in Rosenthal. When they talk about public events, wolf critics in Rosenthal (but also elsewhere) are usually less upset about the treatment of management representatives than about the heated arguments with wolf advocates. While management representatives are usually seen as one-sided, but at least quite rational and moderate in their arguments, wolf

---

32   I have also often encountered confusion among wolf sceptics who mistakenly assumed that some nature conservation organisation is part of wolf management. This distinction seems to be irrelevant in their eyes, as both wolf management institutions and conservation organisations are supposedly working towards similar goals, the reintroduction of wolves to Germany.

advocates are seen as highly emotional, irrational and radical in their aims. While it is possible to try to negotiate with official management (e.g. through petitions and requests for lethal removal), it seems impossible to reach an agreement with *Wolfskuschler* (wolf cuddlers), as wolf advocates are often called in wolf-critical circles.

Finally, the early episodes of events in Rosenthal also show how the dynamics of wolf atmospheres oscillate between consolidation and disintegration. In order to motivate local people to remain engaged in protest, it is not only necessary to have continuous wolf attacks, but also a reasonably stable social organisation of protest. Initially, local people joined forces with anti-wolf movements in other parts of Saxony. It is important to note that both early petitions were embedded in already existing organisations and networks of individual interest groups (of shepherds and hunters). The issue of wolves could thus be linked to other issues of these interest groups and their problems and challenges in today's society. In this way, conflicts with wolves can be linked to conflicts about wolves.

As well as taking part in national protests, anti-wolf activists in Rosenthal have tried to organise local forms of protest, whether by setting up a new hunting association, launching a new petition, or demanding the lethal removal of wolves from the Rosenthal Pack. Although conflicts over wolves and other issues are often presented as expressions of social struggles, such as the perceived opposition between rural and urban areas, the local protests always revolved around Marie and the Rosenthal Pack in particular. This then led to demands for a review of wolf management in general, but always with the view that such a review should change the wolf situation in the immediate lifeworld of Rosenthal and the neighbouring communities.

We can therefore conclude that the temporal stability and consolidation of the wolf atmosphere in Rosenthal depended on the continuous renewal of a certain affective arrangement through a series of wolf attacks and the formation of organised protest. The wolf atmosphere fed off these formations, motivating people's engagement, and they in turn brought new affective qualities to the wolf atmosphere centred on the conflict with the Rosenthal Pack, thereby transforming it. While the particular atmosphere after a wolf attack are quite unstable and can quickly dissipate as the carcasses are removed and the attack is forgotten for a while, organised protest keeps these atmospheres alive and 'dicey' between attacks by retelling and discursively restaging them within their own local community and beyond.

***

A few months later, in July 2018, a new incident further aggravated the situation in and around Rosenthal. In the early hours of the morning, a wolf chased fallow deer through the village of Cunnewitz until a deer crashed into a fence and died there. When the residents woke up and went outside, the wolf ran away.[33] An activist from a neighbouring village remembers the day:

> Then there was this beautiful story in Cunnewitz. In terms of organisation, everything that could go wrong did go wrong. People had called the police, reported everything, while the carcasses were lying around in the sun, two of them about to burst because it was so hot that day. Then a hunter came and removed them. [...] When I was there on Monday, the Landrat was on holiday, neither the reporting chain nor the chain of action worked, not even the game warden was there, nothing. Even the police had no idea what to do after all these years. And I was really interested in how it [the wolf] could run into this village, it was right in the middle of it, it attacked the deer, and how the deer – in its distress – ran here and there, over all the fences, and knocked down a small iron fence [...] where some grandchildren had just camped a few days before. And this fallow deer ran over this fence and would have hit the tent and if the children had been lying there, well, they would have been injured up to their hips. And there was this grandfather, he was in shock, raging and screaming, people were upset [...] they had been up since five in the morning, and they had only heard rumours and screams, and nobody knew what had happened. It was tense. And some people think that kind of thing is normal. The end of the story is that nobody – at least in this village – lets their children camp outside anymore. And that is sad. Because we don't have electric fences that are two metres high, and of course we assume that wolves come through the village at night [...]. Since the wolves have been here, I would never let my grandchildren go out alone, even though they are at the age of five or six – it's just over. And it's so sad. You take away a little bit of freedom from these village children. [...] There is always this feeling of is there something [a wolf] or is there nothing. [...] You have this idea in your head, you can't deny it. And that has nothing to do with Little Red Riding Hood [...].[34]

---

33   "Wolf hetzt Damhirsch mitten in Dorf in den Tod", in: Nordkurier from 31.07.2018.

34   Interview, Rosenthal activist, 04.08.2020.

A month later, Rosenthal's municipal council submitted an application to the Saxon state government to declare Rosenthal a 'wolf regulation zone': "In recent years, many sheep have been killed in the municipality, farmers and shepherds have suffered damage. Most recently, wolves killed fallow deer in the village of Cunnewitz".[35] In the resolution, the municipal council called for the legal protection of wolves to be reduced, for regular hunting of wolves to be allowed, for the wolf population to be reduced, for hunters and livestock owners to be allowed to kill wolves that attack animals, and for wolf reserves to be created outside the municipality. But all these demands were rejected. This did not come as a surprise, as an open statement by the Rosenthal shepherds about the incident suggests:

> In the end, when the Wolf Office was dealing with this case, it became clear to us here in the villages that we were rather a disturbing factor for this institution of the Free State of Saxony. When we finally got hold of someone there, they said they were not responsible. No domestic animals were affected.[36]

By the time the Cunnewitz incident happened, the local population had had several years' experience of wolf attacks on sheep. And although each attack came as a surprise, the people knew they had to expect attacks sooner or later. They were now part of a lifeworld that had become wolf territory. Nevertheless, this event was unexpected and shocking and created an even more tense atmosphere than usual, coupled with concern and anger. What was different this time was that the wolves were not hunting and killing on the outskirts of the village – nor in the woods where they would normally find fallow deer – but right in the middle of Rosenthal's lifeworld, even literally crossing a boundary by coming over the garden fence and into the innermost circle of the home. Normally people (apart from hunters) don't seem to care that much about wolves killing wild animals. But because it happened in a 'domestic' area reserved for humans, the incident suddenly became relevant. *Its necroaesthetics produced what I would call an affective fusion: people realised that it was possible to become 'prey' in this domestic realm*, independently of their own species. Whether the possibility of

---

35   Resolution of the Rosenthal Municipal Council, No. 26–08/2018, 30.08.2018.

36   "Weidetierrisse und kein Ende—Erklärung der Rosenthaler Schäfer", Wolfszone, http ://www.wolfszone.de/01home/000main/texte/rosenthaler%20Sch%C3%A4fer.html (accessed: 30.04.2024).

being attacked by wolves is real or likely for humans is another matter. What is important in this context is that *the sense of potentially being-prey, the sense of one's own vulnerability*, was suddenly given a material reality by the dead body of a fallow deer.

Like the concern of the activist quoted earlier in this chapter, who saw the number of packs increasing and could not imagine where it would all end, the wolf atmosphere feeds on the real and the virtual. *What concerns people is not just what happened there and then, but what could happen or has happened to other people at other times and in other places. It is not just about the Rosenthal Pack, but about the pack as a representative of a species. In terms of affect, everything that 'the wolf' has ever done and is capable of doing becomes a potential for the Rosenthal Pack.* And as the activist in the quote above said, you don't need fairy tales to fire the imagination (as is often claimed by environmental educators who want to combat wolf tales and myths by confronting them with scientific facts). One only needs to consult relevant Facebook groups such as 'Landleben oder Wolf', which provides daily updates on wolves from around the world – including gruesome stories, pictures and videos. It cannot be stressed enough that wolf critics do not usually argue on the basis of fictional stories about wolves. They draw on a wide range of incidents – from the (online) media, from social media sites – and relate them to 'the wolf' in general, as well as to the wolves they have to deal with specifically. Marie and the Rosenthal Pack are thus seen as capable of committing all these atrocities, and it is this potential capacity that frightens some. "There is always this feeling", the activist said. This time it was a fallow deer. But could it be me next, or my grandchild? If I had been here at the wrong time, would they have hunted me? What if …? We see how rational thoughts about possible futures become inextricably intertwined with affects.

***

Meanwhile, wolf attacks on sheep continued. In 2018, four confirmed (C1) and another seven unconfirmed (C3) attacks were counted; in 2019, another seven confirmed (C1) and ten unconfirmed (C3) attacks were counted. The shepherds affected were almost always the same. One was particularly badly affected. Having lost three sheep in 2018, his flock was attacked three more times in 2019. In July, he lost thirty-six sheep in one night. They had broken out of their fences during a thunderstorm and were easy prey for the wolves. In September, he lost another three sheep in a pasture that was protected by an electric fence but not by a fence along the river. A month later I had the opportunity to see the results of another attack.

The events can be reconstructed as follows: In the darkness of the early morning hours, when everyone was asleep, the wolves came across the fields near the village, swam through the Klosterwasser stream and attacked the flock from the unsecured side. The first two sheep were killed, and the rest panicked and ran through the fence, then along the road into the village, the wolves following. On the way, they bit the right hind leg of one sheep, ripping out a large chunk of flesh, skin and wool, and their prey eventually managed to escape into a carport next to a house. Back in the pasture, the wolves killed another sheep and tried to drag it down the stream. But the sheep's wool was soaked with water and became so heavy that they had to leave it dead in the stream before disappearing back into the darkness.

At 6.30am, the shepherd received a call from the owner of the carport, who told him about the injured sheep and the others wandering in the road. When the shepherd arrived and saw what had happened, he called the *Fachstelle Wolf*. A wolf kill expert was sent to investigate and write a report. I arrived at the scene with her at 10:00. We drove to the farm where the shepherd's wife was waiting with her two Border Collies and the injured sheep on a trailer, still in shock and looking rather listless. She was waiting for the vet; her husband was on his way to get a machine to pick up the carcass and remove it from the pasture. The shepherd's wife accompanied us to the pasture and showed us the dead sheep. As we approached, we could see that the rest of the flock was still frightened and huddled in a corner, watching us. The dogs were running around, chasing away a group of ravens who were tampering with one of the carcasses, screeching loudly as they flew away. There were shreds of wool all over the grass, here was the rumen, there were red intestines stretched across the ground like threads. The carcass was ripped open, partially eaten. Lots of flies had settled on it or were buzzing around it. Exposed to the hot October sun that day, it had already begun to smell of decay.

We continued across the pasture to get an overview of the situation. In the stream that ran along the unfenced long side of the pasture, we saw a sheep lying in the water between the water plants. The shepherd's wife barely spoke. Neither did the wolf kill expert, who tried to show both professional demeanour and compassion. "Can I borrow some (disposable-) rubber gloves for me and my husband? [...] I'll bring them back, I promise. Cleaned, of course." The shepherd's wife tried to inject some humour. "Or I'll just put them on the bill", the wolf kill expert joked in return. But apart from these moments, the silence and the presence of the carcasses created a tense and sad atmosphere. The wolf kill expert began taking photographs and measuring the wolf's bite marks on the sheep's throat; I assisted. The shepherd's wife spoke to a local man and his child who had come to the fence to ask what had happened. Meanwhile, the shepherd drove up to the pasture, ready to remove the carcasses. He was even more taciturn than his wife, and in some ways seemed as listless as the injured sheep in the yard. It was the third time this year that they had gone through such a procedure.

Still, I could not understand why, after all they had been through, they had not fenced off the entire side of the stream, more than 100 metres. Under these circumstances, they would not even receive compensation. But when I asked the shepherd, he showed little reaction. Over there (he pointed to some sheep in another pasture across the stream) the wolves had killed one sheep and injured another just three nights before. They were well fenced, but the wolves still managed to get in. So what was the point of fencing properly, then?

After documenting the carcasses and the fencing, we returned to the farm while the shepherd started to remove the carcasses. At the farm we filled in the necessary forms (as this was not the first incident, most of the information could be taken from previous documents). "Is this about fences or animals?" the shepherd's wife remarked, shaking her head in disbelief at the forms. "I don't understand it. I just don't get it". Two men and a little boy in his big electric toy car came over to comfort the shepherd's wife. I told the shepherd's wife that maybe the boy didn't want to see all this. But she replied that children of that age were not that bothered by such sights. And they would hear about it anyway. News gets around. The wolf kill expert thought this was the right time to leave and we said goodbye. Although the situation was not threatening in any way, she was always cautious. There had been another incident here before where a large group of angry locals had turned up and the situation had become uncomfortable for her. People had started to get angry with her and make derogatory remarks about her in Serbian (assuming she wouldn't understand). They only stopped when she replied in Serbian and then someone recognised her and told the others that she was a local.

We got back in the car and drove back to the *Fachstelle Wolf* at the SMUL near the state capital of Dresden. There was a sense of resignation and hopelessness in the air that day. A month later, the shepherd decided to give up.

Figure 19-21: *The necro-aesthetic of a wolf attack: a sheep injured in the hind leg, a half-eaten sheep, and intestines criss-crossing the pasture.*

Source: Author

Shock. Sadness. Listlessness. Sympathy. Fear. Panic. Anger. Resignation. Hopelessness. Tension. The wolf atmosphere that day was a complex mish-mash involving a shepherd and his wife, their flock of sheep, their two dogs, local residents, a vet and a wolf kill expert with her anthropological assistant. The wolf atmosphere drew on the feelings of the sheep (shock, fear), of the people towards the sheep (sympathy, compassion), and of the people amongst themselves (shock, listlessness, anger, but also the sympathy of the residents with the shepherd's family and perhaps distrust or potential anger towards the wolf kill expert). This atmosphere had a strong material anchorage at the site of the killing with its particular necroaesthetic and as visualised here to some extent through the images. It is difficult to avoid a certain horror in the face of these dead animal bodies, and a sympathy for the injured and suffering animals.

The highest intensity of such a necroaesthetic is found in so-called surplus killing, where wolves kill more animals than they can eat at once. As mentioned above, the Rosenthal Pack killed thirty-six sheep in one night in July 2019, and such surplus killing has occurred frequently in Rosenthal in recent years. It is a phenomenon that contributes to the negative image of wolves like nothing else (apart from the rare cases of humans being killed by wolves):

> Surplus killing is still a taboo word in Saxon wolf policy, is supposed to happen only in individual cases, and thus remains without any consequence for the RT Pack. It created a picture of horror in and around Zerna [...], and also caused a herd of cattle including two bulls to leave the pasture at night and flee 400 metres towards [the village of] Gränze. Cattle are flight animals and such a cattle outbreak caused by wolves increases the safety risk strikingly.[37]

In its most extreme form, it is a phenomenon that makes some question the 'naturalness' of such behaviour for a predator and turns wolves into wild beasts that stand out from the rest of the animal world:

> Basically, I had nothing against wolves. It was only a photograph showing the eyes of a sheep, torn open at the belly but still alive, that changed my mind. Just this much, that such behaviour can only be mere lust for killing. Animals

---

37   Letter from the Mayor of Rosenthal to the Landrat, 25 Nov 2019 (provided by the Mayor).

kill for food, but the wolf—depending on the possibility—unfortunately kills for pleasure.[38]

So, the step from the wild beast to the motif of the 'big bad wolf' is not that great.[39] According to this line of reasoning, wolves seem 'bestial' because they behave unlike a real animal, 'unnaturally', acting against the appropriate instincts of an animal, thus showing a high degree of agency, i.e. capacity for action and free will.[40] This makes their behaviour unpredictable and therefore more risky and potentially dangerous. Furthermore, if they have free will and choose to kill when they are not hungry, they must have the intention to cause harm and even enjoy it. Or it is in their 'nature' that they are driven not only by a hunger instinct, but also by a killing instinct, a 'lust for murder', which makes them uncontrollable killing machines? Whichever possibility you think is more likely, both have the potential to spread fear among wolf critics.

However, the horror of *surplus killing* (and to some extent *surplus killing* itself) is man-made, or at least a hybrid phenomenon in which human and animal actions are intertwined. Humans have not only bred animals that cannot effectively defend themselves against a wolf attack, but they also hinder their defence by keeping them in small, fenced-in pastures and perhaps not adequately protecting them. Most importantly, humans interfere prematurely with wolf behaviour by removing carcasses and preventing wolves from returning to the kill site to continue feeding (naturally?) in the days following an attack.[41]

***

---

38   "Mindestens 20 tote Schafe in Schönau bei Rosenthal", MDR, 20.07.2019, https://www.mdr.de/sachsen/bautzen/bautzen-hoyerswerda-kamenz/schafe-gerissen-verletzt-weide-rosenthal-104.html. The quote comes from a comment on this media article—now no longer available online—about the first incident with the 36 dead sheep.

39   See for a detailed discussion on the formation of the big bad wolf stereotype: Jürgens, Uta M./Hackett, Paul M.: 'The Big Bad Wolf: The Formation of a Stereotype', in: Ecopsychology 9.1 (2017), pp. 33–43, https://doi.org/10.1089/eco.2016.0037.

40   See Breyer, Thiemo: 'Bestien—Zur Anatomie des Schreckens vor dem Animalischen', in: Erik Norman Dzwiza-Ohlsen/Andreas Speer (eds.), Philosophische Anthropologie als interdisziplinäre Praxis, Leiden u.a.: Brill | mentis 2021, pp. 194–204.

41   Kruuk, Hans: Hunter and Hunted: Relationships Between Carnivores and People, Cambridge: Cambridge University Press 2002, pp. 50–53.

In November 2019, the municipal council and the mayor of Rosenthal once again asked the Landrat for the lethal removal of the Rosenthal Pack. What was new this time was that they argued primarily for the protection of public safety and the health of residents. The reason for this change in argumentation may be found in a letter to the mayor written by a local activist of the anti-wolf movement, representing both the *Initiative Wolfsgeschädigte und besorgte Bürger* and the *Verein Sicherheit und Artenschutz*. In this letter, she mentioned the response of the District Office to her earlier 'report of imminent danger from wolves':

> As there has been no demonstrable progress on the protection status so far, Landrat X is now concentrating his efforts more on the issue of the threat to people in settlements. The Free State is currently working on a wolf ordinance for Saxony that also takes this point into account [...].[42]

Whether this has become a strategy in the renewed attempt to obtain a permit to remove the pack cannot be said with certainty. But the tone of the mayor's letter to the Landrat was clear. There had been an "escalation of the security situation". The "threatening security situation", "serious danger" and "security concerns" leading to "anger and incomprehension" among residents, are based on several wolf attacks on sheep and wolf sightings in the village near a bus stop used mainly by school children. One of the sheep was even found dead in a garage ten metres away from the house of a family with a child. A shepherd's flock had recently been attacked for the third time this year and some sheep had been "bestially mauled". In the mayor's letter, the feelings of helplessness and powerlessness mentioned earlier is again evident when he writes:

> I no longer have any sympathy for the official trivialisation of wolves. I lack the support from the state. I can only give inadequate answers to the citizens and refuse to take responsibility for the points mentioned, because I alone cannot provide the necessary safety and cannot be held liable for damage caused by wolves.[43]

The local council hoped that they had finally gathered enough arguments for their request. But the answer from the assistant to the Landrat was sobering:

---

42   Letter to the Mayor of Rosenthal, 11.10.2019 (provided by the Mayor).

43   Letter from the Mayor of Rosenthal to the Landrat, 25 November 2019 (provided by the Mayor).

When the [wolf] ordinance comes into force, the *Fachstelle Wolf* will be responsible for assessing the wolf kills and deciding/recommending the removal of the wolf. If they don't make a recommendation, then theoretically we can still order for the wolf to be removed. But that is only in theory, because in practice the wolf lobby will immediately file criminal charges against the Landrat in such a case—a hundred times over. If one of these charges is successful, the illegal killing could be punishable by up to five years in prison and a fine of 50,000 euros. You will be familiar with the consequences of such a verdict under civil service law. For this reason, the theoretical possibility of granting permission to remove the wolf is nothing but hot air. [...] For the above reasons, Mr X [the Landrat] is therefore not the right person to address the public's resentment.[44]

In this section's episode we see the now familiar pattern of the wolf atmosphere consisting of a threat scenario (to sheep and humans alike) coupled with indignation, anger, and incomprehension towards the wolf authorities for allegedly refusing to help. This particular atmospheric ensemble is best exemplified by the 'citizen wolf monitoring' organised by local activists.

Local activists were dissatisfied with the official wolf monitoring because the numbers never seemed to match what they knew. The strict scientific criteria for proper evidence of a wolf presence, such as scat or genetic traces on killed sheep, means that some reported incidents are regularly dismissed for lack of evidence. These reports are not included in the official statistics, which in turn are the basis for debates and decisions on wolf management. But local activists are angry that wolf managers are contradicting what they know from experience. *I have seen a wolf. Why is the wolf management telling me I haven't seen one? Why are they hiding this fact? This must be a deception in favour of the wolf management's agenda*—these are the common complaints.

---

44 Office of the *Landrat* to the Mayor of Rosenthal, email, 12.05.2019 (provided by the Mayor). This is the same Landrat who had already requested the lethal removal twice. However, with the new wolf ordinance of 2019, the distribution of responsibilities for a lethal removal has changed, giving more power to the county administration. Hence the change of mind of the Landrat and his caution in this matter.

Figure 22: Citizen wolf monitoring with photo documentation and maps of reported and unreported incidents.

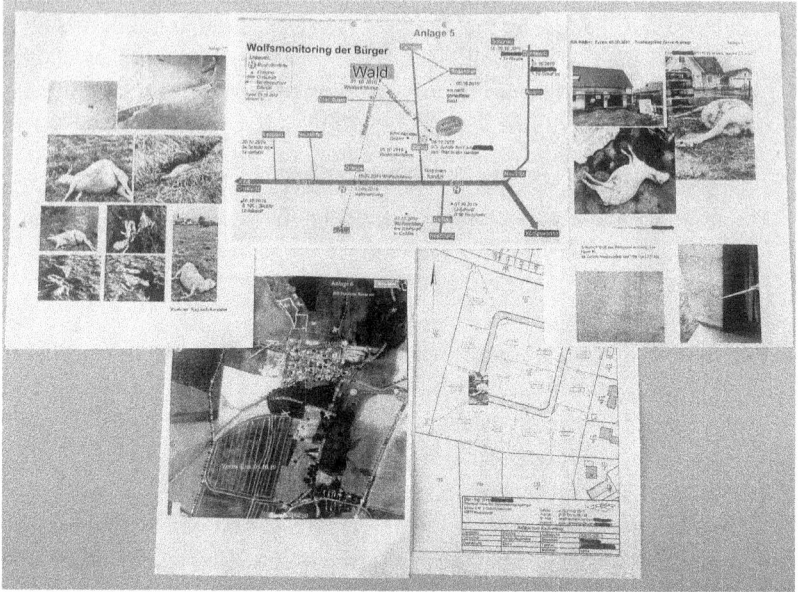

Source: Author

I have already pointed out how the wolf atmosphere feeds on both the real and the virtual, showing how a particular local wolf pack becomes interwoven with the wolf species as a whole. Here we see that it is not only the potential capabilities of the wolf that need to be considered. We also need to revise what is meant by 'the real wolves' at the local level. In this context, it is important to understand that a wolf atmosphere is primarily based on the experiential knowledge of the local lifeworld, rather than purely scientific facts based on C1 evidence. It includes clear evidence (C1), confirmed evidence (C2), unconfirmed evidence (C3), non-assessable signs, unreported signs, and in some circumstances even what the SCALP criteria consider to be false observations. These signs have varying affective intensity and force, but not necessarily along the lines of what is officially considered evidence or no evidence, confirmed or unconfirmed. An unconfirmed sign can be just as affective as C1 evidence. *What really counts is the lifeworldly affect of a sign*: a killed fallow deer in the middle of the village, an injured sheep in the carport, wolf tracks near a bus stop. As all these signs multiply and appear in more and more places, the wolf atmosphere thickens and begins to feel enveloping, intrusive, and unsettling.

***

In the meantime, all was quiet in and around Rosenthal. Unusually quiet, perhaps.[45] Officially, 326 animals were killed by wolves in Saxony in 2020 (after 280 in 2018 and 400 in 2019), but no sheep in the municipality of Rosenthal.[46] Only in nearby Wittichenau were eight sheep killed in February 2020, and there were some incidents with cows, but none of these were confirmed as wolf kills. Overall, the number of animals killed by wolves seemed to be decreasing. Some said this was because almost all shepherds (at least in Rosenthal) had given up. Others said it was because shepherds were reporting losses far less. Maybe it was because all of Marie's pups had probably died in road accidents in 2020 and the year before, so there weren't many mouths to feed. Or maybe Marie had died? After my last visit to Rosenthal in the summer of 2020, I was told to wait for the autumn. It will start again in autumn, as it does every year, when the pups are big enough to go hunting with the others. The people of Rosenthal call it "the time of the [wolves'] hunting school".

In mid-August 2020, I received a WhatsApp message from one of the Rosenthal activists showing two killed sheep from the nearby village of Piskowitz. "Like every year". I forwarded the pictures to the wolf kill expert I knew and asked her for details about the case. She did not know that sheep had been killed in Piskowitz. It had not been reported. But she told me to enlarge the picture: Both sheep were tied up with chains – presumably to a stake in the ground, as was and sometimes still is, customary in Lusatia.[47]

---

45   "Stille graue Räuber: Wölfe in der Oberlausitz bleiben in Deckung", MDR, 18.06.2020. https://www.mdr.de/nachrichten/sachsen/bautzen/goerlitz-weisswasser-zittau/s tille-graue-raeuber-in-der-oberlausitz-100.html (accessed: 18.06.2022, no longer available).

46   However, there were two attacks on enclosed deer in Ralbitz-Rosenthal in December; sachsen. de, https://www.wolf.sachsen.d e/schadensstatistik-4169.html (accessed: 30.04.2024).

47   This chapter covers almost the whole life of the Rosenthal Pack. Since 2020, there have been only three more attacks on sheep in Rosenthal. Marie had more pups until the monitoring year 2021/22, but there have been no signs of her or her pack since then. From 2022/23, the Rosenthal Pack is no longer officially listed as an existent pack.

Towards a concept of wolf atmosphere

In this chapter I have explored not only how a region became a wolf territory, but also how it became a 'landscape of fear' in the experience of local residents and anti-wolf activists. In this conclusion, I will draw together the findings of this chapter to present a multifaceted concept of what I have called a wolf atmosphere, and thereby contribute to our understanding of how complex socioecologies of fear develop from a particular human perspective. The following key points summarise how wolf atmospheres function as affective arrangements:

1. Wolves as atmospheric producers: Wolves, through their lives and actions in their territory, inscribe and engineer the emotional fabric of a shared human-wolf landscape. But so do humans and other animals who, together with wolves, all contribute in their own way to this complex mix of different affective forces. This chapter has shown that wolves affect through their physical presence (sightings) and, even more powerfully, through their powerful affective traces left in the necroeasthetics of wolf kills. However, we have also seen that and how wolf atmospheres are volatile, influenced by continuing wolf attacks and sightings on the one hand, but also by human responses, organised protests, lack of herd protection measures and changing perceptions of the wolf's potential capabilities on the other.

2. The nexus of necroaesthetics: Central to understanding the wolf atmosphere of fear is the concept of 'necroaesthetics', an affective-sensory pattern that emerges from the way wolves hunt, kill and consume their prey. Due to the visceral co-presence of the experiencing subject and dead/injured animal bodies, the wolf-specific necroaesthetic (as exemplified in surplus killing and especially when performed by a whole pack of wolves) is characterised by an unsettling atmospheric immersion in a scene of violence (lots of blood, torn flesh), death, suffering and predation (carcasses and body parts strewn about as signs of pursuit, struggle and fear), which contrasts with the normal (and ideal-idyllic) aesthetics of a pasture or rural village.

3. Variations of fear: The example of Rosenthal shows that a simple characterisation of the local wolf atmosphere as a landscape of fear is too simplistic and reductionist. In this chapter we see that fear is actually expressed in a wide range of affective states, such as caution (not letting the children go into the woods), vigilance (initiating citizen monitoring), worry (about attacks on sheep), anxiety (generally about living in wolf territory), and even panic (the grandfather after a deer pursued by wolves broke through his fence). Developing a more nuanced understanding of fear helps to decipher what 'fear of

wolves' might mean in a given context, and thus to work on more nuanced options for wolf management to address these varieties of fear more specifically.

4. Fear reveals vulnerability: Fear has a dual structure; it points simultaneously outwards (fear-of) and inwards (fear-for). Thus, examining threats inevitably reveals 'what is at stake' for stakeholders. Fear of wolves is connected to a sense of vulnerability, of one's livestock or pets, of one's livelihood, of one's home, or even of one's own life. Some of these vulnerabilities have a material reality, as demonstrated by the necroaesthetics of wolf kills; others are based more on what might happen, feeding mainly on the uncertainties and unpredictability of wolf behaviour.

5. Affective complexity: Emotions rarely come alone, and wolf atmospheres go well beyond fear. Emotions such as shock and fear (of wolves), anger (towards wolf managers), frustration and resentment (towards local politicians) and sympathy (for shepherds and their injured sheep) are all typically involved. The task is then to see how certain emotions, in which constellations and under what conditions become integral dimensions of wolf atmospheres.

6. Transgression of local sensibilities: A wolf atmosphere materialises when the familiar lifeworld of humans is disrupted by the disturbing presence of wolves and wolf attacks on domestic animals. It emerges when wolves cross the boundaries of human domains, challenging the established order and familiarity of these spaces. Local sensibilities – as the emotional backdrop to people's everyday lives – shift from a comfortable sense of home, or 'ontological security', to an unsettling emotional state as individuals grapple with the unfamiliar feelings evoked by the presence of wolves.

7. Shifting axes of conflict: The emergence of a wolf atmosphere is the result of both conflicts with wolves and conflicts between stakeholders over wolves. The latter include 'vertical' conflicts between local stakeholders and official wolf management institutions, and 'horizontal' conflicts between local stakeholders and pro-wolf organisations and their representatives. By looking at these two axes, we can shift our perspective away from focusing too much on the wolf as the sole producer and instead integrate wolves into the structural elements of a wolf atmosphere as a whole. Continuing the line of argument about wolf agency from the last chapter, to describe a wolf atmosphere structurally along its axes is to delineate the fault lines of the atmosphere as an affective arrangement.

8. Local experiential knowledge: Wolf atmospheres are felt and known from the position of the local lifeworld, rather than from a purely rational position based on scientific evidence. Unconfirmed signs, local stories and

personal experience can all contribute to the intensity of the atmosphere. What matters from a lifeworld perspective is how wolves show up in everyday life and how people respond to their presence. This difference between local experiential knowledge and the scientific knowledge used in wolf management is in itself a source of conflict about wolves and thus contributes to the wolf atmosphere (primarily through emotions of anger, resentment or frustration directed vertically at wolf management).

As we can see, fear of wolves could be a good starting point and indicator for studying human-wolf conflicts. However, it is important firstly to unravel, elaborate and be precise about what people actually mean by fear. And secondly, to find out exactly how this fear arises, i.e. what factors contribute to it (who, when, where, why, etc.). In doing so, we shift the phenomenon from being about a subjective emotional state of individual actors and a conflict caused by only one animal (species), to a complex intersubjective, social atmosphere of more-than-human coexistence in a shared landscape of humans and wolves (and other animals).

5. Wolf Feelings

The role of feelings, sentiments, and ethos

In Chapter 3 we saw how coexistence with wolves is affectively charged, accompanied by recurrent emotional outbursts from a wide range of actors in response to wolfish agency. In Chapter 4, I showed how emotionally coloured atmospheres can spread beyond individual actors in a region, persist over time, and thus can shape spontaneous individual emotional experiences. In this chapter, the feelings that shape the relationship between wolves and humans finally take centre stage: I aim to outline and understand the emotional worlds of important groups of actors by a) attempting to capture the repertoire of 'typical' feelings in relation to the wolf; and b) showing how individual, spontaneous feelings are expressions of more enduring affective structures or dispositions. It becomes clear that the opinions, attitudes, and values that are otherwise at the forefront of the public wolf debate are not simply expressions of rational evaluations based on knowledge but are rather to be understood as expressions of *sentiments*, a concept that "connects cognitive processes of forming opinions and judgements with affective dynamics" and which "contain regular patterns, orderly procedures, and rules of how sense is to be made of the world". [1]

So, when I map the emotional worlds of the shepherds, hunters, and wolf friends below, I am not simply listing the emotions, nor measuring the intensity of the emotions, nor judging them as 'positive' or 'negative'. I am trying to understand why, out of the whole range of possible emotions/feelings, only some are typically experienced by a group of actors/stakeholders, and to what extent these feelings can be meaningfully located in their specific lifeworld. In concrete terms, this means that the question of wolf-related feelings is related

---

1   J. Bens/O. Zenker: Sentiment, p. 96.

to the question of **what it feels like to be a shepherd/hunter/wolf friend in general—in this time, in this society, with wolves?**[2] This approach emphasises the fact that the actors are not 'innocently' affected by wolves, but have an affective history – a structure of feelings and sentiments that colour their interactions and inform their responses.

As an anthropologist, I am less interested in individual biographical antecedents than in cultural patterns in the affective structures of the groups of actors. The idea—inspired by practice theory—is that shepherds, for example, as a community of practice[3] and through their shepherding practice, have acquired not only skills, knowledge, and competencies but also the norms, values, and sentiments of their community. In other words, shepherding as a way of life has its own *ethos*, "the tone, character, and quality of their life, its moral and aesthetic style and mood".[4] This does not mean, however, that all shepherds feel, think, and act in the same way (since the individual biographical background mentioned above remains). What is expressed here is a certain spectrum of possibilities, a typical range of affective structures in which individual affective experience occurs and finds expression.

But the methodological question is: how do you identify what is typical for a group of actors? In ethnographic research like this, this is done by collecting and correlating different types of data. Observations are correlated with informal conversations, interviews, official documents from associations, comments on social media, media contributions, and so on, in order to identify patterns across the board (and not just in individual statements). This will also reveal possible differentiations within the community: for example, if there are different views on wolves, rather than one typical view, this will sooner or later appear in several types of data. In interpreting the data I have therefore followed the principle: generalise where possible, differentiate where necessary.

Each of these groups of actors could easily have filled its own chapter, if not a whole book. Treating all three in one chapter was necessary for the coherence of this book, but it means that what follows is not a conclusive overview, but a first approach to the phenomenon. What is important in this context is

---

2   In this chapter, for a better overview of the mapping of emotional worlds, I set indicative emotion terms in bold.

3   On the concept of community of practice, see Lave, Jean/Wenger, Etienne: Situated Learning. Legitimate Peripheral Participation, Cambridge: Cambridge University Press 1991.

4   C. Geertz: Interpretation of cultures, p. 89.

to develop an approach to these affective worlds in the first place and to describe them so that they can be opened up to academic and public discourse. Despite the limitations of having to cover everything in one chapter, I have always aimed for a 'thick description' of feelings. Feelings are not only treated here as emotions—as a culturally normalised category (hate, anger, love, envy, etc.)—but also described in their (phenomenological) experiential qualities. Being angry at wolves or loving wolves can mean many things. Only a thick description establishes the contexts of meaning that are necessary to understand these feelings as typical for a group of actors. It also allows for a more differentiated view of feelings in the wolf conflict: away from simple attributions to emotional categories, towards a complex understanding of the indeterminate, ambivalent, dynamic character of affective experiences. This differentiated view also involves distinguishing feelings directed at wolves from those directed at other social actors in the wolf conflict.

One final point: by now it should be obvious that emotions in wolf issues have a political dimension. Accordingly, adopting a scholarly-critical perspective means repeatedly thematising the political, especially when there is an interest in a certain positive form of external representation, which must be treated as just that—a 'representation', a 'performance'. Here again, the ethnographic perspective is helpful: representations of interest groups can be compared or contrasted with statements of individual actors and observations of events and actions in order to point out contradictions or inconsistencies or to be able to complement what is officially unsaid with what is said elsewhere.

"Loved. Wanted. Sacrificed?"[5]: shepherds, wolves and sheep

Livestock owners are generally considered to be the most affected stakeholder group by the return of wolves, and among them sheep farmers in particular.[6] As sheep account for almost 90 per cent of the wolf-caused mortalities[7], it

---

5   This is the title of a DVD published by the Förderverein der Deutschen Schafhaltung e.V. on the subject of animal husbandry and wolves.

6   Supplementary to my elaborations on shepherds, see a qualitative study co-supervised by me: Ostrowski, Lea: Die Rückkehr des Wolfs in den Leuscheider Wald: Untersuchungen zu Akzeptanz und naturbezogenen Werten im Bereich der Weidetierhaltung, Master's thesis, Hochschule für nachhaltige Entwicklung Eberswalde 2022.

7   As of 2020, according to DBBW, https://www.dbb-wolf.de/wolfsmanagement/herden schutz/schadensstatistik (accessed: 30.04.2024).

makes sense to focus on sheep farmers.[8] They are a heterogeneous group consisting of full-time professional shepherds as well as (and these are the ones I mentioned that allow for a better differentiation) part-time sheep farmers and hobby sheep farmers.

Figure 23: At a demonstration by livestock farmers in Wiesbaden.

Source: Author

It is also important to distinguish them from other livestock keepers and to explore what is special about their situation. It seems important that sheep farmers are a marginal, small group among livestock owners. In the whole of Germany there are about 1.5 million sheep (as of 2021–2023)[9] and about 18,000 sheep farmers, of whom less than a thousand are professional shepherds (as of 2016).[10] They see themselves as 'endangered'—similar to the wolf and similar to

8   Other types of farmers or animal owners are only marginally affected by wolf kills in Germany, but they feel at least potentially affected and threatened. Doing justice to their particular situation would go beyond the scope here.

9   Federal Statistical Office, https://www.destatis.de/DE/Themen/Branchen-Unternehm en/Landwirtschaft-Forstwirtschaft-Fischerei/Tiere-Tierische-Erzeugung/Tabellen/bet riebe-schafen-und-schafenbestand.html (accessed: 30.04.2024).

10   "Schäfer in Not: Zahl der Berufsschäfer jetzt unter 1000!", top agrar online, 06.03.2018, https://www.topagrar.com/management-and-politics/news/schaefer-in-not-zahl-d

some of their old, rare sheep breeds.[11] The former president of the Federal Association of Professional Shepherds explains: "Statistics show declining numbers for the sector. The average age is over 56. Shepherd schools have 10–20 trainees per year. Incomes on farms are at the lower end of the agricultural income scale".[12]

Other problems include a shortage of vets, high vet bills, intense competition, high costs for grazing land, heavy reliance on subsidies, competition for their products from foreign imports, increased bureaucracy, and seven-day weeks with no holidays. The basic ethos among shepherds is therefore one of **existential angst**. "What will tomorrow bring?"—this slogan on a poster at a demonstration by livestock owners and against wolves in Wiesbaden sums up well the deep-seated **insecurity** and **uncertainty about the future** and about how things should go on (now with wolves).

In addition, the social position of sheep farmers has long been marginal: they have neither been visible as a professional group nor have they had a voice to draw public attention to their problems, or the power to make demands—unlike other livestock and animal owners who have relatively powerful interest groups through the German Farmers' Association (DBV) or the German Equestrian Federation (FN).[13] This leads to a widespread feeling among shepherds of a **lack of respect and (social) recognition** for their profession and for what they do with their animals for society and the environment.

However, these feelings are secondary when compared to the importance of the affective relationship that sheep farmers have with their animals. This is illustrated by M., a professional shepherd with about 800 sheep near Neuwied, in the territory of the former Neuwied Pack.[14] He is about to retire and hand over the farm to his daughter. Only once in his life has he been separated from his sheep—while on holiday—and every day he called his daughter to check on

---

er-berufsschaefer-jetzt-unter-1000-9410439.html (accessed: 20.06.2022, no longer available).

11   "Gedanken zur Rückkehr der Wölfe nach Deutschland", Die Schäfer. Bundesverband Berufsschäfer e.V., 19.10.2014. https://www.berufsschaefer.de/news/33/10/152/schafe-wolf-und-artenschutz (accessed: 20.06.2022, no longer available).

12   Günther Czerkus: "Viele Fragen zur Zukunft der Schaf- und Ziegenhaltung", ibid., 24.06.2016. https://www.berufsschaefer.de/news/50/9/152/wo-soll-die-reise-hingehen (accessed: 20.06.2022, no longer available).

13   Hence the attempts to become more publicly visible through grazing animal days, open pasture days, the national sheep show or the European shepherds' procession.

14   Interview, shepherd, from Rhineland-Palatinate, 30.06.2020.

them: whether they had enough food and water and whether everything else was OK. He could not 'let go' of his professional duties, of his sheep. His shepherding was characterised by **care** in a twofold sense: **care for** his sheep and **care about** his sheep. Both forms of care together are constitutive of the practice of shepherding and shape the relationship between shepherd and sheep. This relationship is a reciprocal one, but also a hierarchical one. The practice of herding and the long domestication process of the sheep indicate that there is a clear power relationship and power imbalance in this relationship. The care for and about the sheep is also inextricably linked to their use, which is primarily for meat, milk, wool—and more recently for ecological landscape management or even use as *companion animals* (as companions for oneself or on guided sheep walks for interested city dwellers).

How the relationship between a sheep farmer and his animals is formed in each concrete case depends very much on the way in which they are used. The type of care can become a form of affection and love or more superficial and driven by economic interests. A couple from the Westerwald region, who keep over a hundred goats for landscape conservation and offer goat walks, and whose herd partly consists of formerly neglected and sick rescue goats that have been raised on bottles, have developed a different form of care than a young family father near Bautzen who keeps a few sheep behind the house to provide meat for his family. What both examples have in common is that humans and animals are not necessarily connected in a family, but in a 'household'. As the cultural anthropologists Michaela Fenske and Marlis Heyer argue:

> Those who belong to the household are protected. This makes sense because the household has been an essential basis of successful human economic activity since pre-modern Europe. Of course, this does not mean that the animals in question [...] may not be eaten. [...] However, certain standards are applied with regard to their permissible use, which seem appropriate to the people caring for them. This historically grown, often ambivalent logic characterises rural multispecies work modes and economic communities.[15]

It is this shared household of sheep farmer and animal in the field of tension between care and dominance/use that has to be maintained again and again

---

15   Fenske, Michaela/Heyer, Marlis: 'Wer zum Haushalt gehört. Ethiken des Zusammenlebens in der Diskussion', in: Tierethik 11.19 (2019), pp. 12–33, here pp. 20–21 (translated by TG).

through daily work and whose existence is at stake. This coexistence is characterised by a 'shared vulnerability'[16]—both animal keeper and animal are and become vulnerable in their shared way of life. They depend on each other, especially in shepherding, because sheep have their own vulnerability that distinguishes them from other domestic animals such as cows or horses. In the words of one shepherd, "sheep are built close to death"; "they are always dying of something" and so "you often blame yourself". Caring-for-and-about is therefore an ongoing task.

It is into this affective world that wolves now enter. Their entry might look like this:

[SHEPHERD:] The first time was in February 2010 [...]. The snow was so high that you couldn't get any electricity on the fence. But the guard dog was in there and the guard dog basically pushed the flock into the other paddock, but they [the wolves] still got some [...] Yes, you come out early and see the sheep stuck in another flock and the wolf still there and eating [...].

[INTERVIEWER:] Did you scare him away?

[SHEPHERD:] Yes, we scared him away, we [...].

[INTERVIEWER:] How did you do that?

[SHEPHERD:] We shouted hoo-hoo (laughs). That's the way it is, there's no other way, you've got no other option.

[INTERVIEWER:] What is it like to see an animal killed like that?

[SHEPHERD] It always depends on how many are killed. If it's just one, you can't see it from a distance. You see one lying there, you go and look, maybe it's dead, and then you see if it's a wolf kill, or you see that the fence is down, or ... So I'm not shocked when I see a dead sheep. It would be worse

---

16   Fenske, Michaela: 'Menschen, Wölfe und andere Lebewesen. Perspektiven einer Multispecies Ethnography', in: Lara Selin Ertener/Bernd Schmelz (eds.), Von Wölfen und Menschen, Hamburg: Museum am Rothenbaum 2019, pp. 33–40, here p. 37; see also Arnold, Irina: 'Von traumatisierten Schafen und verwundbaren Lebenswelten: Stimmen von Weidetierhalter*innen aus Niedersachsen', in: Lara Selin Ertener/Bernd Schmelz (eds.), Von Wölfen und Menschen, Hamburg: Museum am Rothenbaum 2019, pp. 41–50.

if there were thirty or forty of them. That would be bad. But thank God I haven't experienced that yet, and I don't want to, because it's shit, it's really bad.[17]

S. has been a professional shepherd for almost forty years and for more than ten years he has worked on a large farm in Lusatia, right in the heart of the territory of the Knappenrode-Seenland Pack. His flock of Coburg chestnut sheep is used purely for landscape conservation and has already been attacked by wolves three or four times in the last ten years, with one or two sheep being killed each time. Considering that S. regularly sees wolves pass by his flock several times a month, his attitude is surprisingly calm and pragmatic. Losses are very limited and his herd protection with electric fences has worked well from the start.

However, when wolves first arrive in a region and encounter unprotected sheep, however, things can be very different, as this shepherd from the Odenwald region, located between Bavaria and Hesse, tells us:

It was a difficult day for me in 2017, it was in November. I will never forget that day. I had 300 ewes, 600 ewes in total, and I was in Hesse with 300 ewes and people called me at seven in the morning and said the sheep were gone. So, I went there because I come from Bavaria, which is 15 kilometres away. When I got to the pasture, I was stunned, eight animals were dead, bitten by wolves. And then I started to look for my animals. They were scattered all over the place. And the strange thing was that I was right next to the kindergarten in the village, so you can't be responsible for that anymore, that can go wrong. So, I went back to look for my animals. Then I called the police. And the police came and called the district office. Then someone from the wolf management came. And then he said it was a stray dog. [...] Then they took DNA samples and after 14 days I got the results. Not from the authorities, and that's such a sad picture, not from the authorities, but from the press I found out that it was a wolf. This is simply impossible. Not even a phone call, how can I help you [...]. I had eight dead sheep, two days later I had two more dead and six badly injured, I needed a vet, I had to find money for that, and then at Christmas I had the stillbirths. One hundred and thirty stillborn lambs! Technically I'm dead, kaput. And I got nothing from the state of Hesse. No phone call, nothing at all [...].[18]

---

17   Interview, shepherd, from Saxony, 16.03.2022.
18   Interview, shepherd, from Bavaria, 15.01.2020.

The wolves left this shepherd in a **state of shock**. **Uncertainty** about the where-abouts of his sheep coupled with extreme **concern** about whether they were well, injured, or even dead, characterise the immediate aftermath of this at-tack. His emotional state is exacerbated by the lack of support from the wolf management. In his view, his suffering is not seen, not acknowledged, no of-fer of help is made. He **feels alone, abandoned** in the face of the tragedy he has experienced.

This example also shows that the affective impact of a wolf attack is not limited to the moment but extends over time. In this case, the wolves did not just come once, they came again two days later. Injured animals had to be treated, the sheep were frightened for days, then there were the stillbirths, the mounting financial losses and the question of what tomorrow will bring. For many shepherds in new wolf regions, therefore, a **diffuse sense of anxiety** is spreading rapidly. Uncertainty about when, where and how wolves might attack again, creates a **sense of vague, anxious anticipation**:

[INTERVIEWER:] Do you know how far away the nearest wolf is?

[SHEPHERD:] You can never be sure. They could be here tonight, they could be here now. It's also possible we won't see any for the whole year.[19]

Anxiety thus becomes a constant companion and changes the shepherds' ethos:

[SHEPHERD:] We have already had attacks here [in the region]. Yes, then of course you no longer have a good feeling, also if you go there in the morning [...]. If you go there with that feeling in your gut, *hopefully everything went well, hopefully he [the wolf] wasn't there*. It's not like he's only going to come once. The fear remains.[20]

Against this background, it sometimes seems incomprehensible that in many places—including my research regions of Lusatia and the Westerwald—herd protection is only hesitantly accepted, and in some cases rejected outright. Es-pecially among keepers of suckling cow herds and horse owners, as well as among side-line and hobby sheep farmers, the **anger** about the return of the wolves (which they never wanted!) seems to lead to **defiance**, which is directed

---

19   Interview, shepherd, from Hesse, 15.01.2020.
20   Interview, shepherd, from Hesse, 15.01.2020.

against the wolves as well as the wolf management and wolf advocates: If you want the wolves here, it should not be me who has to do the extra work, but you! In contrast to other countries[21], protection from predators is apparently no longer considered a natural part of the herding relationship between humans and farm animals in Germany. "Who will protect my animals?" read one poster at the demonstration in Wiesbaden. Some livestock owners see others as having a duty of care when it comes to wolves.

Another reason for the potential rejection of herd protection measures is the pressure from within the livestock owner communities. In the Westerwald, for example, several research participants confirmed to me that the practice of herd protection is seen in the community as an unwelcome sign of acceptance of wolves and wolf management. Livestock owners who practice herd protection are called 'nest foulers' and are subject to hostility. The return of the wolves has brought livestock owners closer together, which requires unity within the group—and also between the different groups of livestock owners. However, the issue of herd protection shows that there is a lack of unity.

Although there are no two opposing camps among sheep farmers, there are certainly differences in sentiment about the wolf, and these are reflected above all at association level. This is illustrated by two position papers on the wolf issue. On the one hand, there is the wolf-critical Action Alliance Forum Nature, which brings together the Association of German State Sheep Breeders' Associations (VDL), the German Hunting Association (DJV) along with the International Hunting Association (CIC), the German Equestrian Federation (FN), the German Farmers' Association (DBV), and the Association of Forest Owners (AGDW). In their position paper, they argue for a reduction of the wolf's protected status; call for hunting, easier removal, and the introduction of a so-called Akzeptanzbestand (accepted maximum number of wolves); and question the current scientific monitoring regime. Sheep farmers who are be part of this alliance are among the most bitter opponents of wolves. Anger and resentment against the wolf and the wolf management that supports it is greatest among them.

On the other hand, the moderate side is the Federal Association of Professional Shepherds together with BUND, NABU, the German Animal Welfare Association, and the International Fund for Animal Welfare (IFAW). Their "Cor-

---

21   For example, in Albania, see Trajce, Aleksander: The gentleman, the vagabonds and the stranger: cultural representations of large carnivores in Albania and their implications for conservation. PhD Thesis, university of Roehampton, UK, 2017.

nerstones for a low-conflict coexistence" recognise the protected status of the wolf and call for no hunting, but for better prevention of wolf attacks, promotion of herd protection, compensation for damage, and greater participation in wolf management processes. But if you are looking for pro-wolf sentiment among sheep farmers, you will not find it here, because even the moderates can do without wolves, show them no affection and are not fascinated by them. They have a right to exist, but they should know their place in the human order of nature, as this quote makes clear:

> We shepherds have many more problems than we need. The decline in sheep numbers and farms is frightening. Now we have the wolf on top of that. The wolf is just one of many animals that cause us additional problems [...]. We really don't need all this! [...] Wolves have no business in our settlements and on our pastures. We need clear boundaries. [...] Successful coexistence is only possible if everyone knows where they belong![22]

In general, it can also be said that the sentiments of sheep farmers towards wolves are far from being consolidated but are dynamically adapting to current developments. For example, there seem to be recent changes in the Federal Association of Professional Shepherds. The former president of the association recently resigned, claiming that the association was becoming more and more aligned with the wolf-critical demands of the Action Alliance instead of taking more initiative on herd protection issues. **Frustrated** with the association, he took matters into his own hands and set up an informal group called "Colleagues Helping Colleagues Protect Herds" on the territory of the Leuscheid Pack to provide practical and rapid support for herd protection among a diverse group of livestock owners, wolf friends, and others.

This brings us back to the question of why herd protection is still rejected by many sheep farmers. The initiator of the collegial help group sees a widespread feeling of **powerlessness, resignation, and hopelessness** among sheep farmers. I first noticed this with the shepherd couple in Rosenthal whom I had visited after a wolf attack (see Chapter 4). As a reminder: Despite several attacks within a few months, the sheep pasture was still not completely fenced when the wolves came for the third time, so the shepherd could not be compensated

---

22   Günther Czerkus: "Der Wolf und die Lämmlein", Die Schäfer. Bundesverband Berufsschäfer e.V., 21.09.2015. https://www.berufsschaefer.de/news/40/10/152/der-wolf-und-die-laemmlein (accessed: 20.06.2022, no longer available).

for his losses. When asked about this, the shepherd would only refer to his neighbour's flock, where even complete protection of the flock had failed to prevent a wolf attack. In the end, the situation for shepherds like him seems hopeless, the protection of the flock futile and useless. The 'Rosenthal Shepherds' Declaration' puts it this way:

> We have improved herd protection as much as we could, but some of the advice and demands of the herd protection advisors were simply not practicable. Failure to follow them was interpreted as bad faith. However, it is known from all wolf countries in the EU that wolves will overcome any fence used in practical animal husbandry as long as this obstacle does not pose a direct threat to them. This does not prevent the Saxon wolf management from now offering a field trial to see if there is a possibility. Where is this supposed to lead? The ultimate wolf-proof fence is in the Moritzburg game park.[23]

In this context, sheep farmers also like to talk about the 'pointless arms race' against wolves. But where do these fatalistic sentiments come from? On the one hand, they are a side-effect of the wolf's legal status as a protected species and its inviolability for the sheep farmers (their only remaining means of defence, as the Lusatian shepherd quoted above reported, is to shout 'hoo-hoo'). They themselves have no means of dealing with the wolf directly. In their self-perception, their hands are tied, they are condemned to passive observation. The fact that they have at least an indirect option for action in the form of herd protection is not seen as such.

But this feeling of powerlessness is also encouraged within their own ranks. While wolf management promotes herd protection and tries to hold out the prospect of a practical solution to the 'wolf problem', the demoralising sentiments come mainly from within their own ranks. People keep telling each other about how bad and hopeless the situation is, confirming each other's fears and at least sharing a common grief. All this is usually done rather

---

23   "Weidetierrisse und kein Ende—Erklärung der Rosenthaler Schäfer", Wolfszone, http ://www.wolfszone.de/01home/000main/texte/rosenthaler%20Sch%C3%A4fer.htm l (accessed: 30.04.2024, translated by TG); Similarly, the latest Open Letter of Saxon livestock owners (with Landesbauernverband, Landesjagdverband, FN etc.) to the Prime Minister of Saxony from May 2022. The ultimate wolf-proof fence mentioned in the quote refers to the fact that wolf fences in enclosures are more than 2 metres high for the safety of visitors and far exceed the minimum heights of fences for herd protection.

casually, but sometimes these sentiments are deliberately stirred up in order to mobilise and facilitate certain political solutions, as I show in detail in the Chapter 6. Those who are resigned and see themselves as incapable of action, so the calculation goes, are all the more likely to look to others for the duty to act. The demand for changes in the law virtually takes the place of one's own duty to protect the flock. While political solutions are being struggled for and herd protection is not being universally implemented, wolves take the opportunity to continue killing sheep. This in turn increases feelings of powerlessness and resignation among local sheep farmers and creates such pressure that herd protection seems inevitable. This was the situation in the Westerwald in the summer of 2022, where the wolf GW1896m had been regularly killing sheep in unprotected flocks for more than a year (more on this wolf in the next chapter).

The issue of herd protection has thus become a focal point for conflicts between sheep farmers and wolves, sheep farmers and wolf management, and among sheep farmers themselves. The picture is completed when the tense relationship between them and wolf advocates is also addressed using the example of herd protection. On the one hand, wolf friends, such as the Wiki-Wolves association, offer help in building fences or providing night guards for the flock. But here, too, cooperation is unthinkable for many sheep farmers, because wolf friends are seen as wolf cuddlers with a 'romantically transfigured', 'trivialising', 'alienated (from nature)' image of wolves. To accept their help would be to take the wolves' presence for granted. The relationship with these supportive wolf friends is made even more difficult by other wolf friends, mainly from the group *Wolfsschutz Deutschland*, who carry out so-called fence inspections on pastures all over Germany to check for the 'correct' condition of wolf-repellent fences and make public what they find.

In Chapter 4, I described the actions of *Wolfsschutz Deutschland* in Rosenthal from the perspective of a Rosenthal resident and activist. The organisation is also active in the Westerwald, where they have been checking fences.[24] The **anger** caused by the confrontation with the sheep farmers is inevitable and is discussed on Facebook or on the spot. The relationship between sheep farmers

---

24   "Große Exklusivreportage NRW: Wölfe im Fadenkreuz zwischen Rotkäppchenhysterie, Anfütterung, Fake-News und geplanter Wolfsverordnung", Wolfsschutz-Deutschland, 23.12.2021, https://wolfsschutz-deutschland.de/2021/12/23/grosse-exklusivreportage-nrw-woelfe-im-fadenkreuz-zwischen-rotkaeppchenhysterie-anfuetterung-fake-news-und-geplanter-wolfsverordnung/ (accessed: 30.04.2024).

and wolf friends can take on an almost sinister turn when livestock owners report threats. A goat farmer from Buchholz (in the area of the Leuscheid Pack), for example, was approached on his pasture late one evening by two strangers who warned him to "keep his feet still" on the wolf issue, after which the two disappeared again.[25] The goat farmer was one of the initiators of a regional WhatsApp group on wolves, where information on wolves is passed on to livestock owners, and his name was known in this context. After this incident, he and his wife became **concerned** and wondered what other threats they might face. From the point of view of most livestock owners, these are all examples of *the* behaviour of wolf advocates as a whole. People don't usually distinguish between WikiWolves, Wolfsschutz Deutschland, the anonymous people who make threats, and other wolf advocates. It is mainly the negative experiences that stick in people's mind and thus determine their general view of wolf supporters. Of course, there are also some positive examples of successful cooperation (such as in the above-mentioned alliance between the Association of Professional Shepherds and nature conservation organisations, or the many actions of WikiWolves, NABU, or the GzSdW), but here, too, established enemy images often have to be overcome first.

"They have no respect!": hunters, wolves, and other wild animals

The hunters, I say, especially the old hunters, still see the wolf as a plague. [...] They don't talk about it, but you can see it in their expressions when they talk about what they have experienced with the wolf, the tone in which it is described, and also the reactions of the hunters, you can see that they are clearly against it. I would say that at the level of the hunting associations and so on, where there is more diplomacy, you hear different tones, although I also believe that it is basically a very critical attitude. I would also like to shoot a wolf. I'm a hunter and it's huntable game [...] normally.[26]

---

25   Interview, two goat farmers, from Rhineland-Palatinate, 05.07.2021.
26   Interview, hunters, southern Brandenburg, 12.10.2019.

Figure 24: At the end of a driven hunt on the military training area Oberlausitz, the oldest wolf territory in Germany.

Source: Author

What does it feel like to be a hunter—in this time, in this society, with wolves? Before I address this question, I would like to briefly provide some information about the hunting community in Germany. The number of male and female hunters has been increasing steadily for years. In 2020–21, there were 403,420 hunting licence holders, 93 percent of them male, with an average age of 57, from a wide range of social backgrounds.[27] When it comes to hunters and wolves, it is important to note that the hunting community as a whole is divided (albeit very unequally)—both in its understanding of hunting and in its relationship with the wolf: On the one hand, there are the 'traditional' hunters, organised in the regional associations of the German Hunting Association (DJV); on the other hand, there are the 'ecological' hunters, organised in the regional associations of the Ecological Hunting Association (ÖJV), in addition to a number of non-organised hunters, whom I will call the pragmatists here. In this chapter I will refer mainly to the 'traditional' hunters, as they not only represent the absolute majority in terms of numbers but are also the most 'explainable' in terms of their relationship with the wolf.[28] The DJV has more

---

27   Facts and figures on hunters. German Hunting Association (DJV), https://www.jagdve
     rband.de/zahlen-fakten/zahlen-zu-jagd-und-jaegern (accessed: 30.04.2024).

28   An early quantitative study on attitudes towards the wolf in the Saxon hunting com-
     munity, see Gärtner, Sigmund/Hauptmann, Michaela: 'Das sächsische Wolfsvorkom-

than 250,000 members, and in some federal states (Bavaria, Rhineland-Palatinate, Lower Saxony) more than 80 percent of the hunters are organised in the DJV.

Although the ÖJV has a total of only about 1,900 members[29] (mainly from the ranks of foresters and private forest owners), it is institutionally well anchored (in forestry agencies, federal and state authorities), so that ecological hunting methods dominate in the state's spheres of influence. The ÖJV was founded in the 1980s as a split from the DJV and under heavy—also public—criticism of 'traditional hunting'.[30] 'Ecological hunting' stands for scientifically based hunting as wildlife management, and it follows the findings of wildlife biology with regard to ecosystem management. From this perspective, the wolf—like other predators—is seen as an important part of functioning ecosystems and its return to Germany is accordingly welcomed.[31] This is reflected, for example, in the ÖJV's good relations with other nature and species conservation organisations, such as in the *Platform for Grazing Animals and Wolves*.[32]

When it comes to conflicts with and about wolves, it is usually the traditional hunters, not the ecological hunters, who are involved. To understand their relationship with wolves, it is helpful to briefly consider the traditional hunters' relationship with wildlife in general.[33] For hunters, there is one category of animals that is at the centre of their interest: *Wild* ('game'), that is, the huntable species of wild animals. They have a special relationship with this game, which is characterised by what is known as *Hege* ('stewardship'). Similar

---

men im Spiegelbild der Jägerschaft vor Ort—Ergebnisse einer anonymen Umfrage', in: Beiträge zur Jagd- und Wildforschung 30 (2005), pp. 223–230.

29   Unsere Mitglieder. Deutscher Naturschutzring (DNR), https://www.dnr.de/mitglieder /organisationen/oekologischer-jagdverband-ev-oejv (accessed: 30.04.2024).

30   See Bode, Wilhelm/Emmert, Elisabeth: Jagdwende: Vom Edelhobby zum ökologischen Handwerk Munich: Beck 1998.

31   See also the contributions to the magazine of the Ecological Hunting Association, e.g. Öko-Jagd 2/2021, p. 5–19.

32   "Wölfe und Weidetierhaltung—wie geht es weiter?", press release, 16.09.2021, in: Öko-jagd 4/2021, p. 45.

33   For more details, see Gieser, Thorsten: 'Hunting wild animals in Germany: conflicts between wildlife management and 'traditional' practices of Hege', in: Michaela Fenske/ Bernhard Tschofen (eds.), Managing the Return of the Wild: Human Encounters with Wolves in Europe. London: Routledge 2020, pp. 164–179.

to the practice of herding or shepherding, this relationship is based on practices of care. Although hunters do not own the 'ownerless' game, they have a so-called right of appropriation, provided the game is in their hunting district, and thus a certain claim to dominance over these animals. Their relationship with game is therefore an ambivalent one, characterised by care and responsibility for its welfare on the one hand and a claim to dominance with the right to 'pursue'—to hunt and kill—the game on the other. Despite this ambivalence, their relationship with game is, from their point of view, quite positive: Hunters identify with their hunting district and the animals in it; they are interested in the welfare of their game population in general and want to promote it (so that individual animals can be killed without endangering hunting as a whole or the population); they are fascinated by animal behaviour and enjoy observing it (the so-called *Anblick*), they improve the habitat of their game by artificially creating wallows or by cultivating crop fields, and they protect their game from (human) poachers and (animal) predators.

The latter refers to the category of animals that pose a threat to 'their' game: the *Raubwild* ('predators'), from birds of prey to martens, badgers, foxes, and wolves. For predators, there is basically no duty of care and so the ambivalence of the hunter-animal relationship no longer applies: it is reduced to the hunting of predators, that is, to the killing of an animal seen primarily as a pest (or 'plague', as in the opening quote). And the wolf is a predator par excellence (all the more so as it is a danger not only to game, but also to their beloved hunting dogs and possibly even to humans)! The relationship with the wolf in hunting practice and hunting tradition is thus clearly defined. It is a negative relationship, somewhere between simple **dislike** and intense **hostility**. The 'proper' way to deal with the wolf is hunting and population regulation (to a minimum level), and the appropriate behaviour of the wolf towards hunters (and humans in general) is shyness (as an expression of respect and fear of the apex predator humans).

Whether it is the DJV in Germany,[34] the European Federation for Hunting and Conservation (FACE) at the European level,[35] or the International Coun-

---

34 https://www.landesjagdverband.de/fileadmin/Medien/LJV/Dokumente/Raubwild/DJ
    V-Positionspapier_Wolf_BJT__19_06_15_wolffinal.pdf (accessed: 30.04.2024).
35 https://www.face.eu/2019/10/green-light-for-hunting-as-a-management-tool-for-wo
    lf/ (accessed: 30.04.2024).

cil for Game and Wildlife Conservation (CIC) at international level,[36] hunting organisations everywhere are actively lobbying to (re)classify the wolf as huntable game, to abolish its protected status, and to start regular hunting. The plan 'Wildlife Management Wolf' of the Action Alliance Forum Nature (under the leadership of the DJV) clearly defines the individual steps:

1. Amendment of the Federal Nature Conservation Act with the possibility of applying 'protective hunting' as a regular exception to §45.
2. Inclusion of the wolf in the hunting laws of the federal states with a simultaneous year-round closed season.
3. Conversion of the year-round closed season into an open hunting season.[37]

In order to achieve this goal, the hunting associations, together with the hunting media, are launching a massive attack on wolf management and wolf science, questioning their credibility and sowing mistrust: "DJV criticises intransparent, outdated wolf figures"; "DJV calls for active wolf management"; "BfN presents study on possible wolf territories. DJV warns against misuse of scientific data".[38] In my more than six years of field research experience with hunters in Germany (first on the relationship between hunters and animals in general, then on wolves, currently on wild boar), I have regularly encountered these arguments in informal conversations during and after social hunts and in interviews with hunters. The formation of opinion on the wolf issue

---

36   The CIC is—like the DJV—one of the co-initiators of the following wolf management plan of the Action Alliance Forum Nature.

37   https://www.pferd-aktuell.de/shop/wildtiermanagement-wolf-handlungsvorschlag. html (accessed: 30.04.2024, translated by TG).

38   Headlines on the DJV homepage of 02.12.2019 (https://www.jagdverband.de/djv-krit isiert-intransparente-veraltete-wolfszahlen), 30. 10.2020 (https://www.jagdverband. de/djv-fordert-aktives-wolfsmanagement) and 06.05.2020 (https://www.jagdverban d.de/bfn-legt-studie-zu-moeglichen-wolfsterritorien-vor). Accessed: 30.04.2024.; on hunting media coverage, e.g. "10 Irrglauben zum Wolf—Oft behauptet, aber gar nicht wahr", in: Jäger 12/2017, p. 29–31, "Wölfe in Deutschland—Obergrenze für Isegrim?", in: Wild und Hund 3/2017, p. 14–21, "Bilanz für einen Rückkehrer—Heimkehrer Wolf in Deutschland", in Pirsch 1/2016, pp. 24–32, "Wolfspolitik—Eiertanz um Isegrim", in: Wild und Hund 15/2020, pp. 60–65; a wolf special issue in Jäger 7/2022 titled: "Wolfs-jagd!—Jetzt wird's ernst" and "Raubwildplage—Tipps und Tricks zum Wolfsmanage-ment", p. 24–39; Wild und Hund 11/2022 headlined "Wölfe in Deutschland—Feuer frei auf Isegrim?", p. 56.

within the hunting community is often conspicuously oriented towards the representations of the DJV and the hunting media.

But let's leave the level of public discourse and look at the direct relationship between hunters and wolves. Let's start with a driven hunt on the military training ground Oberlausitz—where the first wolf in Germany settled more than twenty years ago and where hunters have a lot of experience of hunting game in the presence of wolves. When welcoming the hunters (from all over Germany), the hunting leader from the National Forestry Agency also talks about the wolf:

> I must point out to you that wolves may be present during the hunt. As a rule, the wolf is more uncomfortable with you being there than the other way round. All wolves react differently: some wolves leave the hunt when things get turbulent, others just stay there. In any case, the beaters should draw attention to themselves and that is why we unleash the dogs a little later than usual.

> If you have your dog on a leash and a wolf takes an interest in your dog, which can happen, drive it away with loud clapping, shouting, whatever. [...] And if you are still unsure, better lock your dog in the car. If your dog doesn't want to leave his place, let him stay with you. Dogs know what they are doing and can usually assess the danger. If you feel your dog is interested in wolves, put him back in the car. If your dog points out wolves to you, do not reward him for it. He should not have a positive association with wolves. If wolves are already on the prey, then they have won and we let them have it. However, I assume that most of you will not see any wolves today [...].[39]

As it turned out, quite a few hunters had actually seen wolves during the hunt that day. At the *Schüsseltreiben*, the communal meal after the hunt, the hunters stood in small groups and talked about the hunt and what they had seen. It is customary on these occasions to talk about the *Anblick* ('sight') one had. Sightings of wolves were joined by sightings of red deer, roe deer, and wild boar, and for most hunters it didn't seem all that unusual or worrying. However, one young female hunter with a small hunting dog had had a rather disturbing encounter with wolves. She was posted on a high hunting blind, with her dog waiting on the ground below. At some point during the hunt, a whole pack of

---

39   transcript of the speech, field notes, 13.12.2020.

wolves came and settled about 30 metres away from her, watching her and stay-ing for almost half an hour. After a few minutes she found it so disturbing that she climbed down and took her dog up into the hunting blind with her. The next day she took him up to the blind with her from the start.

This example shows that hunters are in a special situation that distin-guishes them from others and partly explains their special attitude towards wolves. They are the ones most likely to have a real encounter with wolves. They go to the same places as the wolves when they go hunting. They are there at the same time as the wolves, that is, at dusk, at night, and at dawn. They engage in the same activity—hunting—and they hunt the same animals: red deer, roe deer, and wild boar. Under these circumstances, encounters are inevitable and can take more or less disturbing forms from the hunters' point of view: Sightings at a distance, encounters directly at the hunting blind, encounters with a hunting dog, and encounters at the shot animal (also during the 'follow-up search' for shot and wounded animals with a specialist dog). In the example above, I described how most hunters accepted sightings (at a distance) quite calmly. But there were always encounters that caused excitement—even if nothing actually happened (but who knows what could happen). This is also the case in the following account of a hunter during a driven hunt on the military training ground a year earlier:

> I showed Mr X [from the National Forestry Agency] a photo of a wolf from the last driven hunt in November 2018. I photographed him from two me-tres away. He came straight at me. He saw me at 50 metres. It was clear, we looked into each other's eyes. He came within two metres of me [...] while I was standing on the raised platform [...] and marking in front of the platform and then he turned around, he turned his back on me, he didn't even look at me anymore, and I could see him for another ten minutes as he walked away calmly. They are the only animals in the forest that behave like that, I'm sorry [...].[40]

When listening to hunters' accounts of their encounters with wolves, it is strik-ing how often the focus of their stories is on the (to them) abnormal behaviour. Wolves do not behave like other game, not in the way that animals are known to behave: "You have to differentiate: There are predators and wild boar or other

---

40   Interview, Lord Mayor of Bautzen/hunter, from Saxony, 16.12.2019.

game that are not predators. And a predator is unpredictable, has free will and is intelligent".[41]

Wolves seem to have a mind of their own and do not appear to simply follow instinctive behavioural automatisms. They are not even shy, as one would expect from a wild animal—that is, they do not immediately flee when they perceive humans. This is something hunters find very **disturbing**. They usually mention that wolves are 'disrespectful' by not showing shyness. In the example of the encounter on the raised platform, the wolf comes straight up to the hunter, although he has seen him (instead of fleeing head over heels), then marks his territory on the platform (as if to provoke) and turns his back on him (you can't do anything to me anyway!) without 'dignifying' the hunter with a glance. The wolf is thus perceived by the hunter as an animal that does not recognise the superior dominance of the hunter in 'his' territory and simply ignores him. It seems to be a kind of affront.

And this affront is all the more disturbing because hunters, more than any other people I have spoken to in the course of my research, consider wolves to be dangerous. No one else considers wolves to be so dangerous, to game, hunting dogs and even to humans. This alleged danger of wolves to humans is, of course, often used as an argument in the political battle to introduce wolf hunting and therefore needs to be critically questioned. But it seems plausible to me to assume that the hunters are not using this argument for purely political reasons: In their eyes, wolves really are truly dangerous or, in the word of a hunter at a public event I attended, they are *Bestien* ('beasts', although the German word has even more dangerous undertones than the English one—more like 'bestial'). For some, this simply leads to increased caution and vigilance:

[HUNTER:] Basically, I don't want to have anything to do with the wolf. I grew up here in a cultivated landscape where you are at the top of the food chain. And when I was in Africa for the first time and I felt the presence of large predators, I thought to myself, oh, you didn't know that feeling yet. And now I have that here on my doorstep and I have to say it took me a year to get used to it. Now it's routine for me to look at the woods, the fields, the edges of the woods when I walk the dog outside.

[INTERVIEWER:] So you also feel threatened yourself.

---

41   Interview, hunters, southern Brandenburg, 12.10.2019.

[HUNTER:] Yes, I don't feel comfortable with the wolf. I have two terriers. Watson is a cosy, small terrier, nine years old. I also have the opposite, a Border Terrier, two years old, Idefix, who would also mess with big dogs, [...] I know he would also mess with wolves [...]. If I'm out alone in the hunting area and I have my Idefix with me and a wolf comes and attacks us or he's standing in front of me growling, what do I do then? There's nothing I can do. If I take Idefix in my arms, the [wolf] might jump on my arm, I don't know. There have been hunting dogs killed by wolves in Germany.

[INTERVIEWER:] One, right?

[HUNTER:] According to official figures! (Laughter). Up here in the Westerwald, when you drive up here, around Rettersen, in Leuscheid, where many spruce forests have been cleared in the meantime. When I ask the local hunters who come to our driven hunt, [...] I can't get a dog handler to let his dogs jump around [...], I can't get any hunters, they only come with handguns. [...] Yes, really [...].[42]

Although there has not been a single documented wolf attack on a human in Germany, and only one hunting dog has been killed by a wolf in a non-hunting situation, the hunting media, in particular, are fanning the flames of suspicion about these figures and regularly publish reports of alleged attacks on hunters and hunting dogs.[43] A certain **atmosphere of fear** of wolves is therefore widespread among the hunting community (especially in non-wolf regions)—although not everyone shares this and some consider it exaggerated.

Apart from encounters with wolves, hunters are also **concerned** about the mere presence of wolves in their hunting grounds and the effect this has on 'their' game, 'their' hunting grounds, and hunting as a whole. According to hunters, game is behaving differently and has become unpredictable, making hunting more difficult. Roe deer have become more stealthy, rarely showing themselves, and the population has declined considerably. Red deer and wild boar have formed huge *Angstrudel/Angstrotten* ('herds of fear') to protect themselves from the wolf, causing massive damage to forests and fields by their sheer numbers. It is difficult to shoot out individual animals, and so

---

42   Interview, hunter, from Rhineland-Palatinate, 05.07.2021.

43   For example: "Lebensgefahr? – Jagdhunde im Wolfsrevier", in: Wild und Hund 11/2015, p. 30–35.

hunting bags in the area are decreasing and management plans cannot be ful-
filled. These are some of the most common concerns of hunters with hunting
grounds in wolf territory.[44] In turn, these circumstances make the hunting
grounds unattractive: Hunters wonder why they should pay several thousand
euros per year for such hunting grounds. Landowners who want to rent out
hunting grounds cannot find tenants. This was also the case with the Lord
Mayor of Bautzen (himself a hunter), who had problems renting out the town
forest:

> We are in the process of renting out our town forest again. It's 1500 hectares
> of forest and mountain. Until a few years ago, it was one of the richest game
> habitats in East Saxony and I was telling someone, a wolf advocate, at the
> weekend that we only shot the first roebuck this year in a driven hunt in
> November, which is extremely unusual for this area. [...] Three years ago it
> was like this, you could go out in the evening and know that you would be
> back home in two hours because you had three or four deer of which you had
> chosen the right one to shoot. Now, as I said, in the whole hunting year we
> only shot the first roebuck only in November during the driven hunt. This
> is extremely unusual. There were only very few roe deer before that, much
> fewer than in previous years. And that was right at the end of the lease. To
> date, we have not received a single application in response to the call for ap-
> plications. This is also very unusual, because this is actually a very beautiful
> area, also very scenic [...].[45]

Overall, the Lord Mayor sees the wolf ultimately as a threat to hunting itself
and the hunting tradition:

> Of course, on the one hand it is nice to see that the wolves could survive if we
> did not hunt them. But this has a noticeable effect on our hunting tradition.
> I find that quite alarming. Hunting is [...] a tradition as old as mankind itself.
> Of course, in a cultural landscape it is subject to very strong restrictions, and
> in Germany it is extremely strictly regulated. All this is justified. But today we
> have hunting districts where hunting is in principle almost hopeless, where
> there is no chance of shooting anything with any regularity [...]. All in all, the
> hunters feel that hunting has become more difficult because of the wolves,

---

44   Interview, hunter, from Rhineland-Palatinate, 27.04.2020 or interview, three hunters,
      from Brandenburg, 29.07.2021, see also "Folgen für die Jagd – Wenn er da ist", in: Wild
      und Hund 12/2016, pp. 16–22.
45   Interview, Lord Mayor of Bautzen/hunter, from Saxony, 16.12.2019.

and of course it annoys them when they have to hear that this is not true at all, don't make such a fuss, share something with the wolves [...] You can't do anything. I'm not in favour of eradicating the wolves either, but I think we have such a dense population that it can't do any harm if they are now treated according to hunting law, that they can be shot at certain times.[46]

The conflict with the wolf thus seems to be part of a larger conflict that has pre-occupied the hunting community for decades. They **feel under constant attack** from society as a whole, from the state and especially from conservationists.[47] Hunters seem to be **under constant pressure to justify themselves.** Since the 1970s, not only have basic hunting traditions such as trophy hunting or its *Hege* practices been criticised[48], but in the last two decades, hunting itself has also come under public scrutiny. The ethics of animal protection and animal welfare are increasingly being discussed and are no longer a minority position but have found their way into the majority of society. One could say with Michaela Fenske and Marlis Heyer that we are visibly and tangibly redefining our relationship to animals at the beginning of the twenty-first century.[49] Not only is the consumption of animal products no longer taken for granted, but so is the killing of animals, and therefore hunting. Although the number of hunters in Germany is steadily increasing, many hunters **feel that they are socially pillo-ried and disrespected.** Even the *Grauhund* ('grey hound', a.k.a. wolf) is appar-ently preferred to the *Grünrock* ('green robe', a.k.a. hunter), as a commentator in the *Deutsche Jagdzeitung* puts it:

No, it is not a question of painting the devil on the wall. And the government is probably not aiming for a large-scale 'disposal' of the German hunting community. But: The incidents mentioned in the article are neither iso-lated cases nor comprehensible. Strange. And we remember wolves with Italian or French 'passports' that first appeared in NRW or Brandenburg. After thousands of kilometres of migration along motorways and past large cities. They came as if out of nowhere. That is also strange. And then there

---

46   Interview, Lord Mayor of Bautzen/hunter, from Saxony, 16.12.2019.

47   See the cover topic on hunting opponents of Jäger magazine 4/2017, announced on the cover as: "Jagen in postfaktischen Zeiten – Ende der Idylle"; "Drohkulissen: Wer unsere Gegner sind"; "Wahlchancen: Wo die Grünen wegmüssen"; "Kampagnen: Wie wir uns endlich wehren".

48   W. Bode/E. Emmert: Jagdwende.

49   M. Fenske/M. Heyer: Wer zum Haushalt gehört.

are the Greens. In more and more state governments, they are hogging the hunting issue. Then they cobble together new laws that castrate hunting. In return, Isegrim[50] is treated to a contemporary culture of welcome. Strange indeed.[51]

Anger at 'the Greens' is compounded by **envy** of the wolf. From the hunters' point of view, wolves are 'canonised', 'untouchable', and are allowed to live as they please. Wolves are obviously valued more highly than the actual game species of the hunters—even when they are, for example, wiping out the mouflon sheep in the Königshain mountains between Bautzen and Görlitz, which were reintroduced by hunters over a hundred years ago.[52] In addition, wolves are allowed to spread unhindered, while the hunters' beloved red deer are restricted to a few designated red deer areas.[53] Wolves are given preferential treatment, to the detriment of native game, and the hunters themselves.

So, there are many reasons why hunters might get upset about wolves and get involved in the conflict against them. But for some hunters (especially in non-wolf areas) this is all too much, and they don't want to have anything to do with the wolf at all. They prefer to stay out of it and just go hunting. The reason for this is that hunters in general feel potentially threatened if they get involved in any way with wolf issues. Wolf advocates might turn up in their hunting district and snoop around, saw through the posts of hunting blinds or even threaten to sue.[54] As with the shepherds, there is a **diffuse sense of anxiety** in the hunting community of being targeted by these wolf friends. Almost every hunter has heard these stories, in which the diffuse anxiety also had very concrete causes. A hunter from the Leuscheid Pack territory, for example, was the first to tell me about the diffuse atmosphere of anxiety caused by the wolf advocates:

What do I do if a wolf comes at me? I really just run—I sent X a photo—there is my little PKK [pistol], I have it with me, it fits in my jacket pocket. And if

---

50   Isegrim is a cultural reference to a wolf character in the well-known fable of *Reinicke Fuchs*.

51   "Komisch. Grauhund statt Grünrock?", DJZ online from 14.01.2016. https://djz.de/komi sch-grauhund-statt-gruenrock-3777/ (accessed: 30.04.2024, translated by TG).

52   Interview, Lord Mayor of Bautzen/hunter, from Saxony, 16.12.2019; "Muffelwild—Ver- schwinden vorprogrammiert", in: Wild und Hund 5/2022, p. 14–20.

53   Interview, District Hunting Master, from Rhineland-Palatinate, 18.02.2020.

54   Interview, two hunters, from Rhineland-Palatinate, 02.03.2020.

I just fire a warning shot into the ground. [...] But my difficulty is that there is no objective way to deal with it. You can be sure that even if I'm out in the woods with my dog [...] and the wolf attacks my dog or threatens to attack my dog and I feel I have to defend myself and shoot the wolf, then I can be one hundred percent sure that I will definitely be reported to the police because someone will accuse me, even if I didn't want to, of deliberately trying to kill the wolf because it's a thorn in my side. It's as certain as the Amen in church that this would happen, because there is no objective way of dealing with it any more. As a hunter, I now always have to be afraid that if I have anything to do with the wolf, I will be sued and then I [...] will have a trial. I don't need that. It's no longer a rational way of dealing with things.[55]

But then there are also these concrete, non-hypothetical events that fuel this anxiety:

And then two weeks later I was sitting in the hunting blind at night to hunt sows, I think it was 11 p.m., and then I saw, just after I sat down there, I saw people walking across the fields with a torch and shining it into the hunting blind and into the next hunting blind and the next one. Then they stood in front of my hunting blind and said, Are you X? And I said, Yes [...] who wants to know? I thought it was one of the locals, because I actually have a good relationship with the people there, and then I got the answer: 'Watch what you do with the wolf. We're watching you', and then they went away. And I don't need that, I don't need that. They've already slashed my tyres twice and scratched my car and sawed the legs off my hunting blinds. [...] I don't use violence or threats, that's against my nature, with me it's always [...] on a factual basis you can talk to each other and if you disagree, then that's the way it is. But this was really transgressive in a way [...] I didn't tell my wife either, she would never let me out again because she would be afraid for me.[56]

Let us summarise what has been said so far about the ethos of hunters in relation to the wolf: It is typically characterised by a certain anxiety or even fear of (potential or actual) threats from wolf friends; envy of the wolf as an animal that is treated as if it were above one's own game; a general feeling of being blamed and attacked by conservationists and society at large, including the feeling of constantly having to justify oneself as a hunter; Worries about the loss of hunting traditions and hunting itself; worries about the impact of the

---

55   Interview, hunter, from Rhineland-Palatinate, 05.07.2021.
56   Interview, hunter, from Rhineland-Palatinate, 05.07.2021.

wolf's presence on their hunting district and on 'their' game in terms of their *Hege* relationship; aversion to hostility towards the wolf as a predator; and fear of the wolf as a potential danger to their own lives when hunting.

With this in mind, it is easier to understand why there may be strong **feelings of aggression**, or even **hatred** towards wolves within the hunting community. This hatred is fed by the whole range of affects outlined here. It includes feelings towards the wolf, of course, but also feelings towards other social actors, and finally it feeds on the general ethos of how it feels to be a hunter today. In this hatred, the various elements of this affective arrangement mix, reinforce each other, and create the basis for a final possibility: the illegal killing of wolves:

> To put it bluntly: this is how we do it. Full stop. In the past, there would have been no wolves at all; the old foresters would have said: 'Gentlemen, this area is wolf-free. I don't want to hear anything more about it'. That would have been settled quietly [...]. That's why this is so symptomatic of this passivity [...]. You only have to ask why the wolves were exterminated in the past. If you know that, you also know that it must be the same today. You don't need to get tangled up in the details [...]. You just have to argue with common sense. And then they bring in the wolves. And the hunters put up with that too [...].[57]

Here we have the wounded pride, the lost claim to dominance, the need to endure, the dangerousness of the wolves, the wisdom of the old hunters, and the clear, uncompromising action that would provide the solution. The hunter and hunting lawyer Dr. Heiko Granzin is more radical in his hatred. Among other things, he informs hunters about the limits of the legality of shooting wolves in articles in the *Deutsche Jagdzeitung* and offers his legal assistance to those who need it (like the Dutch hunter who shot a wolf during a driven hunt in Brandenburg and was represented in court by lawyer Granzin):

> 'For my sake, let the greyhound go to hell!' Can I say that? Yes, I can! My profession does not deprive me of the right to free speech, and it makes no difference whether PETA or completely confused wolf-huggers wish the plague on me. As a hunter, dog handler, hobby animal keeper, and non-association official, I don't have to 'howl with the wolves' and babble out hypocritical slogans like, 'The hunters' association XY welcomes the return of the wolf'.

---

57   Interview, hunter, from Hesse, 02.11.2019.

No—whenever I read somewhere that one of the greys has been crushed to a pulp on the motorway, a smile flits across my face. But road traffic alone will not stop the ongoing population explosion of this hunting moocher. So why not just pick up a gun? Quite simply: because it is not (yet) legal. But it is not completely forbidden either [...].[58]

If this hatred is accompanied by the right opportunity and the means are available, it is not far to the illegal killing of a wolf, as a hunter from the Lausitz region explained to me after the interview (when the recorder was switched off).[59] It happens when you are hunting wild boar at night, when you are sitting in the dark for hours anyway. Suddenly a young wolf appears instead of a sow (it's always the pups or yearlings, the adults aren't that stupid). Then you seize the opportunity and shoot it. After all, you are well equipped with night vision technology—including the illegal one you got from Dutch hunting guests. No, he has no problems with his game stock, it's great. And no, he has no problems with wolves, he says with a grin.

Get rid of that passivity, get rid of tolerating everything that the Greens, PETA, and others put in front of you, stop swallowing everything quietly, but become active again yourself, solve the problems yourself, assert your claim to dominance in your own territory, make the wolf a huntable game animal, as it has always been, and kill the wolf, as hunters have always done. After all, it is dangerous and a threat to the game you are protecting. Restore 'normality'.

It is the possible extremes of the hunters' affective world that I ultimately wanted to highlight here. Based on six years of research with hunters, I believe that the causes of these feelings and sentiments are widespread; their extremes are not. I hope to have shown that several factors can contribute to the escalation of affective dynamics towards heightened feelings of aggression and hatred. However, these same factors can also help to calm and reduce them.

---

58   "Notwehr gegen Wolf: Wenn Isegrim die Zähne fletscht", in: DJZ 1/2019, p. 8–9, translated by TG.

59   Interview, hunter, from Saxony, 09.03.2022. Yet it remains difficult to assess how serious he really was with his statement. Was he just venting or talking about the possibility? Research into the matter of illegal killings are inherently difficult, see von Essen, Erica/Hansen, Hans-Peter/Peterson, Nils/Peterson, Tarla: 'Discourses on illegal hunting in Sweden: the meaning of silence and resistance', Environmental Sociology, 4 (2018), pp. 370–380, https://doi.org/10.1080/23251042.2017.1408446.

"They touch something deep inside me": wolf friends and wolves

Figure 25: Waiting for wolves in Upper Lusatia

Source: Author

At a vantage point near Hoyerswerda, Lusatia.

I am in the 'Mecca' of wolf friends in Germany, in the territory of the Knap-penrode-Seenland Pack, where probably more wolves have been sighted than in any other place in Germany—probably more wolves than in any other place in Europe. Wolf friends of all kinds can be found here at any time of the year, but especially in the summer months when the pups have left the den and are out and about with the older ones. With naked eyes, binoculars, spotting scopes, or cameras, they keep an eye out for wolves at dawn and dusk. Sometimes there are just a few of them, sometimes up to twenty, standing in a dense row at the very front, their equipment and camping chairs set up, supplied with food and drink, well wrapped up and reasonably protected from the cold in winter, sprayed with Autan to ward off mosquitoes in summer. They stand or sit there for hours, mostly in silence, often without seeing a wolf. Some are happy to see a deer, a wild boar, the cranes, a nightjar, or an osprey. The locals here usu-ally already know each other and greet each other with the question: "Have you seen anything yet? Have any wolves been here yet?" Among them are enthusi-astic wolf fans who seem to spend a lot of their free time here; nature enthusiasts who have found their way to the wolf late in life, or simply people from the neighbouring village who cycle past to see if they can spot a wolf; or the cook from Hoyerswerda who spends his lunch break here in the hope of seeing something; or the shift worker who feels drawn here after work. They are joined by wolf friends who travel from all over Germany. Some come from Berlin for a weekend trip to Lusatia, others stay for a week or two. Still others have booked a tourist wolf seminar or a few days with one of the local nature guides. Most of the time it is quiet here, or you can hear a low whisper from those standing next to you. But when suddenly someone shouts "THERE!", cameras are frantically waved, followed by almost desperate cries of "WHERE? WHERE? I SEE NOTHING!", then life comes to the group and joy breaks out! (Unless it was just a hare or a deer that was mistaken for a wolf from a distance.)[60]

As can be seen from this short vignette, there are—similar to shepherds and hunters—different types of wolf friends. These are not necessarily fundamentally different, but in some respects, they are so different that I will explicitly mention the differences where necessary. They are most visible at the organisational level, where the wolf friends can be found in animal welfare, species conservation, and nature conservation organisations. Animal welfare activists (for example, *Wolfsschutz Deutschland e.V.*) care for and appreciate every single wolf. Because the wolf is important to them as an individual, their relationship with wolves often takes on a deep, personal, and intensely affective character, which is less pronounced in the other two types of organisations. The focus of species conservationists (e.g. the *Gesellschaft zum Schutz der Wölfe e.V.—GzSdW*) is the wolf as a species. Caring for the species can then mean 'sacrificing' individual wolves for the preservation of the species (which in turn is unthinkable for animal welfare activists). Finally, conservationists (e.g. *NABU*) focus on larger ecological contexts in which an individual species only acquires its significance in the network of relationships with other species and their overarching importance for a habitat or ecosystem.

Species conservation and nature conservation usually go hand in hand (but with different emphases) and in their own understanding they distance themselves mainly from the animal welfare movement, which they see as too 'radical'. Conversely, species and nature conservation often does not seem to go far enough for the animal welfare activists. In the case of wolves, it is clear that species and nature conservation organisations are well networked—also with

---

60   Reconstruction of a 'typical day' at the lookout based on field notes from three years.

corresponding organisations of livestock owners or (ecological) hunters, as I have already shown above. Animal welfare activists, on the other hand, tend to be rather isolated and marginalised in the public debate (although they are networked with other animal welfare activists, such as PETA or anti-hunting organisations). During my fieldwork, it was striking that animal welfare activists were the only group that nobody wanted to have anything to do with. I have already mentioned the threat scenarios attributed to them by sheep farmers and hunters.

It is also important to note that wolf friends are generally the most heterogeneous of the three groups of actors. It is not a community of practice like the sheep farmers or hunters who, despite different social backgrounds, develop common norms, values, sentiments, and ethos through a shared practice (of hunting, shepherding). Wolf friends are united primarily by their shared relationship with the wolf, although there is a loose bundle of practices that many share and that provide opportunities for sociality, such as touristic wolf trips, visits to wolf enclosures, reading wolf books, attending lectures or public events or 'wolf seminars', and so on.

So what does it feel like to be a wolf friend—in this time, in this society, with wolves? In order to portray the ethos of wolf friends, I will refer mainly to the sentiments and feelings of three individuals, as their stories express not only their interesting personal relationship with wolves, but also 'typical' elements that are characteristic of wolf friends in general. The first is Jörg, owner of a dog training school, formerly a dog trainer in the German army, and for many years active in nature and species conservation. He is a member of the Senckenberg Society and the GzSdW, among others.[61] Next is Willi, a NABU Wolf Ambassador who spent several years volunteering as a Large Carnivore Officer in Rhineland-Palatinate. He was an intensive care nurse and still works in the care sector. He is also a keen outdoor sportsman.[62] Finally, there is Nicole, who volunteers on the GzSdW board. She has been riding since she was a girl and has learned to love nature on cross-country rides all over Europe. For her, being active and involved with wolves in her work for the GzSdW is a balance to her day job as an accountant.[63]

The best way to explore the ethos of wolf friends is to start with the basics: a felt connection to nature. People who are **fascinated** by wolves are rarely fasci-

---

61   For all quotes below: Interview, 06.07.2020.
62   For all quotes below: interview, 08.11.2019.
63   For all quotes below: Interview, 08.07.2020.

nated by wolves alone. They are usually fascinated by a wide variety of animals, both wild and domesticated (especially *companion animals*, such as dogs and horses).[64] They also tend to **love nature** in general and find **joy in experiencing nature:**

> I am someone who has been in touch with nature all my life. Even as a child, I found nature pleasant. But I really came to the wolf through the dog. [...] It was because I wanted to understand my dog better. The wolf is a wild animal and the dog is a domesticated pet. And because I was interested in the dog, its whole behaviour, I went to the roots, and the roots are the wolf. (Jörg)

> The subject of wolves has always been with me, even in my youth. They have always been animals that have fascinated me. They are such social animals. I come from a social environment, also professionally [...]. Somehow, I thought, this couldn't be true—in 2012 a wolf came to the Westerwald and was shot—that such an animal could come here from Italy and then be shot. That was a reason for me to do something in this direction. (Willi)

> This is a difficult question to answer because I have always found wolves great. I have to go back a long way. The point is that for as long as I can remember, even as a little girl, I thought wolves were great. When we went to the zoo, I can well remember that my parents couldn't get me away from the wolf enclosure. [...] I suppose one of my favourite animals was dogs, which I knew from my personal environment; I didn't have any myself, but there were dogs in the family, there were dogs in the neighbourhood, and I used to walk the neighbours' dogs when I was seven years old. And I think the wolf was like that [...], he had a sense of freedom. It was the big brother from the wild of my favourite animal, the dog. (Nicole)

In all three cases, you can see that the origins of the relationship with the wolf go back to childhood. It is rare for someone to develop a late relationship as an adult. For some it starts with the wolf, for some with the dog, for others with a general love of nature. Whatever the beginning, these three elements usually occur together (so it is not surprising that Willi also has a dog). The role of dogs in this context cannot be underestimated. The two representatives of the species *Canis lupus* create a **feeling of supposed familiarity and closeness**

---

64   For her, wolves accordingly have a 'nonhuman charisma', see Lorimer, Jamie: 'Nonhuman charisma', in: Environment and Planning D: Society and Space 25 (2007), pp. 911–932, https://doi.org/10.1068/d71j.

for both of them through their close (biological-genetic) relationship, conveyed through the dog.

The affective bond with the wolf can also increase when experiences of familiarity and closeness are combined with a kind of identification with the wolves. Willi already alluded to this in his statement when he compared the social, caring behaviour of the wolves with his own. For Nicole, this also plays a role:

> And at the same time, I see a lot of parallels, also in the family, they have their territory, we have our home. They go hunting, we have our jobs. They have their children, we have our children. At some point, when they are sexually mature, the children leave the family, do something on their own, and also start a family. I think there are a lot of parallels.

So, it is not only the similarity between dogs and wolves that provides access to an affective relationship with wolves; wolf friends also see similarities between humans and wolves in their way of life and their sociality. Both forms of similarity, however, are not similarities between equals: The dog is the wolf's 'little brother' and the wolf friend also looks up to the wolf in some way. Nicole was more explicit about this admiration:

> And I think that's also, that's really a very emotional level that I have there, where I really notice that I tend to overreact a bit. It's such an ideal that people read into it. A symbol of wilderness, a symbol of freedom, and at the same time I see that they still live in a family. I think that's what fascinates me about them. This strength and power and this freedom to live in harmony with nature, which we as humans can no longer manage, and the wolf does this quite naturally, as do many other animals, of course.

The last sentence of this quote adds an important qualification to my characterisation of wolf friends as nature-loving (and this clearly distinguishes them from the shepherds and hunters who also see themselves as nature-loving!). **Wolf friends feel close to nature and at the same time alienated from nature.**[65] More precisely, they perceive themselves—on a personal-individual level—as

---

65   I understand alienation with Hartmut Rosa as a "specific form of world relationship in which subject and world are indifferent or hostile (repulsive) to each other and thus inwardly disconnected" (Rosa, Hartmut: Resonanz. Eine Soziologie der Weltbeziehung. Frankfurt a. M.: Suhrkamp 2016, p. 316, translated by TG).

nature-loving but shaped by a society that is perceived as alienated from nature (in this respect, shepherds and hunters tend to distinguish between nature-loving rural people and nature-alienated city dwellers).[66] Their closeness to nature is therefore 'disturbed', as Jörg explains using the example of dog training:

> In my opinion, we humans in our consumer society are not capable of raising a dog in a way that is reasonably appropriate to the species. Very few people can do that in our throwaway society. [...] If something doesn't work, it's usually thrown away immediately and the dog goes to an animal shelter or is beaten or something else.

Willi also believes that our society's relationship with nature is disturbed—for him, the illegal shooting of the wolf Pier-Luigi in the Westerwald in 2012 was an expression of this (see his first quote above)—and he wanted to get involved. There was also something wrong with society's image of animals, as Jörg had already experienced as a child:

> When I finally got involved with the wolf, it confirmed what I had always suspected as a child. As a child, I had to go against what the adults knew. When I was little, they said that animals were stupid and had no feelings. So, in the past you only looked at animals from the outside and didn't see their inner life [...].

The affective bond between wolf friends and wolves therefore depends crucially on seeing wolves as having an 'inner life', an affective world to which they can relate, so that they can affect and be affected by each other. Yet even wolf friends sometimes find it difficult to publicly acknowledge wolves as sentient subjects. The whole wolf debate is very much characterised by a rational, scientific image of wolves, which makes it difficult to treat wolves as subjects. It would too quickly be perceived as 'irrational', and so this aspect is usually raised in private (or it is voiced by animal welfare activists, for whom the recognition of animal subjectivity is central).

The paradox of feeling both close to and alienated from nature ultimately leads them to have a **longing for a more natural life.** One could also say for a 'wilder' life, a connection to nature understood as wilderness—in contrast

---

66   Interestingly, even the hunter from the big city typically sees himself as part of this nature-loving rural population qua his identity as a hunter!

to shepherds and hunters, for whom a nature ordered and controlled by humans, or understood as a cultural landscape, is central. While for shepherds and hunters, humans are still at the centre of their understanding of nature, for wolf friends, humans are only part of a positively perceived whole that is superior to them. With sociologist Hartmut Rosa, one could also say that wolf friends intensely feel the **basic ecological fear of modernity**, namely that nature as a resonance space (for an affective relationship) could fall silent, combined with the simultaneous **hope** that wild animals—and especially wolves as the epitome of wilderness par excellence—can make it resound again.[67]

The return of the first wolves to Germany more than twenty years ago was therefore an affectively charged event for wolf friends that both allayed this basic fear and strengthened their hope for the possibility of a life in resonance with a wilder nature previously unknown in this country. Nicole recalled that time:

> I remember very clearly when [biologist and documentary filmmaker] Sebastian Koerner's film of the pups on the military training ground in Saxony were shown on the news. I sat at home and was deeply moved emotionally because I couldn't believe that these animals were coming home to us again. That touched me like nothing else in my life, because I would never have thought that this could happen [...] in Siberia or Canada, yes [...] that took me away emotionally, in a positive sense [...].

As recently as the 1990s, no wolf friend could have imagined this. The longing for wolves was even greater then, because the geographical distance was greater: wolves existed in Siberia, Canada, or on the fringes of Europe. A NABU wolf ambassador from the Westerwald, for example, wanted to emigrate to Canada as a child (and had already tried to contact the Canadian embassy) to be close to the wolves.[68] Many wolf friends have therefore made expensive trips to Sweden, Slovakia, or Russia to experience what was not possible here in Germany. Jörg is also one of those who had his first encounter with wolves in a distant country—though in his case not during a wolf trip, but during his work as a soldier:

---

67   H. Rosa: Resonanz, pp. 453–472.
68   Interview, NABU Wolf Ambassador, from Rhineland-Palatinate, 09.07.2020.

In Canada, it wasn't one wolf, it was several. It was in Labrador. The US had a strategic bomber command stationed there and when I was there, there was half a metre, [a] metre of snow. We practised parachuting there with the Americans. Then we jumped, were blown away a bit by the wind, came down two or three kilometres away, and then fought our way back to X. And there were five wolves there. And there were four or five wolves there, they were timber wolves, they were all black. [...] They even followed us a bit, but always at a distance, and then we moved on. I'd say they were around us for half an hour, three quarters of an hour.

The return of the wolves to Germany has not only changed nature here, it has also 'rewilded' the cultural landscape. Above all, it offers wolf friends a previously unimaginable opportunity: to live close to the wolves and to be able to meet them 'in real life'—to feel and experience their closeness 'in the flesh':

This is the absolute highlight that everyone strives for. [...] of course, you only know people who have either already seen a wolf or not. And those who have already seen one still talk about it with the greatest enthusiasm years and years later. And those who haven't seen one yet, they all talk about it as the greatest thing they can imagine. That has a very, very high value. [...] But [...] I can't tell you what that does to motivation, because people say they protect what they know. And for me, nothing has changed because I was already committed to protecting them before, [...] for me it's now a golden treasure that I have, I don't need any more. [...] This feverish working towards it, this absolute wanting to have it, that's gone, because I have it [...]. I've always gone on all these trips thinking, hopefully it'll work out [and I'll see a wolf]. (Nicole)

Willi is the only one of the three who has never seen a wolf in the wild. He has also been to Lusatia as part of his wolf monitoring training, but apart from tracks in the sand and wolf scat he has seen nothing there. He also went on wolf trips to Slovakia and Russia to see wolves, but he had no success there either. All the more important for him was the encounter with a wolf in an enclosure during a wolf seminar at the Wolf Centre in Dörverden, where he was even able to touch a wolf. Although he does not see himself as a 'wolf cuddler', he could not resist showing a photo of himself scratching the belly of a polar wolf on the last slide of his presentation at the end of a public talk he gave in the Westerwald. As for Nicole, this encounter was also a kind of 'golden treasure' for him. So there seems to be something about direct encounters with wolves that affects wolf friends more deeply than anything else, regardless of whether the encounter is just a longing in a wolf friend's life, or an actual experience that lingers in memory for a lifetime. We should therefore take a closer look at this experience. First with Nicole:

> Yes, with the [nature guide] last year [...], I have tried for years in other places. I was in Slovakia once, then I was in northern Spain, both in wolf areas, we do trips every two or three years, which are organised by the members, and we go to a wolf territory, and I was there from the beginning. We tried it in the far east of Poland, in the Białowieża National Park, but it didn't work [...]. But I have to say that I had tried it twice before with Stephan [...] and then last year it worked for the first time. I have to say quite clearly that this experience is so emotionally charged for me that I couldn't tell you about it in peace. But it was just unbelievable [...], absolutely unbelievable for me. To actually stand there and look through the binoculars [...], and that was also a relatively long sighting. I always wished that if I ever saw a wolf, it wouldn't be a shoo-and-go! And to have somebody next to me saying, by the way, that was a wolf. That would be a nightmare. Seen, but not really perceived. Please not like that, I don't want that, I would have found that quite horrible. But somehow this wish was granted. We spent a total of about five or six minutes [...], at the closest point it was about four, five hundred metres. That's quite close.

A little later in the interview, she finally found the right words to describe the 'indescribable':

> It was really very feverish, it was total longing and wanting to have an experience, with an incredible urge behind it [...]. I have to say quite clearly that in my whole life there has never been anything that has touched me as deeply as this wolf sighting, not by a long shot [...], it touches a part of our soul that is extremely primal, and I think that releases a special emotion [...]. It just appeals to a part of our inner being that has become very atrophied in our modern world, and I just find that it makes such a 'Whoa!' when it's addressed in this way, because it doesn't know that it's being addressed, [...] It's something deeply rooted in us and our actual humanity, not this functional thing that we have in the modern world, we used to be hunters and gatherers and part of the forest and the wilderness and the nature that we live in, and I think this emotional thing is this moment where for a fraction of our life or a moment we come back into a unity with something that we used to be one with, but today in the modern world we are no longer [...], this is a feeling of euphoria [...].

Jörg found it as difficult as Nicole did to find the words to describe this deeply moving experience, and first kept his description of his first wolf encounter in Germany, in Lusatia, short: "It was on a military training ground, I was walking along the path all alone, and suddenly a wolf stood there and looked at me, quite simply, and a short time later it disappeared".

I then asked him if his encounters in Canada and in Lusatia had had any special meaning for him:

[JÖRG:] Yes, of course. When you love nature and animals in the wild, it always triggers something. I would say very pleasant feelings. I don't want to say it was a feeling of love, but at least it was a feeling of joy. Not a euphoric joy, a quiet joy, a confirmation. It was pleasant, and of course it still arouses curiosity.

[INTERVIEWER:] What do you mean by confirmation?

[JÖRG:] Well, confirmation that it has been said that free-roaming animals, in the wild, live much more quietly, more pleasantly, more contentedly than animals in an artificial world, as it is in our society. They don't need golden taps, they just need peace and quiet. If it's not about eating and being eaten, there is peace and contentment in nature, and I'd even say respect and love, which are no longer so present, or very little, in our artificial world. [...] For me it's always new excitement, experiencing something new, but it's always different what you experience. There is always a certain anticipation and a certain tension. I'm a very optimistic person, I have a lot of fun and laugh a lot, and when I go to the countryside and I get away from this accelerated society and this hectic pace and find myself in nature and then experience something pleasant [...] it's always nice, it's exciting and you always want to experience more of it.

An encounter with wolves thus offers wolf friends, as is impressively demonstrated here, a space for **resonance experiences**: *"the (momentary) shining forth, the lighting up of a connection to a source of strong valuations in a predominantly silent and often also repulsive world"*.[69] This experience of resonance is characterised by complex feelings (**pleasure, excitement, curiosity, anticipation, quiet joy, euphoria, Whoa!**) that are deeply affective and even transform the deep-seated dissatisfaction with living in the modern world (the functional, golden taps,

---

69   H. Rosa: Resonanz, p. 317 (translated by TG, emphasis added).

hectic, no respect, no love), with its sense of alienation, and instead bring to life a sense of connectedness. In other words, in resonance with the wild animal wolf, wolf friends can, as it were, feel themselves in their 'being-animal' and 'being-wild'.

For those who are simply wolf friends in private, their ethos may already be sufficiently described here. But even this group of people may sometimes have the **uneasy feeling** that the return of wolves is threatened and that there are wolf critics who want them dead. If one is a committed wolf friend and actively campaigns for wolves in the public sphere, then one certainly cannot avoid going into another dimension of that affective world, that which is fed by the social conflict with other groups of actors. The threat scenarios described above by shepherds and hunters are not one-sided. Some wolf friends also face hostility. Volunteers like Willi, who publicly campaigns for wolves, are often verbally attacked by livestock owners or hunters. In his opinion, this also affects the public relations work of NABU wolf ambassadors. Their work is considered particularly important in places where emotions are running high, but often there is no one to 'step into the lion's den' and do it. One Wolf Ambassador from North Rhine-Westphalia, for example, received a phone call from a hunter after an event, insulting her. The wolf biologists at the LUPUS Institute have also been insulted and threatened many times.[70] Among other things, hunters took them to court for using soft-catch traps to tag wolves as part of Saxony's state monitoring programme.[71] A Large Carnivore Officer in the Westerwald was threatened with legal action for setting up camera traps for monitoring purposes. And the chairwoman of *Wolfsschutz Deutschland* reported that her tyres were slashed, and the bumper of her car damaged when she went into the territory of the Leuscheid Pack to check the fences of local sheep farmers.[72]

Especially among animal welfare activists, there seems almost a **sense of being in a kind of 'state of war' with the wolf critics**, as can be seen regularly in various Facebook groups. Since every single wolf counts for them, so does every single sheep farmer, hunter, or other wolf critic. Inevitably, the conflict becomes personal and therefore more intense: wolves are deeply loved, and

---

70   Interview, biologist, from Saxony, 03.08.2020.

71   "Kein Vorsatz beim Einsatz von Fallen", Jäger 3/2016.

72   "RLP—Leuscheider Rudel: Angriff auf Vorstand von Wolfsschutz-Deutschland e. V. bei Recherche", Wolfsschutz Deutschland, 30.04.2022, https://wolfsschutz-deutschland. de/2022/04/30/rlp-leuscheider-rudel-angriff-auf-vorstand-von-wolfsschutz-deutschl and-e-v-bei-recherche/ (accessed: 30.04.2024).

when someone acts against these beloved animals, they provoke correspondingly **strong outrage, anger or even hatred**. This is especially true in the extreme case of the illegal killing of wolves, as can be seen from this commentary on an illegal killing published on the website of *Wolfsschutz Deutschland*:

> I had always thought it was impossible that I could ever hate. But that has now changed, because I now I HATE the murderers of the wolves to the core. In the new [eastern German] states it seems to be all about getting their way, no matter by what means, they do not shy away from murder, lies, and spreading fake news. The wolf is a social, wonderful animal and has many advantages over humans. I'd rather meet a wolf than a human, especially the kind that are vicious, vile murderers, and there seem to be far too many of them in the East!!!! These murderers MUST be caught and punished severely, very severely, just murderers!!!![73]

For animal welfare activists, there is also not much difference between the illegal killing of a wolf and the legal 'removal' of a wolf. Both end in what they see as the unjust death of a beloved animal. Accordingly, legal removals are regularly challenged in court. In Lower Saxony, for example, the hatred directed at those responsible in such cases has ensured that removals are only made public to a limited extent before they are carried out, which has led to accusations that the Ministry of the Environment is acting in undue 'secrecy'.[74] This in turn fuels the conflict between the official wolf management and wolf protectionists in particular and wolf friends in general.

Despite these tense conflicts between wolf management on the one hand and livestock owners and hunters on the other, the return of wolves has been a cause for celebration for wolf friends. In recent years, however, their mood may have become a little **more depressed and worried** as the wolf critics have become more vocal and seem to have found a more sympathetic ear in the political arena. *Is the public mood turning against wolves and their friends?* One thing

---

73   Comment by Marga, 01.08.2018, 8:34 am, https://wolfsschutz-deutschland.de/2018/0 7/11/grausame-toetung-einer-jungwoelfin-10-000-euro-belohnung-fuer-die-ergreifu ng-des-taeters-ausgesetzt/ (accessed 30.04.2024, translated by TG).

74   "Auskunftsklage zu Wolfs-Entnahmen—Doods: 'Von Geheimniskrämerei kann keine Rede sein'", Niedersächsisches Ministerium für Energie, Bauen und Klimaschutz, Presseinformation 149/2021, https://www.umwelt.niedersachsen.de/startseite/aktue lles/pressemitteilungen/auskunftsklage-zu-wolfs-entnahmen-doods-von-geheimnis kramerei-kann-keine-rede-sein-206506.html (accessed: 30.04.2024).

is clear: politics is an affective affair and affects are political, so it is not surprising that wolf management is also a kind of affect management. And that is the subject of the final chapter.

6. Wolf Management as Affect Management

The affective dynamics of wolf management

In the last chapter, I outlined the subjective experience of wolf-related feelings for different actors and placed them within the larger intersubjective affective structures (ethos, sentiments) of the respective social movement or community of practice. This has allowed me to show how attitudes and opinions about wolves are affectively coloured and how conflicts with wolves and about wolves are subject to affective dynamics.

The purpose of this chapter is to clarify the extent to which these affects outlined above are not only structurally shaped by ethos and sentiments but are also 'made' in a very different way. For affects are not only subjectively experienced as something given with a vital dynamic of its own; they can also become an object (to be controlled), something that can be modulated, directed, transformed, governed. In other words, the affective dynamic becomes something that can be intervened by means of management measures. Accordingly, the aim here is to describe and understand wolf management and its practices as a kind of affect management.

In Germany, wolf management is organised at state level under the overall guidance of the Federal Ministry for the Environment, Nature Conservation and Nuclear Safety (BMUV) and the Federal Agency for Nature Conservation (BfN). Overall, the legal framework is based on the strict protection status of Annex IV of the EU Habitats Directive, which has so far been strictly adhered to (in contrast to Sweden and France). The reasons for this German approach can be found firstly in the high value placed on nature conservation in general and wolves in particular (in contrast to most Eastern European countries); secondly, and on this basis, Germany was one of the main drivers of the Habitats Directive and had a vested interest in seeing it applied to the letter; and thirdly, it was discussed and signed in the late 1980s, early 1990s, when wolves (and potential conflicts) were still unthinkable in Germany. This strict approach is also reflected in the general, unquantified objective of wolf management, which is to achieve a 'favourable conservation status', i.e. to establish and maintain a viable wolf population (in contrast to Norway, Sweden and France, which have defined a maximum number of wolves). Germany also has a coexistence or land-sharing policy (partly in contrast to the Fenno-Scandinavian countries with their 'wolf-free' reindeer areas), based on the belief that wolves and live-stock farming should be possible with a minimum of conflict. Although the details vary from federal state to federal state, it can generally be said that wolf management uses a mix of instruments to ensure coexistence, focusing mainly on subsidies for the implementation of protection measures, compensation for livestock losses and guidelines for dealing with potential 'problem wolves', in-cluding their 'lethal removal'.

As can be seen from this summary, wolf management is a deeply political endeavour that must address and reconcile not only species conservation but also conflict resolution. Wolf management is political not only in the narrower sense (i.e. as part of an institutionalised political field, operated by professional political actors), but above all in the broader sense, as part of a broadly con-ceived sphere of the political, "where human individuals and collectives deter-mine—either jointly or adversely—what their finite earthly existence will ulti-mately look like: the how of their living together and relating to one another".[1] Wolf management is a special case, however, because it is not only human ex-istence that is being negotiated, but also a more-than-human coexistence be-tween humans and animals. In these negotiations, power relations (both be-tween human actors and between these actors and the wolves) and ideas about cultural norms and values are manifested. In the words of Jonas Bens and col-leagues: "The political usually entails negotiating, debating, or at least posi-tioning oneself with regard to 'right' and 'wrong' or 'good' and 'bad' in a given context".[2] Accordingly, in wolf management (or in society as a whole) there is much room for negotiation and interpretation about how wolves and humans should live together. However, in contrast to the Fenno-Scandinavian countries in particular, the German *Länder* have so far been reluctant to adopt participa-tory models of co-management that would involve stakeholders in decision-

---

1   Slaby, Jan/Bens, Jonas: 'Political Affect', in: J. Slaby/C. v. Scheve (eds.), Affective Soci-eties, p. 349.

2   Bens, Jonas et al.: The Politics of Affective Societies – An Interdisciplinary Essay. Biele-feld: transcript 2019, p. 19, https://doi.org/10.14361/9783839447628.

making processes. There are consultation mechanisms, such as informal round tables, to which the ministries invite, but overall, the opportunities to have a real influence on institutionalised wolf management are very limited.

The power of wolf management in Germany can thus be seen as concentrated in the hands of state institutions. In some previous work on wolf management, governance and policy in countries such as Switzerland, Norway or the USA, 'official' (state-institutionalised) wolf management is often understood in Foucauldian terms as a disciplinary regime of power and surveillance, and wolves as more or less passive 'objects' of power.[3] The practice of wolf monitoring is used as an example to show how wolves are made visible through the collection of scientific data, through methods of classification and categorisation, and made controllable and thus governable through such regimes of knowledge that feed into concrete management actions. When wolf management is thus seen as part of a broader biopolitical (in terms of wildlife population management) or necropolitical (in terms of hunting or removal of wildlife) regime, one might get the impression that a wolf management regime has total control over wolves and that their management is merely a translation of theory (policy) into practice. However, the state wolf management regimes in Germany share certain characteristics that are hard to reconcile with such a pronounced claim to power on the part of the state: few staff, centralised (rather than locally dispersed) administration, outsourcing of work to volunteers, a passive monitoring regime, hardly any GPS-collared wolves, hardly any dietary analysis of wolf scat, hardly any scientific wolf research, and so on. Ultimately, the strength of wolf management depends largely on the allocation of resources, as wolf management is only one element in a suite of conservation measures, as the ecologist Nicolas Schoof and his colleagues have recently argued.[4]

3   See Rinfret, Sara: 'Controlling animals: Power, Foucault, and species management', in: Society and Natural Resources 22 (2009), pp. 571–578, https://doi.org/10.1080/089419 20802029375; Nustad, Karin/Swanson, Heather: 'Political ecology and the Foucault effect: A need to diversify disciplinary approaches to ecological management?', in: Environment and Planning E: Nature and Space, 5 (2022), pp. 924–946. https://doi.org/10.1 177/25148486211015044; Stokland, Håkon: 'Conserving Wolves by Transforming Them? The Transformative Effects of Technologies of Government in Biodiversity Conservation', in: Society and Animals 29 (2020), pp. 1–21.
4   Schoof, Nicolas et al.: 'Der Wolf in Deutschland. Herausforderungen für weidebasierte Tierhaltungen und den praktischen Naturschutz', in: Naturschutz und Landschaftsplanung 53.1 (2021), p. 10–19, https://doi.org/10.1399/NuL.2021.01.01.

A spokesman for the Rhineland-Palatinate Ministry of the Environment described the situation at a public event as follows:

> With regard to scenarios, I can tell you that we were of course surprised—and you know this—by the return of the wolf to Germany and Rhineland-Palatinate. It is also a fact that we basically—and here I also speak for the other federal states—that we basically don't know what the wolves are doing 95 percent of the time in the federal states—because you have to remember that not all wolves have transmitters ... That means they move around in our landscape, they move around in the forests, they are also inconspicuous 95 percent of the time. We don't see them. Even if a wolf is encountered from time to time, is detected by a wildlife camera, those are the only points where we see them. So we cannot say that this and that is the scenario of how they [the wolf population] will develop. Retrospectively, it's easy to show that when you recapitulate the data you have. But many of the occurrences of wolves are sudden. For example, there was the one alpine wolf that appeared in the national park a few weeks ago and has since disappeared. We don't know where the animal is, if it has migrated to Belgium, [...] and Wolf Billy has been run over or shot in France, I think [...] we always find out about that much later. In that respect, such scenarios [...] would imply that one has a detailed overview all the time, and quite frankly one does not have that.[5]

If we want to better understand human-wolf conflicts in Germany, we must therefore turn the previous power- and knowledge-focused perspectives on their head: While it seems conclusive that the production of knowledge about wolves feeds into regimes of power over and management of wolves, we must acknowledge how patchy and incomplete this knowledge is. The wolf management regime faces the challenge of establishing governability largely on the basis of scarce scientific knowledge and scarce resources. In relation to wolves, this means that management institutions have difficulty accessing wolves at all. Any access is primarily a challenge to those exercising power, not to the ('resisting') wolves!

If we want to stay with a Foucauldian concept of power in relation to wolf management, we need a different reading that foregrounds the discontinuities, the fragility, the inconsistencies of political processes, as well

---

5   Species Protection Officer (*Referent*) of the Rhineland-Palatinate Ministry of the Environment in the Q&A session of a public information event on the wolf in Neitersen, 22.06.2021.

as the need for constant renewal and confirmation or perpetuation of the power structures.[6] This precarious 'order of the discourse', or perhaps more accurately the ordering efforts of discourse, become apparent when we turn to the actual practice of management and emphasise its corporeal and affective foundations. In other words, we need to understand wolf management as affect management.

Such an approach is not only consistent with the conceptual framework that underlies this book but is also crucial to understanding a central problem of wolf management. Affective dynamics have a life of their own and can counteract the goals of management. This destabilising potential of affects is well known to wolf managers and was recognised as a problem early on. For example, a 2007 publication by the Federal Agency for Nature Conservation (Bundesamt für Naturschutz, BfN) summarised the social acceptance of wolves as follows:

The vast majority of the population has a positive attitude towards wolves. There is little public interest in wolves in Germany, the level of knowledge is low, and the interest in further information on wolves is not very high. The overwhelmingly positive opinion of the respondents is not very consolidated and there is a *risk that the mood will tip into the negative if major problems arise.*[7]

We can therefore see that wolf management is always confronted with an affective dynamic that has the potential to jeopardise the conservation of wolves and therefore requires some form of management or, one might say, *affective governance.*[8]

Affect management as *affective governance* is primarily an attempt to establish governability by taming 'negative' and promoting 'positive' affective dynamics. In doing so, wolf management proceeds in an immersive-spreading manner, i.e. it attempts to establish its field of power over a large area by multiplying its control mechanisms over several levels, thereby involving as many of the relevant actors as possible or minimising their power by excluding them. In many federal states, for example, various actors have a say in the development of wolf management through their participation at so-called round ta-

---

6   See Chrulew, Matthew/Wadiwel, Joseph (eds): Foucault and Animals, Leiden: Brill, 2017.

7   Reinhardt, Ilka/Kluth, Gesa: Leben mit Wölfen – Leitfaden für den Umgang mit einer konfliktträchtigen Tierart in Deutschland (= BfN-Skript 201), Bonn: Bundesamt für Naturschutz 2007 (translated by TG).

8   J. Slaby/J. Bens: Political Affect, p. 345.

bles, to which hunting associations, associations of livestock owners, and nature conservation associations are usually invited. Radical voices, however, are rarely heard. The exclusion of animal welfare organisations such as *Wolfsschutz Deutschland* from the round table has already standardised the range of acceptable intensities of affect. Only moderate affects—those regulated and tamed by reason—are supposed to contribute to rational management and be considered conducive to the goal. In this way, it is hoped that extreme antagonism between the parties involved, which could lead to violent outbursts of affect, can be countered.

As long as there is public support for the return of wolves and the attempt at coexistence, this interest, this opinion, this (precarious and changeable) mood must be stabilised and transformed into lasting dispositions, attitudes, and sentiments. In the words of Jan Slaby and Jonas Bens:

> The wielding of power, either in order to govern or to resist, is fundamentally an affective process. Insofar as politics is about the creation, maintenance and use of power, political actors understand the relevance of the creation of relatively stable affective dynamics to further political projects, both as a target for destabilization when it comes to their political opponents, as well as a goal to achieve for themselves.[9]

This is to be achieved primarily through the construction of general institutionalised legal frameworks, rather than through targeted individual interventions in affects. In this way, the protection of wolves as a species is meant to be removed from the volatility of the affects of individual actors or groups of actors. It is intended to create a 'path dependency' of coexistence-friendly sentiments and moods that, once established, would carry them into the future.[10] The most important of these path-dependent frameworks is the nesting of various nature conservation laws on the wolf as a protected species, ranging from the global level (Bern Convention) to the EU level (Flora-Fauna-Habitat Directive), to the national and state levels (federal and national nature conservation laws). This nesting of legal levels has proven to be particularly successful against applications for the removal of individual 'problem wolves' and has usually led to the rejection of the applications. However, the example of Olaf Lies, the former Environment Minister of Lower Saxony, who pushed through

---

9   J. Slaby/J. Bens: Political Affect, p. 345f.
10   Krzysztof Niedziałkowski: Between Europeanisation and politicisation.

several permits for the removal of wolves, often on shaky legal grounds, shows that resistance is possible within this *affective governance* regime if only the political will is there. However, this stable legal basis is accompanied by a still ambiguous and unconsolidated interpretation of the law, which can be creatively worked on by willing actors.

Affect management in the legal sphere therefore also includes a) the mere possibility, b) the threat, or c) the actual legal action in court—especially by nature conservation associations.[11] Moreover, it is precisely these possibilities for legal action that indicate that wolf management itself is an affective expression of a socially accepted and normatively understood value of species protection which is to be publicly enforced by the wolf management regime, but which is also open to public criticism if wolf management does not take this value seriously enough. *In a sense, conservation can be understood here as an institutionalised affect—that is, it is Sorge, a German word with two meanings: that of 'concern' or 'worry' (Sorgen-machen) and that of 'caring' (Fürsorge).* In this reading, wolf management as an affect-led institution aims to socially establish and consolidate concern for the conservation of the wolf species, that is, to 'communitarise' it among citizens, so that they care about wolves and their conservation.[12]

Rationality as a guiding principle

Understanding species conservation as an affective value and wolf management as affect management may, however, be difficult for wolf managers. As in all administrative processes, affects have no real place here and are often ignored in the whole public-political discourse. The political scientist Nicolas Demertzis states:

> The marginalization of emotion in political analysis was to a large degree owed to: (a) the stripping of the dimension of passion from the political because it was associated with romantic and utopian conceptions unrelated to the modern public sphere as well as because of the more or less instrumental and neutral-procedural conception of politics, a popular view at the end of the 1960s as well as today [...]; (b) the supremacy of 'interest' as opposed

---

11   In Chapter 4 I mentioned the example of the Bautzen Landrat who did not want to order the removal of a wolf because of possible lawsuits from wolf supporters.

12   '[A] certain striving for communalization' of political emotion' (T. Szanto/J. Slaby: Political Emotions, p .14).

to 'passion' as an explaining factor of political action [...] ; (c) the dominance
for many years of the rational choice paradigm across a very large number of
political science departments in the United States and Europe, in the context
of which emotions are either conceived as irrational elements or are taken as
objective traits which do not affect the actor's, by definition, 'rational' thinking [...].[13]

The discomfort of having to deal with affect in a wolf management regime is
thus structurally and historically embedded. The value of nature conservation
and species conservation underlying wolf management is not understood as
an affective value, as suggested earlier, but as a rational value, and is seen to be
underpinned by scientific research and knowledge. Thus, the guiding principle of 'rationality' is binding for both wolf management and public discourse
on wolves in general. Rationality is a cultural matter of course, a value in itself,
and is generally taken for granted by all parties to the wolf conflict, claimed for
themselves and denied to the other party. This goes hand in hand with the de-
valuation of emotionality in any form: it can quickly be used to reprimand participants in the debate, who are then accused of being overly emotional (where
any deviation from rationality is usually already considered 'overly' emotional).
Rationality thus frames and shapes the discourse, seeking to exclude the irrational, to suppress expressions of emotion, to steer contributions to the debate
towards rationality, and to enforce an orientation towards scientific knowledge.

According to this view, wolf conflicts are primarily fuelled by emotion on
the one hand, and by a lack of factual knowledge on the other. Conflict resolution strategies in public relations, for example, therefore, often focus on the
logical and rational communication of 'factual knowledge' (often referred to as
'education'). But this does not always go down well with wolf critics. The example of a public lecture event in the Westerwald illustrates the problem.

The Heimatverein Holzhausen—a local organisation that aims to promote
both the local community and the local *Heimat,* including local nature conservation—has asked a fellow Westerwälder to give a talk on wolves. A retired zoologist and member of the Society for the Protection of Wolves, he had worked
with various canids in a local game park and is also a sought-after 'wolf expert'

13   Demertzis, Nicolas (ed.): Emotions in Politics. The Affect Dimension in Political Ten-
      sion. Basingstoke: Palgrave Macmillan 2013, p. 1f.

for wolf management. He knows the wolf critics in his region from many public debates in which he often engages in heated emotional arguments (albeit on
a familiar first-name basis). Wolf experts like him and the anti-wolf and pro-
wolf groups in a region usually know each other. You always meet 'old acquaintances' when you go to a wolf event, he told me. His introductory words set
the tone for his talk: "Most discussions between so-called wolf opponents and
so-called wolf cuddlers [...] are very emotional, very heated, but often without
knowledge of the facts. And today I just want to give some facts, so that we can
have a factual discussion".

Over the course of the evening, he provides a lot of facts on the biology and
ecology of wolves, on the history of wolves in the Westerwald, and on herd protection and the impact of wolves on hunting. On the last two topics in particular, he spends more time on the arguments of the wolf critics, refuting them
one by one with scientific facts.

From a purely factual point of view, his arguments do not appear to be
open to attack, and there is no criticism from the ranks of the wolf opponents
present. Only on the subject of herd protection does a concerned horse owner
speak up and ask:

[HORSE OWNER:] I am a horse owner [...] and we are so desperate because
we say we would like to fence in but we are not allowed to. The building
regulations don't allow us to protect our animals and that's ridiculous. I keep
horses that have been rescued from slaughter, bad husbandry, confiscation,
and so on....

[SPEAKER:] How many horses have been killed [by wolves] in Germany?

[HORSE OWNER:] No, it's bad about every single one.

[SPEAKER:] Yes, of course. Of course, but there is no total protection.

[HORSE OWNER:] Yes, but it must be possible for us to protect our animals.

[SPEAKER:] How many horses have been killed in Germany?[14]

---

14   Public information meeting, Holzhausen, 05.03.2020, author's minutes.

The discussion goes on for minutes until the horse owner finally gets so annoyed that she gets up, pushes her way through the narrow row of chairs, and leaves the event.

Such a scene is not uncommon. I have seen similar scenes at other events during my fieldwork. Again and again, it became apparent that rationality and emotionality meet and come into conflict, with rationality prevailing, at least in the short term and superficially, but without being able to convince the affectively irritated. On the contrary, affects rarely seem to be appeased by rationality; they are often intensified precisely by the confrontation with an affect-negating rationality. In the above example, the horse owner's concern at the wolf expert's answers (the constant recourse to the statistics on the number of horses killed by wolves) is intensified into annoyance. In other words: emotions are difficult to explain away—with a few (but important) exceptions.

I have already mentioned the results of an acceptance study which showed that most Germans neither know much about wolves nor are very interested in them. When these people live in areas where wolves then appear for the first time, some of them are affected by the newcomers: they may feel a little insecure (due to the potential danger and their ignorance about wolves) and worried (whether they can still go for a walk in the woods, walk their dog, etc.). At information events, these worried people regularly come to the wolf experts for advice and are usually reassured by factual, science-based answers. This is the group of people who is receptive to this kind of affective public relations work based on rationality.

But when it comes to people with more intense emotions, when the level of concern is higher, mere rationality does not seem to get you very far. It does not help if wolf management has no strategy beyond rational argumentation to address and influence affects in its favour. Wolf management as affect management is usually exhausted in the attempt to de-emotionalise the conflict and is carried out more implicitly than explicitly. This leads to inconsistencies in practice, to a narrowed perspective on what affect management could mean, and therefore leaves a lot of room for *affective resistance;*[15] in other words, affective dynamics can easily evade *affective governance* and go their own way with their own means. An expanded understanding of wolf management as affective management must therefore follow multi-layered and directionally ambivalent dynamics. It must take into account both state actors and an overall situation (an affective arrangement, in other words) in which a variety of actors

15   J. Slaby/J. Bens: Political Affect, p. 345.

attempt to regulate and modulate affects, feelings, atmospheres, moods—on both small and large scales, by individuals, groups, and society as a whole. I will explore this in more detail below, using the practices of what is known in German as *Sorgen und Ängste ernst nehmen* (taking concerns and fears seriously), *Stimmung machen* (stirring mood), and *Dampf ablassen* (blowing off steam).

"We take your concerns and fears seriously"

A wolf conference in Hachenburg, Westerwald, in August 2019. After the first resident female wolf was confirmed in the Westerwald in early 2019, there was a need for discussion in the region. Wolf management organised a wolf conference to bring together experts and local residents to discuss wolf issues. In the workshop 'Wolf and Society', questions could be asked to a wolf biologist. A Ministry of the Environment spokeswoman, who moderated the workshop, introduced it as follows:

> Of course, you should be able to tell us your concerns and fears. [...] The ultimate goal for me would be to perhaps get an impression of the mood here. You now have the wolf at your door now, so to speak, but that's not the case in Mainz [the state capital and seat of the ministry], and maybe we're missing some things that are going on here. Please be honest, tell us your concerns and we will see that we include them.[16]

A long discussion ensued about whether you could still go hiking in the forests, whether you had to be even more careful when disposing of sandwiches at rest areas, whether there were special rules of conduct for dog owners, whether children could still camp in the garden, and so on.

'Taking concerns and fears seriously' has recently, at least since the so-called refugee crisis in 2015, become a maxim for action for many politicians and administrations and is now applied in all kinds of policy areas—including, and especially, in matters concerning wolves. Behind this maxim, however, there was initially a rhetorical trick by right-wing populist parties to reinterpret negative, socially sanctioned affects—such as hatred—as socially recognised affects—such as concern and fear. As Ulrich Bröckling has noted:

---

16   Wolf conference, Hachenburg, 09.09.2019, minutes of the author.

As a speech act, the sentence 'I am afraid of foreigners' has different effects from the phrase 'I hate them': those who refer to their fear claim to be taken seriously; but no politician, no matter how concerned, would think of demanding that we take people's hatred seriously and therefore tighten up refugee laws.[17]

I mentioned in Chapter 5 that (the public expression of) hatred of wolves is rare among sheep farmers or hunters. Although it can be assumed that it is certainly present among some wolf opponents, it is not expressed publicly, because hatred—unlike fear—does not find social acceptance and support. In the course of my research, I have often experienced how even wolf friends who are actively involved in wolf conservation do not know how to deal with the concerns and fears of wolf critics. These emotions are there, they cannot be argued away. This makes them a 'killer argument' and gives those concerned a strategic advantage: "Those who play the fear card undermine any criticism. He cannot be refuted because he insists on the authenticity of his feelings. To every objection he replies: 'But I *have* my fear! Who would want to deny it to me? Affect immunises against facts".[18] What is lost in this way of looking at affects is the fact that affects can be managed, even by those who are affected.[19] They are not a given natural fact.

The wolf conference in Hachenburg shows that wolf management has an ambivalent relationship with the concerns and fears of the public. On the one hand, efforts are being made to acknowledge them. On the other hand, it is already evident that a distinction is being made between justified and unjustified concerns—namely on the basis of their 'factuality'. In their view, unjustified concerns are based on misinformation, on 'wolf myths' and 'fairy tales', and should be countered by communicating scientific facts. This was the tenor of the whole 'Wolf and Society' workshop. Unjustified concerns (i.e., those that stand up to the facts), on the other hand, should be reduced through management measures, such as herd protection or financial compensation for losses.

---

17   Bröckling, Ulrich: 'Man will Angst haben', in: Mittelweg 36 (2016), pp. 3–7, here p. 5, translated by TG.

18   U. Bröckling: Man will Angst haben, S. 4, translated by TG.

19   Brezger, Jan: 'Muss man die Ängste und Sorgen der BürgerInnen ernst nehmen? Die aktuelle Asyl-Debatte und der Fall Bremgarten', Theorieblog, 19.08.2013, https://www.theorieblog.de/index.php/2013/08/muss-man-die-aengste-und-sorgen-der-buerger innen-ernst-nehmen-die-aktuelle-asyl-debatte-und-der-fall-bremgarten/ (accessed: 30.04.2024).

But there is a third way of dealing with concerns and fears, especially when it is difficult to determine exactly what is justified: when taking concerns and fears seriously becomes a method of affect management itself. It consists of three explicit and one implicit stage. First, it means an openness on the part of wolf managers to become affected by the voiced concerns and fears. This is done by providing a space where these feelings can be expressed. Secondly, it is about making people feel that they are being listened to. Third, understanding is expressed, and the authenticity of their feelings is acknowledged. In the logic of the person concerned, a fourth step should follow from this, namely that this recognition should lead to an action that takes care of their concerns so that, as a result, all the concerns are dealt with. The fact that this 'promise' is implicitly and potentially held out without being explicitly promised is what makes it so attractive for politicians and wolf managers. After all, you are not really promising anything if you take the concerns and fears seriously, and if this is so (positively) received by those affected, then it is a useful side-effect in addition to the goodwill shown to them.

It is doubtful that this method can be effective in terms of affect management if the fourth step is not explicitly followed up. However, I would argue that wolf management in general does not even attempt to address all concerns and fears. On the contrary, a certain undercurrent of negative affect is accepted as an inevitable part of any political negotiation process. It is the large outliers of affective intensity that need to be appeased.

In any case, the method has a significant side effect: the very focus on negative affect as something that needs to be given space, listened to, and acknowledged, has the effect of framing many public debates in a negative way. The primary mode in which wolves are discussed is as a problem and a conflict, and thus a trigger for negative emotions. Even in presentations by wolf management or conservation organisations, a considerable amount of time is spent discussing concerns and fears, even if only to show them to be unfounded in a completely 'rational' way. At the end of such an event, however, it is still mainly concerns and fears that have been discussed, and not much else. Taking these feelings seriously is therefore a double-edged sword: on the one hand, wolf management tries to manage affects this way. On the other hand, wolf critics definitely manage to set the coordinates of the debate in their favour.[20]

This is what happened, for example, with the so-called wolf resolution of the municipality of Asbach in the Westerwald. To briefly continue the story of

---

20   Ibid.

the return of the wolves to the Westerwald: It turned out that the male of the former Neuwied Pack, GW1159m, had indeed formed a new pack with the female GW1415f in the Leuscheider Wald area. Shortly afterwards, however, he disappeared and was replaced by the now 'notorious' male GW1896m. He had already attracted attention during his migration through several federal states by regularly killing sheep. Finally settling in the Leuscheider Wald in the spring of 2021, he began a series of sheep kills (all but one on unprotected sheep) that continued as of this writing (January 2024). The sheer number and consistent regularity of these kills, occurring almost every week, caused lasting anxiety and discontent among livestock owners in the region.

In an online information event organised by the municipality of Asbach, the official wolf management, in the form of two representatives of the newly founded Lynx and Wolf Coordination Centre (KLUWO), tried for almost four hours to answer all the questions of the local residents and to allay most of their concerns. But the wolf critics in the region apparently felt that they were not being taken seriously enough and kept up the pressure, flooding the mayor with concerned letters. Eventually, the municipal council met to pass an (anti-)wolf resolution, which was passed unanimously. The resolution states:

> In recent weeks and months, there have been an increasing number of wolf sightings and wolf attacks in the area of the Asbach municipality. These developments and circumstances have not left our population unscathed. Farmers, hunters, livestock owners, as well as walkers and other members of the public have contacted us as a municipality to express their justified fears, worries, and concerns as well as a multitude of questions about the wolf issue. We have received a large number of photos and some video footage from members of the public clearly showing the wolf in the municipality of Asbach both during the day and at night. The municipality of Asbach takes the concerns and needs of the population very seriously and sees itself in this situation as a representative of the interests of agriculture, livestock farmers, walkers, and all people who are concerned about the wolf.[21]

As we can see, taking concerns and fears seriously is indeed an important part of wolf management and is indeed demanded by those concerned. However, if

---

21   Resolution of the Association Municipality of Asbach/Westerwald, https://www.vg-as bach.de/nachrichten/2022/03/vg-ratsitzung-03-03-2022/resolution-wolf-vg-asbach.p df?cid=ldm (accessed: 10.08.2022, translated by TG, no longer available).

the crucial fourth step of taking concerns seriously is missing, affective resistance will form. People try to find alternative caretakers. In the case of the wolf resolution, these were sympathetic local politicians who were unwilling to distinguish between justified and unjustified concerns and fears; a former professional shepherd organised a heterogeneous group called 'Colleagues helping Colleagues', consisting of livestock keepers, representatives of wolf organisations (WikiWolves, NABU and GzSdW), and others to offer livestock owners quick and unbureaucratic support in protecting their flocks and herds; other livestock keepers networked in a WhatsApp group to exchange 'factual' information on the wolf issue, as they felt they were not taken seriously by the wolf management; an alternative wolf expert addressed livestock farmers' concerns about 'dubious' results of the genetic sampling of kills ordered by the ministry and offered her services.

Attempts to manage affects thus criss-cross society and in turn send affective impulses into wolf management. It seems almost impossible to keep track of such a confusing situation, and even more impossible to manage it. However, I would like to conclude this section with an example from my fieldwork in Saxony that shows what I consider to be successful affective management. To be more precise, it is about affect micromanagement.

A few years ago, the region around the village of Krauschwitz in Lusatia repeatedly made the headlines for several wolf attacks on dogs and other domestic animals. Between Christmas and New Year 2017–18, a wolf had killed two dogs, one of which was tethered in a yard and the other running free near the house. The wolf was then killed or 'lethally removed' and the necropsy revealed that it was seriously ill. Then, in August 2019, another wolf killed a dog 200 metres from a farmhouse. A month later, a neighbour of Mrs. S. saw a wolf running along her garden fence in the afternoon.

Mrs. S. lived with her husband and three dogs on the outskirts of Krauschwitz, in the last house in the village bordering the forest. She used to walk her dogs in the forest every day, but not any more. Her neighbour across the road had seen a wolf and just a week later she had a strange experience that frightened her. Her husband was out of town and she was expecting a friend to visit her that evening. By the time she heard her friend's car outside the house it was already dark, so she took a solar garden torch and went to the gate to greet her. As the two women met at the gate, they suddenly heard a menacing 'wolf-like' growl from behind the hedge and were so frightened by it that they quickly ran back into the house.

The next day, Mrs S. contacted the LUPUS Institute for help and advice. Someone came and set up photo traps in the garden and outside the house to see if there really was a wolf prowling around. Over the next few weeks, a LU-PUS biologist checked the photo traps with her again and again, but no wolf could be photographed. In the meantime, Mrs S. had installed more solar lights in her garden, stopped taking her dogs into the woods (other dog owners had confirmed to her that they had sometimes seen a wolf on their walks), and even kept her youngest and oldest dogs on a lead when they played in her garden.

The situation was so scary, she told me when I visited her together with a LUPUS biologist. She still has no idea what it was. Was it really a wolf? What else could it have been? She had not imagined the sound. After all, these attacks on dogs had happened nearby before and her neighbour had seen a wolf right over there. Yes, of course, the dog owners in the area are worried. But on the other hand, she says, it is also a bit exciting to find out if there is a wolf around. In fact, she always looks forward to checking the pictures from the photo traps. She has also seen foxes in her garden and wild boar in the hedgerows. No, she would not be frightened if a wolf was actually photographed in her garden. In fact, she would be happy. After all, she loves animals.

Whether the threatening growl that evening was really a wolf is unclear. But the LUPUS biologists had to react. As the official partner in Saxony's wolf management, they have to follow up and investigate reports like the one from Mrs S. If a wolf shows threatening behaviour in close proximity to a human, this would possibly be interpreted as problematic and dangerous behaviour, making the wolf a 'problem wolf' that might have to be lethally removed. As there was no evidence to support such an interpretation, the case could have been closed fairly quickly. But there was more to do than possibly identifying a problem wolf.

It struck me that the LUPUS biologists were spending a lot of time on this case, which did not seem particularly serious to me. They spent many hours visiting Mrs S., setting up photo traps, talking to her. What they were doing could be described as *affective micromanagement*. According to the biologist I accompanied, they are always on the lookout for such cases and try to allay peoples' concerns and fears by listening, talking and, above all, acting. By treating the small 'seeds of anxiety', she said, they can prevent them from growing and spreading.

Wolf management practices can therefore be found at a number of levels: from the international to the national, state, regional and local. Wolf management 'on the ground', in the midst of people's lives, seems particularly challenging, and yet this is where many wolf-related affects arise and need to be recognised and 'managed'. Mrs. S's story shows how a small incident, embedded in a wolf atmosphere of several previous incidents, can affect the everyday lives of people in the countryside: small changes in garden lighting, changes in dog walking routes, an unsettling feeling in their familiar lifeworld. But it could have been worse if no one had intervened and taken them seriously. Not being taken seriously, not seeing anyone taking preventative measures and 'caring', could easily have turned into anger at wolf management, the creation of wolf-critical WhatsApp or Facebook groups, the signing of anti-wolf petitions, and so on.

But such small-scale interventions involving micromanagement of affects are rather rare. In Saxony, the LUPUS Institute has been commissioned to deal with such issues and is equipped with the necessary human and financial resources. In Rhineland-Palatinate (as in other states), the wolf management regime does not have these resources and in some cases does not see the need to micromanage affects.[22] Before I went to the public lecture by the well-known wolf opponent in the Hunsrück, described in Chapter 3, I received a phone call from someone from the official wolf management asking me if I would go and tell them how it went. They themselves, as described above, did not want to send a representative there because the situation was 'too heated' for them, and they suspected that their presence would have a counterproductive effect and only add fuel to the fire. Would they talk to the people in person and offer help, I asked? No, they would only act if asked—for the same reasons.

Whether affects are officially recognised and managed or not, they have an impact on human-wolf coexistence. When wolf kill experts in Saxony arrive at the scene of a sheep kill in their big, white, expensive-looking SUV, they make an impression. When another expert measures a sheep farmer's fences with perfect accuracy and finds that one point is just one or two centimetres short of the specified height that determines compensation for a killed sheep, his behaviour also makes an impression. If, as described above, hunters report a roebuck killed by a wolf and want the Large Carnivore Officer (LCO) to take the whole carcass for genetic analysis, contrary to the usual regulations, and

---

22   In Rhineland-Palatinate, this has changed with the establishment of the *Koordinationszentrum Luchs und Wolf* (KLUWO) in 2021. For the first time, there are employees who are able to work and act exclusively on wolves and lynx.

the LCO gives in to the situation and leaves the carcass temporarily in the forest, where the hunters unfortunately find it again, then the LCO has created a story that will haunt him even years later. When an amateur nature photographer in the Westerwald started tracking and photographing the new Leuscheid Pack a little too enthusiastically, the wolf management discussed whether they should intervene—especially since the stalking of wolves is against nature conservation law. The photographer then received a call from a local LCO he knew, asking him to tone down his enthusiasm and leave the wolves alone.

Both the success of wolf management and the acceptance of wolves stand or fall with each of these small management interventions. The general mood of society as a whole towards wolves is largely fed by the successes and failures of this affective micro-management, both on a small and a large scale. It seems inevitable that a wolf management regime will usually not have the capacity for an all-encompassing affective micromanagement, with the result that smaller negative swings on the mood barometer will be accepted—if only the overall mood does not change. The latter, in turn, tends to be steered by special framework conditions (preventive measures, compensation, legal regulations) into calmer waters where individual outbursts of affect make fewer waves. Whether such a management strategy can prevail in the long run seems at least doubtful in view of the challenges and conflicts with and about the wolf—especially since the official management wants to deal with the conflicts in an emphatically 'factual' and rational manner, and thus marginalising or even ignoring the power of the affective dynamics inherent in the conflict. However, the fact that affects can combine to form larger intersubjective atmospheres and moods should serve as a warning: Affective dynamics at the micro level of individual local cases can affect the macro level of societal affect management as a whole. This is the subject of the next section.

"You also have to stir the mood"

Fifteenth of January 2020, Wiesbaden/Hesse. Shepherds and other livestock owners from Hesse and neighbouring states announced a demonstration for animal husbandry and against wolves for that day. About 200 demonstrators marched loudly, with whistles and cowbells, from the train station to near the Hessian parliament, where a stage had been set up for the final rally. The demonstrators held up signs that read:

Wolves!—Tormented sheep—sleepless nights—unbearable costs
Is one species above all others?
We love our animals!
Wolf—we don't need you here!
The wolf comes ... we go
Wolf no thanks—Who protects our animals?

Next to the stage, a pen was set up with sheep in it and signs emblazoned with photos of killed sheep and captions such as: "Are we the next wolf food?" and "Where's my mum?" One livestock owner had brought his alpacas. On stage, there were greetings and political demands from various livestock owners' associations, which were greeted with applause and cheers from the demonstrators. A young shepherdess read a poem about wolves:

Dear people, if it were only hunger,
he would take just one and then go wander.
But the grey hound in the night kills without a single thought.
He rips the first one's throat apart, grabs the second from behind.
Blood is everywhere, the lambs are crying.
So he kills five little ones besides.
Plays the game till he can't catch his breath
and tomorrow the next twenty will meet their death.
Herd protection is priority one, but no solution seems to come.
Higher nets, solid fences, preferably a stall at night,
Dogs to guard, or why not the shepherd himself, alright?
Pain in the soul and financial ruin
Your own idiocy will lead you there soon.

One of the following speakers, a representative of the farmers' association, then got to the heart of why they were all there and what such a demonstration was for:

We are here today to create a mood among the masses. And when I was asked, when we as the farmers' association were asked, we clearly said of course, also as the farmers' association we are clearly behind the shepherds, behind the livestock owners, because today, we as the farmers' association have also learned, it's not enough to talk all the time, *you also have to create a mood* [...].

The Hessian Minister for the Environment then had to find out exactly what this meant when she took to the stage to explain the state's policy on wolves on stage and answer questions from the demonstrators—mostly amid persistent boos, whistles, and the ringing of cowbells. [23]

This example shows that a demonstration is never only—in the literal sense of the word—about making one's opinion known publicly and thus contributing to a public rational discourse. The quote from the representative of the farmers' association shows that a demonstration is also an affective practice that does not seek to convince through argumentation; rather, by creating a mood, it seeks an alternative way of influencing public opinion and generating political pressure for action through the affective dynamics of the mood. [24]

But what is a mood anyway and how are moods produced? In Chapter 4, I already introduced (with reference to Gernot Böhme) the concept of atmosphere as an intersubjective, diffuse affective arrangement that colours the subjective experience of those affected by it emotionally in a specific way. In the relevant literature, the terms atmosphere and mood are usually used synonymously. When we speak of mood here, I mean a special form of atmosphere that is predominantly produced and experienced by people, requires an effort (of stirring or producing or performing), and that therefore has a more intense and condensed affective impact than atmospheres. Producing moods then refers to the conscious production of an affective intensity in which the mood itself becomes the object to be worked on, which in turn is also to be experienced subjectively by the producers. However, creating a mood can also take on a performative character, as in the case of the demonstration described above, aimed at affecting an audience which becomes affectively 'tuned' by this mood. The mood is thus much more than a mere experience or entertainment; its affective dynamics are heightened to the point of producing tangible effects: The minister is supposed to be 'shaken' by the concentrated anger of the animal owners and to be transformed in her attitude towards the wolf in the light of this anger. The affective attitude of the livestock owners

---

23   Field notes and photo documentation, 15.01.2020.

24   There are parallels here to the media strategies of right-wing populism. The media scientist Christian Helge Peters summarises these with the phrase, 'why use facts when you can use affects?', Peters, Christian Helge: 'Medienökologie II. Wozu Fakten, wenn es auch Affekte tun? Zur Medienökologie des Rechtspopulismus und seinen Strategien der Affizierung', in: Behrendt, Gianna/Henkel, Anna (eds.), 10 Minuten Soziologie: Fakten (= 10 Minuten Soziologie 2), Bielefeld: transcript 2018, pp. 97–108, here p. 97, http s://doi.org/10.14361/9783839443620-008.

should rub off on the minister. Ultimately, this felt mood should create in her the affective urge to become active on their behalf.

As can be seen from this example, creating a mood has an inherently ambivalent character: the fact that the mood is created rather than just occurring naturally always raises the question of the motivation, the purpose, and thus the 'authenticity' of the performance (is it all just an act?). In the demonstration in Wiesbaden, at least two levels come together: Affects that were already present in the individual participants before the event in various compositions and weightings (the feelings and sentiments, the ethos) are bundled, selected, and concentrated into a collectively produced and directed mood. The mood is thus never a simple reflection of the participants' affects on a larger scale, but an ephemeral affective re-arrangement adapted to the specific moment, which also has its own idiosyncratic dynamics.

The moods present in the wolf conflict are therefore best approached with a critical attitude. They are not only experienced subjectively, but also used as a political tool.[25] In Chapter 3, this was expressed in the WhatsApp message of the district hunting master, who wanted to prove the imminent danger of wolves with increased evidence of wolves and thus create pressure for action. As shown in Chapter 4, wolf critics from Rosenthal tried to use fear of wolf attacks (rather than actual wolf attacks) as a means of obtaining a 'removal' permit. In this chapter we have seen how anti-wolf sentiment was stirred up in the municipality of Asbach, which eventually led to the formulation of a 'wolf resolution'. Only rarely do the actors reveal their motives, as the representative of the farmers' association did at the demonstration in Wiesbaden. All these examples are isolated, local manifestations of moods. But moods can be contagious and become more persistent. Like the forms of *affective governance*, the *affective resistance* of the anti-wolf groups aims to achieve lasting changes in affective structures. It is one thing to generate political pressure to obtain individual removal permits for the wolf Marie in Lusatia or GW1896m in the Westerwald. Achieving lasting changes in the law, such as the regular hunting of wolves and the downgrading of the wolf's protection status, is another. For this to happen, these isolated, local manifestations of mood would have to combine and spread in order to tilt the overall mood in society towards wolves in a negative direction. To make matters even more difficult, the spread of mood depends on the power of the affective impulse. For example, if a wolf resolution passed by a local council is to have an affective impact on its march through the institutions

---

25   J. Hiedenpää/J. Pellikka/S. Ojalammi: Meet the parents.

to Brussels, it is not just the resolution as a written document that needs to be transported, but also its affective power—without the affects running out of steam and losing 'pressure'.

However, since moods tend to be ephemeral, it is difficult for wolf critics to perpetuate them. Perpetuating them means performing them over and over again and being able to motivate one's own ranks to do so over a long period of time. This is underpinned by the fact that moods not only affect an audience witnessing it, but also affects the producers themselves. As an *Erregungsgemein-schaft* ('excitement community'),[26] it can modulate the affective states and responses in ways that help to promote affects that are beneficial to its own cause, to foster in-group motivation and group identity. This is the case for both wolf supporters and wolf opponents.

An example of this is a public event in the town of Niedert in the Hunsrück region, which I briefly mentioned in Chapter 3. Following alleged sightings of wolves and the suspected killing of a calf, local livestock farmers organised a wolf information event for farmers in the region. A well-known shepherd and wolf critic from North Rhine-Westphalia was invited as speaker and wolf expert. He gave a two-hour talk in a farmer's barn to an audience of about a hundred people (almost all local farmers and a few hunters).

He began by explaining the biology of wolves. With a shoulder height of 120 centimetres, wolves are huge animals, he said, with long legs that make them excellent runners, with top speeds of up to 65 kilometres per hour and the ability to jump 4 metres high. They are also excellent swimmers. They can smell up to 2.8 kilometres against the wind, hear up to 15 kilometres in open country, have excellent night vision, and a wide field of vision. This animal surpasses all other predators. It can do anything, the speaker concluded his introduction.

As predators, wolves are even more dangerous, he continued, because they typically do not hunt alone, but in packs. And although humans are not their typical prey, they can certainly become prey—as has been shown in other parts of the world. They even use diversionary tactics, and some packs in eastern Germany specialise in tracking down game killed by hunters and claiming it before hunters get there—leading to critical situations during the hunt.

These predators are spreading rapidly, and are hardly an endangered species, he said (there are 400,000 wolves in the world!). With a series of calculations, he showed that Germany would soon be overrun by wolf packs. If you want to walk your dog then, it won't be very nice". Later in his talk, he

---

26   U. Bröckling: Man will Angst haben, p. 5.

returned to the subject of wolf population growth. He cited several ecological studies modelling potential wolf habitats in Germany. He showed that the Hunsrück region was considered an ideal habitat, and that 1400 packs could live in Germany.[27] He repeated: "You won't be able to go outside anymore!"

He then debunked several 'myths' propagated by wolf management and conservationists about the ecological value of wolves and their supposed positive role in maintaining ecosystems. Instead, he stressed that wolves mainly prey on domestic animals, as shown by studies in Italy, the Alps, and France (where 15,000 domestic animals were killed there in 2019!).

Another problem was wolf hybrids, he continued. It is not so much the hybrids themselves that are a problem (both wolves and wolf hybrids are dangerous to domestic animals), but the fact that wolf management denies that there are any in Germany. The Senckenberg Institute has a monopoly for the genetic identification of hybrids and alternative investigations by laboratories such as the private ForGen Institute in Hamburg are not officially recognised. In this way, the wolf management tries to prevent competing statements and findings about hybrids in order to retain the sole authority to decide whether a domestic animal has been killed by a wolf or a hybrid.

This fits into the larger framework of what wolf management is really about, he said. It is not about managing wolves (they can do whatever they want), it is about managing people. They use 'framing' methods to tell their lies without anyone noticing ("I hate this!"), such as using the word 'wolf management' when "it's us they really want to manage!" They used the word 'wolf advisers' when they obviously do not advise the wolves. The wolf kill experts are not really experts in the legal sense. Finally, they lie about 'the favourable conservation status' of wolves: "Only when every village has its own wolf will the favourable conservation status be achieved".

The last point of his speech was a criticism of herd protection measures. "I'll show you the only thing that really helps". And behind him on the screen appeared the image of a sheep with a helmet and a big gun in its hooves. Fences? Wolves can jump. You'd have to make them higher and higher, but that wouldn't really help. Llamas or donkeys? They would soon be eaten. Dogs? Well, there are more than 7,000 guard dogs in France and it still doesn't work. But what does work then, someone in the audience asked. Again, he referred to France and

---

27   He refers here to the following study: Kramer-Schadt, Stephanie et al. Habitatmodellierung und Abschätzung der potentiellen Anzahl von Wolfsterritorien in Deutschland, Federal Agency for Nature Conservation (=BfN-Skripten 556) 2020.

its principle of 'reciprocity'. Wolves have to learn that it is dangerous for them to attack domestic animals. Shepherds there have the right to shoot them.

Wolf management would have to change drastically. National management plans would have to be drawn up, internationally coordinated monitoring regulations and much more. And if nothing changes?

> Then there will be an uprising. I think in military terms. You have to make a fist. [...] You have to show what we can do and what our power is. [...] I would put it a little more cleverly. I would say: The rural population must take the solution to their problems back into their own hands. If someone says: 'What do you mean?' Then I say: 'You know what I mean'. The state has a monopoly on force. If they don't help us, if they don't protect our property, which is their constitutional duty, then they need to be reminded of that. [...] Perhaps we are heading for such times. [...] I don't know what would happen then [...].[28]

If we look at the content of this talk, we see the same typical topics that appear in most talks about wolves, regardless of who is actually giving the talk: wolf biology and ecology, reproduction, habitats and territories, food, problems of wolf hybrids, wolf management, and herd protection. However, a look at the rhetoric of this lecture shows that these topics are presented in such a way as to lead the audience to a particular solution through a series of affective impulses. As there were no other 'wolf experts' in the audience, no one could really question or refute the interpretation of the facts. Was the audience logically convinced by the speaker's argument? Hard to say. But we should interpret his talk not only in terms of content, but also in terms of rhetorical affect. The story that was told that evening might go something like this:

The wolf is a dangerous super-predator to be feared. This super predator will soon be everywhere and in large numbers in your area. You will no longer be safe outdoors and your animals will be in danger. If you think the authorities will help you, you are on the wrong track. They cannot be trusted, they lie and are not interested in helping you. Instead, they see you as a problem to be dealt with. They will not protect you and you cannot protect your animals by any means. Nothing works, nothing helps. It is all hopeless. There is only one solution left. Only one way out ...

The lecture thus creates a mood of danger and fear, destroys trust in institutions, invokes a sense of hopelessness and despair, and finally offers only one

---

28   Public wolf event, Niedert, 04.07.2020, minutes and audio recording.

way of hope and one solution to the conflict. The audience was ready to listen and be affected by what the wolf expert had to say. They trusted him. He was introduced by the organisers as 'one of us'. He was a shepherd and farmer, but one with a university degree, which made him both a colleague and a trusted 'expert'. But he was not quite 'one of us'. He was a shepherd, and the audience was mainly (cattle) farmers. As explained in Chapter 5, there are different types of livestock owners and there is also a hierarchy among them, with shepherds being a rather marginalised group within this community. Perhaps this was the reason why the audience did not really warm up to his 'one and only' solution and did not feel as affected as he intended. Although the audience seemed to respond to the sense of danger, the fear of wolves and the distrust of institutions (which farmers knew from their experience of agricultural politics), as farmers they had other options: the Farmers' Union, a powerful lobby. So their response to his call to arms was not to reach for the pitchforks, but to ask if and how the farmers' association could help.

Letting off steam, taking pressure out of the system

How does state wolf management deal with such attempts at *affective resistance*? If appeals to rationality or taking concerns and fears seriously in all their forms do not work, other means have to be found to counteract the stirring up of moods and the resulting political pressure to act. A wolf manager from Rhineland-Palatinate gave me a crucial hint as to how this might work.

An information event on the subject of wolves was held in Neitersen, Westerwald. Experts were invited to give presentations, followed by a question-and-answer session in which the experts on the panel answered questions from the audience. After the event, I spoke to one of the wolf managers about how the evening had gone. Everything was as expected, including the emotional outbursts at the end. That was normal at such events, he said. Discussions always follow a pattern. In the first phase, people come forward with real questions and also want to hear real answers. When all the real questions have been answered, the discussion shifts to the second phase, where people just want to vent their anger. No real answers are expected; it is just a matter of 'letting off steam'. But that is what such events are good for.

In other words, such information events are not only about conveying information, but also about providing a public space where not only opinions but also feelings can and even should be expressed. However, this should not be done in any form and with any intensity, but within the framework of socially accepted norms of public discourse (rationality, politeness, respectful interaction, etc.) and to a socially acceptable degree. Not all expressions of emotion are considered appropriate (concern or anger yes, rage and hatred rather not), and only some are considered 'not excessive' (*expression* of feelings yes, *outburst* of feelings rather not).

At this information event, for example, a horse owner whose farm lies in the core zone of the Leuscheider Wald Pack spoke up. Wolves regularly pass by her farm, and a wolf is said to have attacked one of her horses. A long discussion ensued about the genetic samples, which apparently only proved that a 'dog-like animal' (canid) had attacked, but not clearly that it was a wolf. The Ministry spokesman then explained how genetic testing works, but the horse owner refused to believe it and continued to doubt the results. The moderator then intervened and ended the discussion:

> [MODERATOR:] All right, I'll take it from here: genetic evidence takes precedence over conjecture.
>
> [HORSE OWNER:] No, but the results showed it wasn't a dog but a dog-like animal.
>
> [MODERATOR:] But genetics were found and there is a result and we'll leave it at that for now.
>
> [HORSE OWNER:] No, no. [gets louder]
>
> [MODERATOR:] The gentleman in front here is next.
>
> [HORSE OWNER:] You get shut down here when you say a wolf is a dog-like animal! [now shouting]
>
> [MODERATOR:] We take note of that. OK, now the gentleman here up front is next.

One can see here how the moderator of the event not only moderates and modulates the course of the evening, but also its affective dynamics, guiding it into rational channels, cutting off 'exaggerated' outbursts, and generally ensuring that the rules of social interaction also apply to the conflict about the wolf. He was supported in this by the panel of experts in the background and by the audience in general—as representatives of social values and norms, so to speak.

The idea that such events are also about letting off steam is also supported by the timing of these events. After all, they do not take place at just any time and in any place, but precisely when and where tempers are running high and moods are boiling up or threatening to boil over—as in the area of the Leuscheider Wald, where the wolf GW1896m has proven its affective agency again and again with almost weekly kills. Preventive information events in areas without wolves were almost non-existent during my fieldwork.

The motivation for wolf management to provide such spaces for the expression of feelings is, of course, to maintain some control over the public mood and its affective dynamics. If livestock owners themselves organise an information event by and for livestock owners with their own wolf expert (as happened in the Hunsrück region, described in the last section), the wolf management has no influence on the affective dynamics on the ground: expressions of feelings can turn into escalating outbursts, concern can turn into anger, rage, or hatred, and the event can ultimately also provide incentives for illegal actions. Nevertheless, wolf management felt that it had also intervened here in a regulating way by deliberately not being present in order not to escalate the affective dynamics of the event. But even the absence of wolf management representatives can affect the dynamics: at many events I have been told by livestock owners that it would have been nice if wolf management representatives had 'dared to come here'. They would have expected nothing less, but a visit would have been received positively. The same goes for wolf supporters. Whether or not representatives of NABU, the Society for the Protection of Wolves, or similar organisations attend events organised by livestock owners always has some kind of affective impact.

But when even non-presence and non-action have an affective impact, it is easy to see in detail how complex and difficult affect management can become. The very concept of management itself suggests that we are dealing with controllable situations and processes, but we must be aware that the return of wolves to Germany always produces an *excess of affects* that poses a major challenge to any attempt at management. While it is possible to intervene selectively in affective dynamics, their multiple entangled directions, scales, participants, and unintended consequences as an affective arrangement guarantee that affect management is an interplay of various forms of *affective governance* and *affective resistance*, and that the results of management attempts are always only short-term, unstable, and in transformation. The same applies to the wolf-induced mood of society as a whole, which is crucial for securing public support for the protection of the wolf species in Germany.

Ultimately, the central challenge of wolf management as affect management is a question of temporality. On the one hand, it is a matter of selective, timely intervention in (still) locally limited affects. On the other hand, it is about taming the volatility and 'wildness' of affect, of civilising it and transforming it into durable, stable affects and values that are favourable to species conservation. But wouldn't this also require managing the affects of the wolves themselves?

EXCURSUS: affect management of wolves

To what extent can wolf management also be understood as a form of managing wolf affects?[29] In this section I want to look at various common management measures and how they can be seen to affect wolves, i.e. to alter their behaviour or at least to try to communicate to them what we want.[30] When using the term 'management' for these measures, it is implied that it is a one-way process, from humans down to wolves as passive recipients. If, however, wolves are really active agents of a shared more-than-human society, affect management becomes more of a two-way process, a negotiation, or in the words of philosopher Baptiste Morizot, a diplomatic mission[31]. But how diplomatic is wolf management in Germany? In this context, it is worth looking at how so-called problem wolves are dealt with. Problem wolves are declared a problem because of 'conspicuous' behaviour. The official DBBW guideline, *How to deal with bold wolves*, defines this type of behaviour as follows:

---

29   For an encompassing recent assessment of different management interventions on large carnivore behaviour, see Lorand, Charlotte/Robert, Alexandre/Gastineau, Adrienne/Mihoub, Jean-Baptiste/Bessa-Gomes, Carmen: 'Effectiveness of interventions for managing human-large carnivore conflicts worldwide: Scare them off, don't remove them', in: Science of the Total Environment, Volume 838, Part 2 (2022), 156195.

30   See von Essen, Erica/Drenthen, Martin/Bhardwaj, Manisha: 'How fences communicate interspecies codes of conduct in the landscape: toward bidirectional communication?', in: Wildlife Biology (2023): e01146, doi: 10.1002/wlb3.01146.

31   Morizot, Baptiste: Wild Diplomacy: Cohabiting with Wolves on a New Ontological Map, Albany: State University of New York Press 2022.

Conspicuous behaviour in the sense of this report refers to a behaviour of wolves towards humans that seems to be outside the range of behaviour shown by most individuals of this species. Conspicuous behaviour covers the entire range from unusual or undesirable to bold behaviour. [...] Bold (problematic) behaviour in the sense of this report is behaviour which may become dangerous to humans if it escalates. Such behaviour at the least requires attention but can also be deemed serious or critical [...].[32]

So, we see that conspicuous behaviour always has an (inconspicuous) background against which it can first be noticed as something unusual. But how can someone who encounters a wolf correctly assess wolf behaviour when encounters are so rare that most people cannot have no clear idea of the range of 'normal' behaviour? Many cases of supposedly conspicuous behaviour therefore resolve themselves as they turn out to be based on a lack of knowledge of 'normal behaviour'. It is in this context that the dual function of wolf monitoring becomes apparent. Not only does it serve to record the (genetic make-up of the) wolf population and its geographical distribution, but 'monitoring is also a useful tool for the early detection of 'bold' wolf behaviour and, if necessary, for taking measures to counteract it'.[33] The collected and documented sighting reports in their entirety represent the range of 'normal' behaviour during encounters, a kind of 'background noise'[34] that can be used for evaluation by experts.

In terms of affect management, this means first of all that wolf affects are only relevant to management when they are directed at humans (including their animals). Wolves are free to act out their affects among themselves and other wild animals, and only need to adhere to the wolf-specific 'discipline' of affects that living together in a pack requires of each individual wolf. *But it is when living together with humans that wolves are expected to keep their affects under control, and a disciplinary regime is in place to ensure that they do.* In the official guideline, *How to deal with bold wolves,*[35] an increasing disciplining of affect can be seen in several steps. The management protocol begins with measures that do not directly affect the wolf. The public is informed about 'normal' wolf behaviour and encouraged to report sightings in order to find and remove potential 'triggers', to correct misconceptions about conspicuous behaviour (e.g.,

---

32   Reinhardt et al.: How to deal with bold wolves, p. 9.
33   Ibid, p. 17.
34   Ibid.
35   Ibid, p. 22–27.

that an encounter at a distance of less than 30 metres is not 'abnormal') and to communicate rules of behaviour in encounters.

Further interventions to manage wolf affects can then take several forms: a) direct interventions aimed at the wolf itself; b) indirect interventions aimed at the 'conspicuous' wolf, but also at human affects and behaviour; and c) indirect interventions aimed at humans only. The latter include, for example, the various measures presented earlier in this chapter, particularly those targeting public mood. The Protocol confirms that *"public sentiment* also influence[s] the way problematic animals are dealt with. The more people are familiar with the occurrence and behaviour of wolves, the more trust they have in the experts consulted, the more likely they are to accept the experts' recommendations".[36] Ultimately, even in the case of wolf affect management, it is true that on the one hand it is an intervention in the lives of wolves (or the wolf population at large), but on the other hand it is also an intervention in the lives of people and their 'being affected by wolves'.

> The aims of these recommendations are: a) to ensure that people in Germany are not injured or killed by wild wolves; b) to foster and maintain public trust in wolf management authorities in wolf regions; c) to ensure that people's fear of wolves does not increase; and d) to enable wolves to spread further in Germany without causing serious conflicts between wolves and humans.[37]

But how concretely can wolfish affects actually be managed in the sense of being tamed, influenced, disciplined? Here the official guideline draws on the principles of classical ethology. Behaviourism, already criticised in Chapter 2, is used both to explain conspicuous behaviour and to justify management measures. In this scheme, abnormal behaviour is usually explained by excessive 'habituation' or 'positive conditioning' (usually 'food conditioning'). The ethologist Klaus Immelmann defines habituation as "the ability of an animal to become accustomed to and no longer react to repeatedly occurring stimuli that are associated with neither positive nor negative consequences".[38] According to him, positive conditioning refers to the positive stimulus reinforcement of spontaneously occurring behaviour in order to solidify it into a recurring pattern of behaviour.

---

36   I. Reinhardt/G. Kluth: Leben mit Wölfen, p. 113 (translated by TG).
37   Reinhardt et al.: How to deal with bold wolves, p. 7.
38   Immelmann 1982, quoted from ibid. (translated by TG).

In both cases, wolves appear as passive, stimulus-driven beings who cannot help but reflexively follow the automatisms of stimulus and response. We have already encountered such arguments in the context of *surplus killing* (Chapter 4). According to this, wolves cannot help but follow the movement impulses of frightened sheep and kill more than they can eat (at once) out of 'lust for murder', a 'killing impulse'. However, I have described the apparent irrationality of this behaviour—and thus the apparent logic of an inherent killing impulse—as being a result of human intervention, which removes the killed animals so that the wolves have no chance of returning to them, thus constructing the 'irrationality' of the killing in the first place. The same is true of the stimulus-induced 'killing impulse' claimed in this context. The framing of conspicuous wolf behaviour in classical ethological terminology thus has consequences that can directly affect the perception of conspicuous behaviour. For if wolves are indeed 'affect-driven' and these affects can be escalated through the smallest stimuli (according to the rules of habituation or conditioning), how is it possible to control conspicuous behaviour at all?

The answer is again couched in classic ethological terminology. Problematic habituation or positive conditioning can be changed with 'aversive conditioning', i.e. by repeated exposure to 'punishing stimuli' (shooting with rubber bullets, setting off firecrackers or rocket flares, etc.). However, this 'hazing' is anything but easy to implement, as it has to follow the undesired behaviour directly as a negative stimulus (in its original temporal and spatial context) in order to elicit an appropriate response and behavioural adjustment from the wolf. Furthermore, to be effective as conditioning, it must be repeated. In other words, to be *effective*, deterrents must be *affective*, not only in the sense that they must be 'noticeable' to the wolf, but also that the affective dynamics of the deterrence must be evident: the wolf must be affected, and it must be clear by whom.

Communication scientist (and hunter) Michael Gibbert explains this problem in an interview using the example of the so-called Lupara, a sawed-off shotgun traditionally used in Italy to ward off wolves.[39] At close range (less than 30 metres), it can be lethal. At longer ranges, the lethality of lead pellets decreases rapidly, but they can still hurt and can therefore theoretically (though not necessarily legally) be used to scare away wolves. Unlike a long-distance

---

39   Duchet, Laura/Gibbert, Michael: 'Managing a "Wicked Problem": A Conversation with
        Michael Gibbert', in: Marlis Heyer/Susanne Hose (eds.), Encounters with Wolves: Dy-
        namics and Futures, Sorbisches Institut: Bautzen 2020.

shot from the cover of a hunting blind, when a wolf is shot with a Lupara, it is always clear to the wolf who is causing it pain. Hazing with the Lupara could therefore act as negative conditioning.

This raises the question of whether people outside official wolf management are also using deterrent measures to discipline wolves according to their own ideas. For example, some hunters in the Westerwald appeared to be considering the possibility of using hazing to drive out the local pack. In a (presumably half-serious) WhatsApp message with the title "We will visit our wolf pack on 24.04.2021 please be there", they called for people to join them:

> We visit our wolves! A large turnout is requested, pre-registration is not required. Whether on foot or motorised, please be there. Yes, shooting is allowed, but only with the camera, the gun stays in the cupboard. Or loaded with salt, of course. Current location: Leuscheider Wald or forest near Flammersfeld. Time: Dusk to night, so: night vision devices. They [wolf friends] don't have any, so we'll see them before they see us. Have fun.[40]

As research participants from the region later confirmed to me, some wolf critics did indeed turn up, but no action was taken because wolf supporters were also there. However, the call shows that there are other illegal ways to 'teach wolves to fear humans' (a well-known appeal in hunters' circles regarding wolves' alleged lack of shyness) than illegal shooting.

Another form of deterrence is herd protection measures—both in the form of 'wolf-deterrent' fences and guard dogs. Although it is also possible to protect livestock from wolves in the pasture with a fixed fence, which is merely a physical barrier to the wolf's prey, the electric fence is considered to be the most effective form of protection. The electric fence works through its electric shocks and the pain it causes, which is said to negatively condition the wolf. Encounters with guard dogs can also deter wolves through the sheer physical force of the confrontation. But even greater is the affective impact that the presence of the dogs (as a constant aversive stimulus) is supposed to have.

Finally, there is an affective dimension to the last resort in dealing with wolves exhibiting bold behaviour – lethal control. Given the problem in wolf management practice of clearly identifying a particular wolf as a 'problem wolf' at the time of removal, the new legal framework, as amended in 2019, has created the possibility of generally removing wolves in the region in question until

---

40   A WhatsApp message forwarded to me, received 22.05.2021.

the problem wolf has been killed or until the deterrent effect/affect on the surviving members of the pack is such that the problematic behaviour ceases.[41] In this way, lethal removal can be seen as the ultimate affect management; it is fatal for the wolf in question, but it can and should continue to have an affective impact on the rest of the pack—even after the 'problem wolf' has died.[42]

With all these measures in place, however, the question arises as to whether 'conditioning' as a concept and method does not fall short of understanding wolf behaviour. The management model assumes that there is a) an undesirable behaviour, which b) can be influenced by human intervention, leading to c) a change in wolf behaviour in the future. The wolf's response is clearly determined: Hazing can only lead to an increase of fear of humans. But is this the only possible response? Hunters often point out that wild boar in wolf territory have become more defensive and aggressive, more likely to confront and fight hunting dogs. In this view, wild boar have not simply responded with fear to the stimulus of wolf attacks. For a sentient, affective creature, hunting (by wolves or humans) raises the question of how it affects the animal (and this must be asked not only at the species level, but also for family units and even individuals). An (aggressive) attack may cause fear, but it may also cause counter-aggressions, anger, or a willingness to fight. And the wild boar's affects 'conditioned' through wolves can then also influence not only encounters with wolves, but also with hunting dogs or even with hunters. *Rather than thinking in terms of a rigid causal determinism, it seems more appropriate to consider the possibility of multiple, behaviourally open responses in both boar and wolves. Taking the agency of wolves seriously also means keeping an eye on the variety of possibilities in their complex behaviour.*

---

41   The four wolves legally removed in Lower Saxony in spring 2021 can serve as an example of this. In all four cases, in four different packs, a wrong wolf was killed. see Information on species protection exemptions and wolf removals in Lower Saxony, Lower Saxony Ministry for the Environment, Energy, Building and Climate Protection, https://www.umwelt.niedersachsen.de/startseite/themen_im_fokus/der_wolf_in_niedersachsen/informationen-zu-wolfsentnahmen-in-niedersachsen-197937.html (accessed: 30.04.2024).

42   This management tool seems to underlie the wolf management regime in Washington State, US, for example. See Anderson, Robert/Charnley, Susan/Epstein, Kathleen/Gaynor, Kaitlyn/Martin, Jeff/McInturff, Alex: 'The socioecology of fear: A critical geographical consideration of human-wolf-livestock conflict', in: Can. Geogr., 67 (2023): 17–34. https://doi.org/10.1111/cag.12808.

Furthermore, we have to consider that there is a high possibility for mis-communication, especially when it comes to attempts to induce a general shy-ness (towards humans) in wolves through hunting, removal, or hazing. Re-search in sensory ecology supports this caution, as when Elmer et al. argue that

> Not only do we need to predict what sensory cues and signals an animal will respond to at a particular time, but also how that animal will respond in its given condition and environment.[43]

When the authors here point to the 'given condition' of the animal, we can con-clude that behaviour is not only bodily performed but also consciously experi-enced and processed by the animal. Condition here is not just a physiological condition but also a matter of *what the animal feels like*. Regardless of whether we can gain access to this subjective experience of the animal, the question of what the wolf knows and how it experiences an encounter is one of the most exciting and at the same time fruitless questions that can be asked about animals. And as Thomas Nagel[44] has already convincingly argued, we do not have a satisfac-tory answer to it. But heuristically, this question helps us to bring something into focus: We may not know *what* a wolf knows, but we know *that* it knows something; we may not know *how* it experiences a situation, but we know *that* it experiences it. In other words, wolves have consciousness and affective aware-ness; they are rather opaque subjects to us, but they are subjects, nonetheless.

In this context, the philosopher Jens Soentgen reminds us that ecology as a relational science has long been an explanatory ecology of objects, neglect-ing an ecology of subjects (the 'interior' of ecological relations, as he calls it). He therefore suggests that hermeneutic approaches to ecology should com-plement explanatory approaches. In this context, he reminds us that in the formative period of ethology, animal psychological models were also part of the fledgling science. In recent years, some ethologists seem to remember this

---

43   Elmer et al.: 'Exploiting common senses: sensory ecology meets wildlife conservation and management', in: *Conservation Physiology*, Volume 9, Issue 1, 2021, coab002, https://doi.org/10.1093/conphys/coab002, p. 18.

44   Nagel, Thomas: 'What Is It Like To Be A Bat?', in: The Philosophical Review 83.4 (1974), pp. 435–450, https://dx.doi.org/10.2307/2183914.

early alliance and are now paying more attention to *animal personality*, including in relation to the wolf. [45]

However, behavioural research with wild wolves is rare and therefore it is concentrated on a few cases of wolves in captivity. Nevertheless, there seems to be a gradual realisation that the classical ethological behavioural models of habituation and conditioning have reached their limits, and that behaviour needs to be understood differently. In their report on wolf attacks on humans, John Linnell, Ekaterina Kovtun, and Ive Rouart also state that the concept of habituation loses its explanatory power when wolves live in highly anthropogenic landscapes such as those of Europe. [46] The documented wolf attacks also show that habituation is not nuanced enough as a concept to account for the diverse situational conditions of such attacks. Hopes are therefore pinned on animal-psychological *character trait models* to help explain the influence of character types on problematic behaviour. In terms of affective wolf management, these findings should then be used for more differentiated conditioning. Ultimately, however, the authors of the report have to admit that the effectiveness of deterrent measures is still unclear and therefore undetermined.

How will biologists and wolf managers explain and respond to problematic wolf behaviour in the future? Linnell and colleagues seem to present two alternatives at the end of their report: One is to continue with the old explanatory models and advocate the study of even more and more accurate data from GPS-collared wolves. The other alternative, as I understand it, potentially opens up a hermeneutic path that seeks to understand situationally emerging affective dynamics between humans and wolves by analysing accounts (and video footage) of such encounters in much greater detail (see Chapter 2). I

45   Blumstein, Daniel T.: 'Habituation and sensitization: new thoughts about old ideas', in: Animal Behaviour 120 (2016), 255–262, https://doi.org/10.1016/j.anbehav.2016.05.0 12; Wolf, Max/Weissing, Franz J.: 'Animal personalities: Consequences for ecology and evolution', in: Trends in Ecology and Evolution 27.8 (2012), 452–461, https://doi.org/10 .1016/j.tree.2012.05.001; Hansen Wheat, Christina/van der Bijl, Wouter/Temrin, Hans: 'Dogs, but Not Wolves, Lose Their Sensitivity Toward Novelty With Age', in: Frontiers in Psychology 10 (2019), article 2001, https://doi.org/10.3389/fpsyg.2019.02001.

46   This is why the wolf biologists Reinhardt and Kluth distinguish strong habituation from normal habituation, in order to distinguish bold, undesirable behaviour as exceptional behaviour, see Reinhardt, Ilka et al: How to deal with bold wolves. See also the scales of habituation in Baker, Rex O./Timm, Robert M.: 'Coyote attacks on humans, 1970–2015: implications for reducing the risks'; in: Human-Wildlife Interactions 11.2 (2017), 120–132, https://doi.org/10.26077/jy37-p271.

hope that this chapter has shown that qualitative interpretations of encounters make sense in a complex behavioural ecology of subjects and need to be recognised in wolf management regimes.

7. Epilogue: towards a resting pulse of coexistence

Intentional and unintentional consequences of following wolves as method

How do you, as a reader, feel about living with wolves at the end of this book? On the whole, much of it revolved around the conflicts with and about wolves. The affects that accompany them excite, agitate, sometimes disturb, and often overlay more subliminal affects in the public perception that could also show wolves in a different light beyond the conflicts. As the guiding principle of my research was to 'follow the wolves', this ethnography inevitably had to take up and address what the wolves pointed out to me. Due to the great challenges of following wolves (see Chapter 2), I have certainly missed some aspects, and I feel similar to the speaker from the Ministry of the Environment (see Chapter 6), who had to admit that we really do not know what the wolves are doing most of the time. So this book can only shed some light on some aspects of life with wolves and has to leave a lot in the dark. And that's a good thing, because the 'transparent wolf' would be just as suspicious to me as the 'transparent human'.

The picture of wolves drawn here is therefore more conflict-laden than it should be.[1] For example, the wolf critics got a whole chapter, while the wolf friends did not. But this was necessary, because the accusations against wolves are serious, the emotions are intense, and the potential for conflict is high. Understanding how and why wolves can create such charged atmospheres is therefore a priority. At the same time, these charged atmospheres provide an

---

1   This seems to be an inevitable side effect of following Donna Harraway's dictum of 'staying with the trouble', see Making kin in the Chthulucene (= Experimental futures Technological lives, scientific arts, anthropological voices), Durham/London: Duke University Press 2016.

opportunity to show that they are never created by wolves alone. Wolves get entangled and become part of socio-cultural processes and negotiations in a society that we might call 'more-than-human', despite the fact that animals rarely appear in public discourse as agents in their own right. Hopefully this book has shown how different groups of human actors, as well as a variety of domestic and wild animals, are entangled in wolf atmospheres and that it is precisely the interplay in this affective arrangement that makes atmospheres so powerful. As a result, we can now take a different, anthropologically informed critical look at 'wolf-critical' atmospheres.

In this book I have also tried to take a look at the wolves beyond the conflicts. Chapter 2, for example, begins as an 'animals-only' story, with humans only appearing in the last part of the chapter. In this way, the chapter offers a first approach to a quasi-wolf perspective, showing what else wolves do when they are not in conflict with humans, but also how a spontaneous encounter with humans in their everyday lives can very quickly become the seed of a conflict (I could have mentioned that the encounter described here was not the only one in the area and that there were also deterrent actions by the very rudimentary wolf management at the time). The etho-ethnological perspective adopted here has precisely this advantage: it makes us think of wolves as agents with the power to act and have an impact in a very concrete way, and it encourages us to question our anthropocentric view where necessary.

The 'resting pulse of coexistence' and the 'queasy sometimes-feeling'

There has been a shift in the scientific literature on wolves over the last twenty years or so towards an emphasis on coexistence rather than conflict. Constructively, this work reflects a desire to prevent science itself from creating or exacerbating conflict by treating the wolf exclusively in the context of conflict. Instead, the perspective is shifted to what is being sought: successful coexistence in the future. Something similar can be observed with the return of wolves to Germany: Wolf managers and supporters are keen to emphasise the possibility of (peaceful) coexistence, while wolf critics and the media focus on the conflicts. In the three years of my research, the conflictual version of living with wolves seemed to dominate – I explained why with the concept of affect management in Chapter 6. From an anthropological point of view, it makes little sense to try to redress this 'imbalance' (i.e. overly one-sided and insufficiently complex views) simply on principle, or even to replace the concept of conflict with that of coexistence by purely rhetorical means.

The question is rather: How did this imbalance, this hardening of public discourse towards conflict rather than coexistence, come about? Apart from the many reasons that I hope have become clear in the course of this book, it is important to remember that the return of wolves to Germany is not a sin-gular event, but a process that has been going on for more than twenty years and is far from complete. Wolves have not repopulated the country all at once, but year by year and region by region. In each new region, the wolf can cause excitement, livestock owners are usually unprepared, knowledge about wolves is low, uncertainty is high, and wolf critics stir up the mood. Because of this lack of preparation, the likelihood of wolf attacks is quite high, and so many of the conditions are in place that initially often lead to a state of permanent affective excitement in the region. It is therefore not surprising that the pub-lic discourse as a whole is under *sustained affective fire*, fed as it is by so many small regional conflicts, at least one of which is always boiling over somewhere. The picture that emerges is of a conflict-ridden, never-quiet coexistence with wolves suggesting that successful coexistence is impossible now and in the fu-ture. However, this is an unlikely scenario as we can expect habituation effects to develop, including a habituation in how we deal with wolf-related affects. We should therefore ask: What is the *resting pulse of coexistence with wolves* once they have arrived properly and their presence is no longer perceived as new and alien?

I would like to answer this question and thereby conclude this book with a brief look at a small town that has had twenty years of experience with wolves. Neustadt, in the municipality of Spreetal in Saxony, is located right next to the military training area Oberlausitz, where the female wolf GW0006f and the male wolf GW001m founded the second pack in Germany in 2005: the Neustadt Pack (now called the Neustadt/Spremberg Pack).[2] The female settled in the area as early as 2002 and attracted the attention of the Neustadt residents by reg-ularly appearing on the outskirts of the village during the mating season and howling through the nights in vain search of a mate. In the absence of a male wolf, she eventually mated with a male dog and produced Germany's first wolf hybrids. However, two of the pups died early, while the others were caught in

---

2   The first years in and around Neustadt are described in detail in Stoepel, Beatrix: Expeditionen ins Tierreich: Wölfe in Deutschland, Hamburg: Hoffmann und Campe 2004.

elaborate driven hunts using arrays of flags to direct the wolves. It was not until male wolf GW001m arrived from Poland the following year that a litter of pure wolf offspring was born.

Throughout the 1990s, individual wolves passed through the region from time to time, but these were the first to settle. Their arrival caused a great deal of excitement in and around Neustadt. In the region, it was mainly the hunters who mobilised against the wolves. There were not many livestock owners in the municipality (apart from people with chickens in their backyards, a shepherd, and a cattle farmer), but anger quickly ignited when the first sheep were killed. The shepherd eventually calmed down though as he quickly learnt to deal with the wolves' presence with new herd protection measures and the support of the Society for the Protection of Wolves, local wolf friends, and two biologists who had come to Neustadt to study the wolf population. But for some, the dual presence of wolves and wolf friends was a double thorn in the flesh. Two women from Neustadt remember the early years:

[Resident 1]: It really boiled over at the beginning. It was really bad; it had been really bad for many years. And because of the fact that they were so active here, [the two wolf researchers] from LUPUS ...

[Interviewer]: Did it then boil up here like this because LUPUS was active here?

[Resident 2]: They were the buffers. They were seen as the bad guys ...

[Resident 1]: They were the foster parents of the wolves ...

[Resident 2]: They introduced them here ...

[Resident 1]: That's just how it was presented [...]. Yes, the two LUPUS women received quite a few threats [...].

[Interviewer]: Did you get the impression that it was really about the wolf? Or was it about something else and the wolf was just an excuse?

[Resident 1]: No, no ... it really was about the wolf.

[Resident 2]: Otherwise, there wouldn't have been these discussions. It was really ... it was about that.

[Resident 1]: Yes, yes, it was about the wolf, that the wolf is here as a competitor [...].

[Resident 2]: And as a danger [to humans] ...

[Resident 1]: As a danger ... yes, the fear of it. But the fear was also stirred up a lot, a lot by the hunters. They wanted to get those who had nothing to do with hunting on board.

As in Rosenthal many years later, hunters were the driving force against the wolves. According to my interviewees in Neustadt, one in particular, the chairman of the association *Sicherheit und Artenschutz* (Security and Species Protection), which was founded near Kamenz in 2004 (and later also became active in Rosenthal), was always stirring things up and trying to win over the entire population of the region to his cause—sometimes with success.

So, while the local hunters were increasingly agitating against the wolf and the wolf researchers of the newly founded LUPUS Institute in the first few years, a completely different development started in parallel, which made Neustadt *the* wolf town of Germany (unnoticed by most Neustadt residents themselves). From the beginning, the wolf attracted scientists and journalists from Germany and abroad who wanted to learn more about the first wolves in Saxony from the Neustadt researchers. Then began the official wolf monitoring training courses, which have attracted participants from all over Germany every year since. The courses were developed and run in collaboration with one of Germany's leading animal trackers. His seminars attracted more and more interested people to Neustadt and Lusatia, and since then courses on tracking, environmental education, and much more have been held there several times a year in his wilderness school. Many course participants return here again and again, sometimes with their families, to learn more about wolves and the other wildlife in Lusatia. Two local nature guides (one from Neustadt, the other from nearby Hoyerswerda) have also been involved in wolf issues from the beginning, supporting the researchers' work and still offering walks in the wolf area and wolf seminars. Considering that tourism in this coal region would be an important economic factor for the post-coal era, it is surprising that the small-scale wolf tourism has gone unnoticed, even by the mayor of the municipality.

As the owner of the local guesthouse explained to me, this is probably because the wolf tourists tend to have little contact with the people of Neustadt and are 'very focused' on the wolves and their nature hobbies. The only time they attract attention is when they walk barefoot through the town or when whole groups (of trackers) meet under the bridge to find otter or beaver tracks in the wet sediment, much to the amazement of the people of Neustadt. More conspicuous is the local nature guide who moved here many years ago and built a camp with log cabins and a campsite on the River Spree. His house and his 'wild garden' look very different from the neat houses and front gardens that you usually find in Neustadt. The 'wolf people' are sometimes 'unpleasantly' conspicuous in this sense; they have a reputation for not wanting to 'fit in' and integrate properly (and of course the locals know exactly who the handful of Green Party voters are who are now—unfortunately—present in their otherwise more conservative community).

But over the years, people have got used to both wolf friends and wolves. The hunters still don't like the wolf, but they keep their anger largely to themselves. The out-of-town hunting guests, who came to Neustadt less frequently for a few years, are now coming more often again. There haven't been any wolf kills for a long time (there is almost no animal husbandry, apart from chickens, and the fight against hawks and foxes is more important here), although Neustadt is currently surrounded by three packs (the Neustadt/Spremberg Pack, the Mulkwitz Pack, and the Milkel Pack). Most of the people of Neustadt have never seen a wolf. Wolves are simply too unimportant to the everyday lives of the people here, and those who do not spend their nights out in the woods do not have much chance of seeing them.

It could be said that life with wolves in Neustadt and the surrounding area is no longer so triggered by the great highs and lows of public affects, atmospheres, and moods that were the subject of this book. The resting pulse of coexistence is by and large low—albeit with a discontented grumble from the hunting community. Wolves raise this resting pulse mainly in a certain affective mode: as a *queasy feeling*. By this I mean an unpleasant emerging feeling of diffuse anxiety that is not yet fully formed. This queasy feeling pulls you out of a world that feels familiar and draws your attention to something potentially threatening. Here is a brief example from the life of a woman in Neustadt:

> When I had my children, we didn't behave any differently. We told them, 'please go into the forest' instead of saying, 'stay at home'. But they don't go of their own accord [...], they're so scared, they're afraid someone might come. They are more afraid of people, that something might happen. Children are so sensitised to this nowadays. They don't go into the forest because

they think they might meet a stranger. But that they are afraid of wolves ... Although I have to say, I usually say, you don't have to be afraid and it's not all that bad. But once we went into the woods to get a Christmas tree [...] in the direction of the military training area [...], and we went there, the children were still quite small, and we spotted wolf tracks [...] and there were quite a few of them, so we made sure that we got the tree and went home. We didn't know how old they [the tracks] were, if the wolves were still there or if they were from a few days ago [...]. And the children, too, they noticed it immediately, 'Carry me!' I had to pick up the little one, and the big one, my husband had to carry him and the tree. But yes, it was a bit strange. You know it's nonsense, but somehow ...

We can see how even wolf tracks in the snow can fill you with an uneasy sense of foreboding and a desire to escape the situation. So one could say that a queasy feeling is somehow part of living with a large predator like the wolf. However, this does not mean that there is a constant queasy atmosphere in wolf country and that the queasy feeling is a constant companion in the lives of the people who live there. Rather, this queasy feeling is a *sometimes-feeling* that usually lies dormant in the background and only stirs up under certain conditions. The wolf-specific queasy feeling is also just one manifestation of a general feeling that has very different addressees. People may feel queasy in the forests not only because there are wolves there, but also because the forest is generally regarded a place of queasiness in Germany's cultural memory.[3] Encounters in the forest with potentially dangerous 'strangers' can also cause queasiness, as can encounters with large dogs on the loose, or with wild boars. The occasional queasy feeling seems to be part of life—including life with wolves. So one of the central questions that needs to be answered about the coexistence with wolves is: How much queasiness can we tolerate as a society? How much queasiness are we willing and able to allow on the fringes of our lifeworld—knowing full well that we are not necessarily entitled to a life free of queasiness?

Coexistence with affect-guided thinking, sensibility and resilience

These questions once again illustrate one of the central concerns of this book, which is to show that affects (including the queasy ones) are not simply

---

3   See Lehmann, Albrecht: Von Menschen und Bäumen: Die Deutschen und ihr Wald, Reinbek: Rowohlt 1999.

'there' and should not be taken for granted. Affects are not only dynamic and therefore in a constant state of change, but they can also be worked with and shaped—both on a social and on an individual level. Successful coexistence does not depend solely on technological solutions (e.g. herd protection), but is above all a form of relationship building. This also includes how we actively deal with affects. *How we are affected by wolves does not follow any natural law but can be modulated by cultural and individual forms of sensitivity and affect regulation. How much we allow ourselves to be affected by wolves, how sensitive we are to their affective impacts, and under what conditions we try to control our affects (to show composure, not to lose our composure or to face the queasy with courage) will be revealed, developed, and negotiated in the coming years through our coexistence with wolves.*

Is this book then another appeal to take affects (a.k.a. concerns and worries) seriously? Or a counter-appeal from science to always return to rationality and reason? It is neither. The main purpose of this book is to overcome the speechlessness that has paralysed our discourse on wolves and affects for years, and to present a conceptual apparatus with the help of which one can think constructively not only *about* affects (from a seemingly neutral, objective, and unaffected distance), but *with affects*. Such *affect-guided thinking* requires attention to affective dynamics—in oneself and in others—but without passively letting them wash over one. *What is required is an active, reflexive attitude, one that allows itself to be guided by affects without being driven by them.* This attitude does not require sympathy [*Verständnis* in German] for those affected but an understanding [*Verstehen*] of how they affect and are affected by each other: Affect-guided thinking should make the affects themselves explicit, their arrangement-like connections visible, and their meanings comprehensible to the actors affected by them. This facilitates new discussions that can transcend the conventional dichotomy of rationality vs emotion instead of reproducing it along established lines.

This book has shown why affects are everywhere in the debate; why they nevertheless lead a shadowy existence; how the cultural value of rationality hinders a constructive approach to affects; in what manifestations affects occur; that affects are unfinished, processual, ambivalent; how individual affects are part of larger structures; how affects are felt both subjectively and intersubjectively and can themselves become an object to be processed; how affects are socio-culturally conditioned and what conditions intensify or diminish affects.

It is my hope that the path I propose here can contribute to a successful coexistence with wolves in two ways. It can help us to reflect carefully on and refine our sensitivity to the affective dynamics of coexistence, so that we as a society become more adaptable to the new realities in times of the Anthropocene. For old, outdated notions of separate worlds of humans and animals, or culture and nature, with each living side by side in their respective allotted spheres, have proved obsolete. Whether we like it or not, the lifeworlds of humans and wild animals are becoming more and more entangled. Whether songbirds and moles in the garden, pigeons and raccoons on the roofs, ducks and nutrias in the rivers, wild boars in the playgrounds, red deer in the cornfields, or even wolves roaming through the suburbs of big cities and through villages: Our society is and has always been a more-than-human society, human life has always been a living-together with animals and other living beings. Sharing this society not only with beloved pets or useful farm animals, but also with wild animals that can sometimes become unpleasant, demands a lot of us humans: on the one hand, a *sensibility* for the right closeness and distance of this diverse coexistence and the coordination of our life rhythms; on the other hand, a *resilience* that enables us to let affects bounce off us from time to time, and that puts a stop to our sensibility when it degenerates into unhelpful irritability. For a successful coexistence with wolves in a more-than-human society, we must learn to distinguish when an increased sensitisation or when a desensitisation to wolf affects is the best response.

8. Appendix

Figure 26: National damage statistics (Anzahl Übergriffe = Number of attacks; Anzahl
Tiere getötet/verletzt = Number of animals dead/injured)

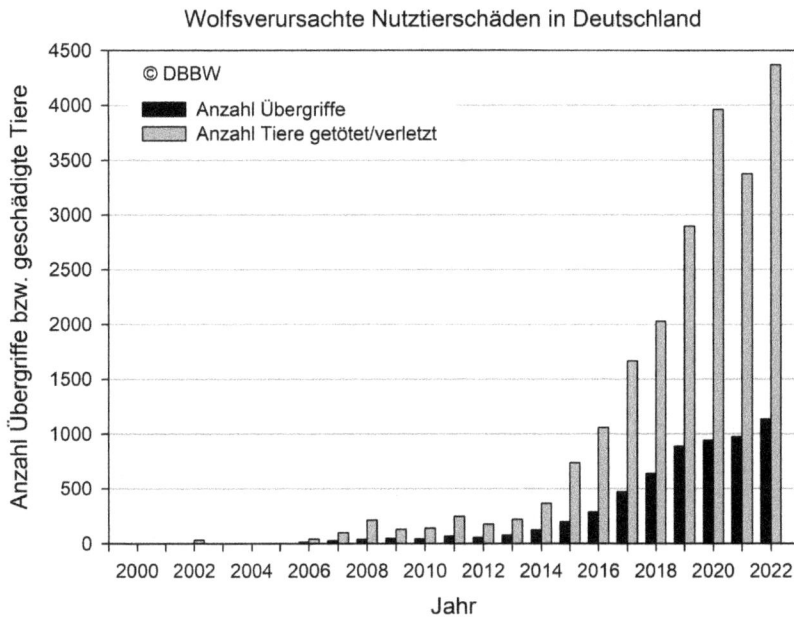

Wolfsverursachte Nutztierschäden in Deutschland

Entwicklung der wolfsverursachten Nutztierschäden in Deutschland von 2000 bis 2022.
Seit 2000 gibt es reproduzierende Wolfsrudel in Deutschland.
© DBBW Dokumentations- und Beratungsstelle des Bundes zum Thema Wolf

Source: Federal Documentation and Advisory Centre on the Wolf (DBBW)

Figure 27: Occurrence (occupied grid cells) of wolves in Germany in the 2022/23 monitoring year

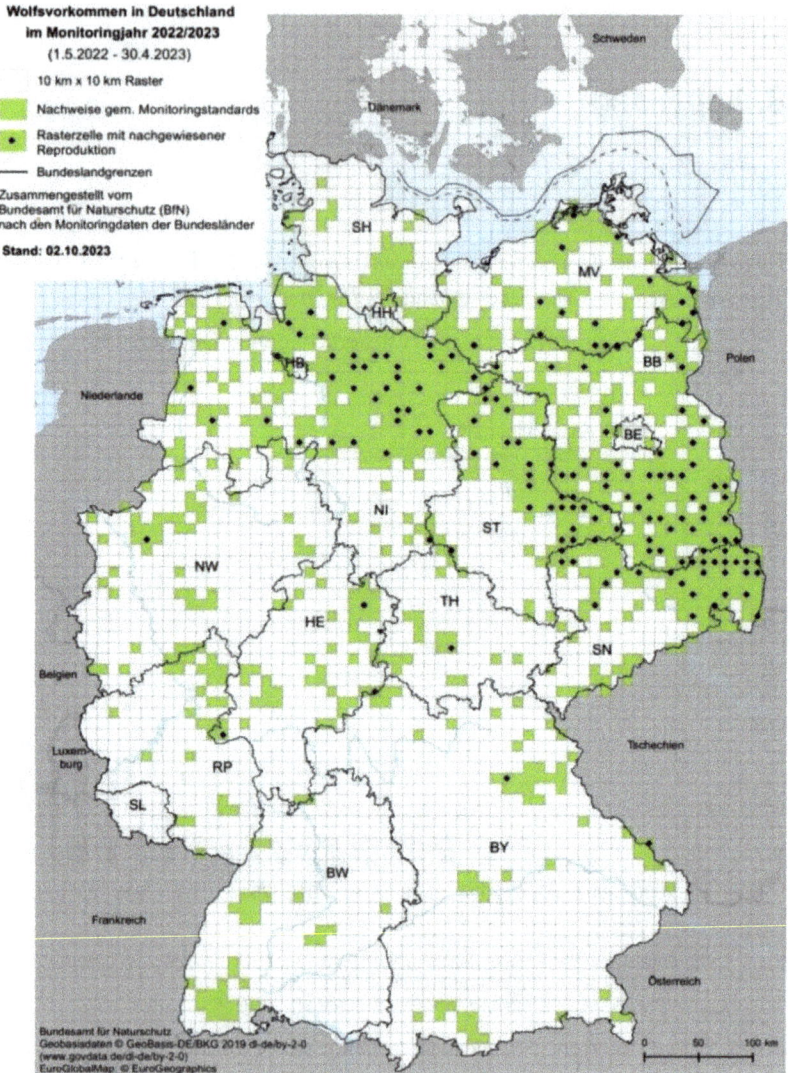

Source: Federal Documentation and Advisory Centre on the Wolf (DBBW)

Figure 28: Wolves found dead – statistics of causes of death (illegal killing, management, natural cause, unclear, road accident, open, other)

1062 Totfunde von Wölfen in Deutschland seit 1990

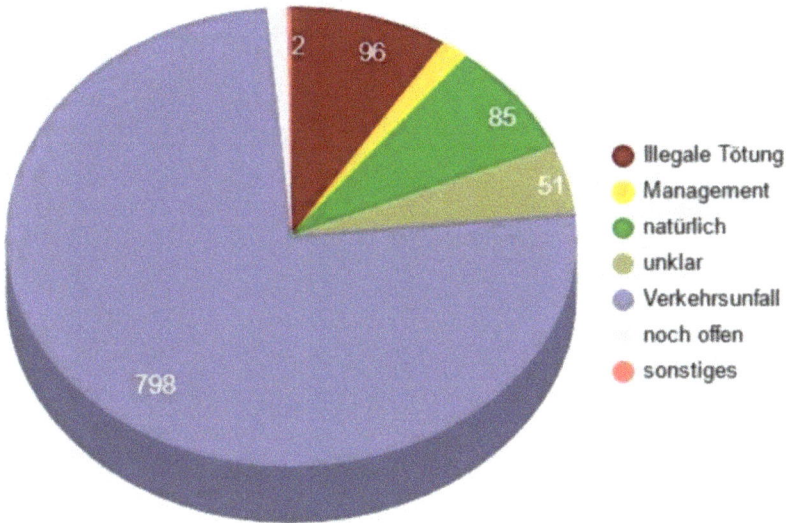

Legend:
- Illegale Tötung
- Management
- natürlich
- unklar
- Verkehrsunfall
- noch offen
- sonstiges

Values shown: 2, 96, 85, 51, 798

Source: Federal Documentation and Advisory Centre on the Wolf (DBBW)

9. Bibliography

Ahne, Petra: Wölfe. Ein Portrait (= Naturkunden, No 27), Berlin: Matthes & Seitz 2017.

Alexander, Justine S. (ed.): Large carnivore conservation and management. Human dimensions (= Earthscan Studies in Natural Resource Management), London/New York: Routledge 2018.

Amann, Klaus/Hirschauer, Stefan: Die Befremdung der eigenen Kultur. Ein Programm, in: Amann, Klaus/Hirschauer, Stefan (ed.), Die Befremdung der eigenen Kultur: Zur ethnographischen Herausforderung soziologischer Empirie, Frankfurt a. M.: Suhrkamp 1997, pp. 7–52.

Ameli, Katharina: Multispecies Ethnography, Bielefeld: transcript 2021, https://doi.org/10.14361/9783839455326.

Anderson, Ben: Encountering affect. Capacities, apparatuses, conditions (= An Ashgate Book), London/New York: Routledge 2016.

Anderson, David G.: 'Humans and Animals in Northern Regions', in: Annual Review of Anthropology 46 (2017), pp. 133–149, https://doi.org/10.1146/annurev-anthro-102116-041556.

Anderson, Robert/Charnley, Susan/Epstein, Kathleen/Gaynor, Kaitlyn/Martin, Jeff/McInturff, Alex: The socioecology of fear: A critical geographical consideration of human-wolf-livestock conflict. Can. Geogr., 67 (2023): pp. 17–34. https://doi.org/10.1111/cag.12808.

Arbieu, Ugo et al.: 'Attitudes towards returning wolves (Canis lupus) in Germany: Exposure, information sources and trust matter', in: Biological Conservation 234 (2019), pp. 202–210, https://doi.org/10.1016/j.biocon.2019.03.027.

Arbieu, Ugo et al.: 'The positive experience of encountering wolves in the wild', in: Conservation Science and Practice 2.5 (2020), article e184, https://doi.org/10.1111/csp2.184.

Arnold, Irina: 'Von traumatisierten Schafen und verwundbaren Lebenswelten: Stimmen von Weidetierhalter*innen aus Niedersachsen', in: Lara Selin Ertener/Bernd Schmelz (eds.), Von Wölfen und Menschen, Hamburg: Museum am Rothenbaum 2019.

Ausilio, Giorgia et al.: 'Ecological Effects of Wolves in Anthropogenic Landscapes: The Potential for Trophic Cascades Is Context-Dependent', in: Frontiers in Ecology and Evolution 8 (2021), article 577963, https://doi.org/10.3389.

Badmington, Neil/Thomas, Julia (eds.) The Routledge Critical and Cultural Theory Reader, London: Routledge 2008.

Baker, Rex O./Timm, Robert M.: 'Coyote attacks on humans, 1970–2015: implications for reducing the risks', in Human-Wildlife Interactions 11.2 (2017), pp. 120–132, https://doi.org/10.26077/jy37-s271.

Barua, Maan: 'Bio-Geo-Graphy: Landscape, Dwelling, and the Political Ecology of Human-Elephant Relations', in: Environment and Planning D: Society and Space 32.5 (2014), pp. 915–934, https://doi.org/10.1068/d4213.

Barua, Maan: 'Encounter', in: Environmental Humanities 7 (2016), pp. 265–270, https://doi.org/10.1215/22011919-3616479.

Bassi, Elena et al.: 'Attacks on hunting dogs: the case of wolf-dog interactions in Croatia', in: European Journal of Wildlife Research 67.1 (2021), pp. 1–9, https://doi.org/10.1007/s10344-020-01451-5.

Baumgartner, Hansjakob: Der Wolf. Ein Raubtier in unserer Nähe, Bern: Haupt 2008.

Beatty, Andrew: Emotional worlds. Beyond an anthropology of emotion (= New departures in anthropology), Cambridge: Cambridge University Press 2019.

Behdarvand, Neda/Kaboli, Mohammad: 'Characteristics of Gray Wolf Attacks on Humans in an Altered Landscape in the West of Iran', in: Human Dimensions of Wildlife 20.2 (2015), pp. 112–122, https://doi.org/10.1080/10871209.2015.963747.

Bens, Jonas et al.: The Politics of Affective Societies—An Interdisciplinary Essay. Bielefeld: transcript 2019, https://doi.org/10.14361/9783839447628.

Bens, Jonas/Zenker, Olaf: 'Sentiment', in: J. Slaby/C. v. Scheve (eds.), Affective societies, pp. 96–106.

Bisi, Jukka et al.: 'The good bad wolf—wolf evaluation reveals the roots of the Finnish wolf conflict', in: European Journal of Wildlife Research 56.5 (2010), pp. 771–779, https://doi.org/10.1007/s10344-010-0374-0.

Bjerke, Tore/Reitan, Ole/Kellert, Stephen R.: 'Attitudes towards wolves in southeastern Norway', in: Society and Natural Resources 11.2 (1998), pp. 169–178, https://doi.org/10.1080/08941929809381070.

Blumstein, Daniel T.: 'Habituation and sensitization: new thoughts about old ideas', in: Animal Behaviour 120 (2016), pp. 255–262, https://doi.org/10.101 6/j.anbehav.2016.05.012.

Bode, Wilhelm/Emmert, Elisabeth: Jagdwende: Vom Edelhobby zum ökologischen Handwerk, Munich: Beck 1998.

Böhm, Alexandra/Ullrich, Jessica: 'Introduction—Animal Encounters: Contact, Interaction and Relationality', in: Dies. (ed.), Animal Encounters. Contact, Interaction and Relationality, Stuttgart: J.B. Metzler 2019, pp. 1–21.

Böhme, Gernot: Atmosphären. Essays zur neuen Ästhetik, Frankfurt a.M.: Suhrkamp 2013.

Braun, Stephan/Geisler, Alexander (eds.): Die verstimmte Demokratie. Moderne Volksherrschaft zwischen Aufbruch und Frustration (= SpringerLink Bücher), Wiesbaden: VS Verlag für Sozialwissenschaften; Imprint: VS Verlag für Sozialwissenschaften 2012.

Brettell, Jonathan: 'Exploring the multinatural: mobilising affect at the red kite feeding grounds, Bwlch Nant yr Arian', in: Cultural Geographies 23.2 (2016), pp. 281–300, https://doi.org/10.1177/1474474015575472.

Breyer, Thiemo: 'Bestien—Zur Anatomie des Schreckens vor dem Animalischen', in: Erik Norman Dzwiza-Ohlsen/Andreas Speer (eds.), Philosophische Anthropologie als interdisziplinäre Praxis, Leiden: Mentis 2021, pp. 194–204.

Brezger, Jan: 'Do we have to take citizens' fears and concerns seriously? Die aktuelle Asyl-Debatte und der Fall Bremgarten', Theorieblog, 19.08.2013, https://www.theorieblog.de/index.php/2013/08/muss-man-die-aengste-und-sorgen-der-buergerinnen-ernst-nehmen-die-aktuelle-asyl-debatte-und-der-fall-bremgarten (accessed: 20.06.2022).

Bröckling, Ulrich: 'One wants to be afraid', in: Mittelweg 36 (2016), pp. 3–7.

Bronlow, Alec: 'A wolf in the garden. Ideology and change in the Adirondack landscape', in: C. Philo/C. Wilbert (eds.), Animal spaces, beastly places, pp. 141–158.

Brown, Joel S./Laundré, John W./Gurung, Mahesh: 'The ecology of fear: optimal foraging, game theory, and trophic interactions', in: Journal of Mammalogy 80.2 (1999), pp. 385–399, https://doi.org/10.2307/1383287.

Brox, Ottar: 'Schismogenesis in the Wilderness: The Reintroduction of Predators in Norwegian Forests, in: Ethnos 65.3 (2000), pp. 387–404, https://doi
.org/10.1080/00141840050198045.

Buller, Henry: 'Animal geographies I', in: Progress in Human Geography 38
(2014), pp. 308–318, https://doi.org/10.2307/1383287.

Buller, Henry: 'Animal geographies II', in: Progress in Human Geography 39.3
(2015), pp. 374–384, https://doi.org/10.1177/0309132514527401.

Bussemer, Thymian: Die erregte Republik: Wutbürger und die Macht der Medien. Stuttgart: Klett-Cotta 2014.

Cassidy, Rebecca: 'Lives With Others: Climate Change and Human-Animal Relations', in: Annual Review of Anthropology 41 (2012), pp. 21–36, https://do
i.org/10.1146/annurev-anthro-092611-145706.

Charlier, Bernard: Faces of the wolf. Managing the human, non-human boundary in Mongolia (= Inner Asia book series, vol. 10), Leiden: Brill 2015.

Chua, Liana et al.: 'Conservation and the social sciences: Beyond critique and
co-optation. A case study from orangutan conservation', in: People and Nature 2.1 (2020), pp. 42–60, https://doi.org/10.1002/pan3.10072.

Creel, Scott et al.: 'Elk Alter Habitat Selection as an Antipredator Response to
Wolves', in Ecology 86.12 (2005), pp. 3387–3397, https://doi.org/10.1890/05
-0032.

Cromsigt, Joris P. et al.: 'Hunting for fear: innovating management of human-
wildlife conflicts', in: Journal of Applied Ecology 50.3 (2013), pp. 544–549, h
ttps://doi.org/10.1111/1365-2664.12076.

Dale, Rachel et al.: 'The influence of social relationship on food tolerance in
wolves and dogs', in: Behavioral ecology and sociobiology 71 (2017), article
107, https://doi.org/10.1007/s00265-017-2339-8.

DeCesare, Nicholas. J. et al.: 'Wolf-livestock conflict and the effects of wolf
management', in: The Journal of Wildlife Management 82.4 (2018), pp.
711–722, https://doi.org/10.1002/jwmg.21419.

Demertzis, Nicolas (ed.): Emotions in Politics. The Affect Dimension in Political Tension. Basingstoke: Palgrave Macmillan 2013.

Demmering, Christoph/Landweer, Hilge: Philosophie der Gefühle. Von Ach-
tung bis Zorn, Stuttgart/Weimar: J.B. Metzler 2007.

Derrida, Jacques: The Beast and the Sovereign, Volume 2, Chicago: Chicago
University Press 2011.

Despret, Vinciane: 'Responding Bodies and Partial Affinities in Human-Animal Worlds', in: Theory, Culture and Society 30 (2013), pp. 51–76, https://d
oi.org/10.1177/0263276413496852.

DiNovelli-Lang, Danielle: 'The Return of the Animal: Posthumanism, Indigeneity, and Anthropology ', in: Environment and Society 4 (2013), pp. 137–156, https://doi.org/10.3167/ares.2013.040109.

Elias, Norbert: The Civilising Process, Oxford: Blackwell 2000.

Elmer, Laura/Madliger, Christine/Blumstein, Daniel/Elvidge, Chris/ Fernández-Juricic, Esteban/ Horodysky, Andrij/Johnson, Nicholas/ McGuire, Liam/Swaisgood, Ronald/Cooke, Steven: Exploiting common senses: sensory ecology meets wildlife conservation and management, Conservation Physiology, Volume 9 (2021), https://doi.org/10.1093/conphy s/coab002.

Federal Documentation and Advisory Centre on Wolves (DBBW): Wölfe in Deutschland—Statusbericht 2019/2020, p. 1–34.

Duchet, Laura/Gibbert, Michael: 'Managing a 'Wicked Problem': A Conversation with Michael Gibbert', in: Marlis Heyer/Susanne Hose (eds.), Encounters with Wolves: Dynamics and Futures, Bautzen: Sorbisches Institut 2020.

Eberlein, Undine (ed.): Zwischenleiblichkeit und bewegtes Verstehen—Intercorporeity, Movement and Tacit Knowledge (= KörperKulturen), Bielefeld: transcript 2016, https://doi.org/10.14361/9783839435793.

Eriksson, Max/Sandström, Camilla/Ericsson, Göran: 'Direct experience and attitude change towards bears and wolves', in: Wildlife Biology 21 (2015), pp. 131–137, https://doi.org/10.2981/wlb.00062.

Ertener, Lara S./Schmelz, Bernd (eds.): Von Wölfen und Menschen (= Mitteilungen aus dem Museum am Rothenbaum, Neue Folge, vol. 52), Hamburg: Museum am Rothenbaum 2019.

Essler, Jennifer L./Marshall-Pescini, Sarah/Range, Friederike: 'Domestication Does Not Explain the Presence of Inequity Aversion in Dogs', in: Current Biology 27.12 (2017), 1861–1865.e3, https://doi.org/10.1016/j.cub.2017.05.06 1.

Fenske, Michaela: 'Menschen, Wolfe und andere Lebewesen. Perspectives of a Multispecies Ethnography', in: L. Ertener/B. Schmelz, Von Wölfen und Menschen, pp. 33–40.

Fenske, Michaela/Heyer, Marlis: 'Wer zum Haushalt gehört. Ethics of living together under discussion', in: Tierethik 11.19 (2019), pp. 12–33.

Flaßpöhler, Svenja: Sensibel. Über moderne Empfindlichkeit und die Grenzen des Zumutbaren, Leipzig: Lagato Verlag 2021.

Foucault, Michel: Die Ordnung der Dinge, Frankfurt: Fischer Verlag 1991.

Fox, Camilla H./Bekoff, Marc: 'Integrating Values and Ethics into Wildlife Policy and Management-Lessons from North America', in: Animals 1 (2011), pp. 126–143, https://doi.org/10.3390/ani1010126.

Frank, Beatrice/Glikman, Jenny A./Marchini, Silvio (eds.): Human-wildlife interactions. Turning conflict into coexistence (= Conservation biology, Vol. 23), Cambridge, UK/New York, NY: Cambridge University Press 2019.

Frank, Elisa: 'Follow the wolves: Reflections on Ethnographic Tracing and Tracking', in: Marlis Heyer/Susanne Hose (eds.), Encounters with Wolves: Dynamics and Futures, Bautzen: Sorbisches Institut 2020, pp. 99–114.

Frank, Elisa: 'Multispecies Interferences: Taxidermy and the Return of Wolves', Ethnologia Europaea 49 (2020), pp. 79–97, https://doi.org/10.16995/ee.143 4

Frank, Elisa/Heinzer, Nikolaus: ' Wolfish infiltrations of nature and culture: orders and spaces renegotiated', in: Groth, Stefan/Mülli, Linda (eds.), Ordnungen in Alltag und Gesellschaft. Empirisch-kulturwissenschaftliche Perspektiven, Würzburg: Königshausen und Neumann 2019, pp. 93–124.

Fuentes, Agustin: 'Naturalcultural encounters in Bali: Monkeys, Temples, Tourists, and Ethnoprimatology', in: Cultural Anthropology 25 (2010), pp. 600–624, https://doi.org/10.1111/j.1548-1360.2010.01071.x.

Galipeau, Steven: 'Dancing with Wolves', in: Jung Journal 7 (2013), pp. 34–47, https://doi.org/10.1080/19342039.2013.759061.

Gärtner, Sigmund/Hauptmann, Michaela: 'Das sächsische Wolfsvorkommen im Spiegelbild der Jägerschaft vor Ort—Ergebnisse einer anonymen Umfrage', in: Beiträge zur Jagd- und Wildforschung 30 (2005), pp. 223–230.

Gazzola, Andrea et al.: 'Temporal changes of howling in south European wolf packs', in: Italian Journal of Zoology 69.2 (2002), pp. 157–161, https://doi.o rg/10.1080/11250000209356454.

Geertz, Clifford: The interpretation of cultures. Selected essays, New York: Basic Books 1973.

Gesing, Friederike et al.: NaturenKulturen. Denkräume und Werkzeuge für neue politische Ökologies (= Edition Kulturwissenschaft, Vol. 146), Bielefeld: transcript 2019, https://doi.org/10.14361/9783839440070.

Gieser, Thorsten: Wolfsbegegnungen – eine Annäherung des Fremden. in: Uzarewicz, Charlotte/Gugutzer, Robert/Uzarewicz, Michael/Latka, Thomas. (eds.) Berühren und berührt werden – Zur Phänomenologie der Nähe (Neue Phänomenologie 35). Baden-Baden: Verlag Karl Alber, pp. 309–332.

Gieser, Thorsten/von Essen, Erica: Wolves, ecologies of fear, and the affective challenges of coexistence', Society and Space, 6 September 2021, http s://www.societyandspace.org/articles/wolves-ecologies-of-fear (accessed 18.06.2022).

Gieser, Thorsten: 'Beyond Natural Enemies: Wolves and Nomads in Mongolia', in: Heyer, Marlis/Hose, Susanne (eds.), Encounters with wolves: dynamics and futures, Bautzen: Sorbisches Institut 2020, pp. 50–62.

Gieser, Thorsten: 'Hunting wild animals in Germany: conflicts between wildlife management and 'traditional' practices of Hege', in: Michaela Fenske/Bernhard Tschofen (eds.), Managing the Return of the Wild: Human Encounters with Wolves in Europe. London: Routledge 2020, pp. 164–179.

Glikman, Jenny et al: 'Coexisting with different human-wildlife coexistence perspectives', in: Frontiers in Conservation Science 2 (2021), pp. 1–6, https://doi.org/10.3389/fcosc.2021.703174.

Gomille, Axel: Deutschlands wilde Wölfe, Munich: Frederking und Thaler 2018.

Hackländer, Klaus: Der Wolf. Im Spannungsfeld von Land- & Forstwirtschaft, Jagd, Tourismus und Artenschutz, Graz/Stuttgart: Leopold Stocker 2019.

Hall, Edward T.: The Hidden Dimension. Garden City, N.Y.: Doubleday 1966.

Hansen Wheat, Christina/van der Bijl, Wouter/Temrin, Hans: 'Dogs, but Not Wolves, Lose Their Sensitivity Toward Novelty With Age', in: Frontiers in Psychology 10 (2019), article 2001, https://doi.org/10.3389/fpsyg.2019.02001.

Haraway, Donna J.: Staying with the trouble. Making kin in the Chthulucene (= Experimental futures Technological lives, scientific arts, anthropological voices), Durham/London: Duke University Press 2016.

Haraway, Donna J.: The companion species manifesto. Dogs, people, and significant otherness (= Paradigm, Vol. 8), Chicago, Ill.: Prickly Paradigm Press 2012.

Hartigan Jr, John: 'Knowing Animals: Multispecies Ethnography and the Scope of Anthropology', in: American Anthropologist 123.4 (2021), pp. 846–860, https://doi.org/10.1111/aman.13631.

Hartigan Jr, John: Shaving the Beasts: Wild Horses and Ritual in Spain, Minneapolis/London: Minnesota University Press 2020.

Hastrup, Kirsten: 'Dogs among others. Inughuit companions in Northwest Greenland', in: Robert J. Losey/Robert P. Wishart/Jan P.L. Loovers (eds.), Dogs in the North. Stories of cooperation and co-domestication, London/New York: Routledge 2018, pp. 212–232.

Heberlein, Thomas A./Ericsson, Göran: 'Ties to the Countryside: Accounting for Urbanites Attitudes toward Hunting, Wolves, and Wildlife', in: Human

Dimensions of Wildlife 10.3 (2005), pp. 213–227, https://doi.org/10.1080/1 0871200591003454.

Heinzer, Nikolaus: 'Der Wolf M64 im Lötschental: Ethnographische Schlaglichter aus einem Wolfsdurchzugsgebiet', in: Schweizer Volkskunde 106 (2016), pp. 62–66.

Heinzer, Nikolaus: Mensch-Umwelt-Relationen in Bewegung. An ethnography of wolf management in Switzerland, PhD thesis, Zurich 2020.

Helmreich, Stefan: Listening against Soundscapes, in: Anthropology News 51.9 (2010), p. 10, https://doi.org/10.1111/j.1556-3502.2010.51910.x.

Heurich, Marco (ed.): Wolf, Luchs und Bär in der Kulturlandschaft: Konflikte, Chancen, Lösungen im Umgang mit großen Beutegreifern, Stuttgart: Ulmer 2019.

Heurich, Marco: Die Rolle der großen Beutegreifer im Ökosystem, in: M. Heurich (ed.), Wolf, Luchs und Bär in der Kulturlandschaft, pp. 71–94.

Heurich, Marco: 'Was ist Wildtiermangagement?', in: M. Heurich (ed.), Wolf, Luchs und Bär in der Kulturlandschaft, pp. 96–98.

Hiedanpää, Juha/Pellikka, Jani/Ojalammi, Sanna: 'Meet the parents. Normative emotions in Finnish wolf politics', in: Trace. Journal for Human-Animal Studies 2 (2016), pp. 4–26.

Hovardas, Tasos: Large Carnivore Conservation and Management. Human Dimensions (= Earthscan Studies in Natural Resource Management Ser), Milton: Routledge 2018.

Hübl, Philipp: Die aufgeregte Gesellschaft. Wie Emotionen unsere Moral prägen und die Polarisierung verstärken (= Onleihe. E-Book), München: C. Bertelsmann Verlag 2019.

Huizinga, Johan: Homo Ludens. Vom Ursprung der Kultur im Spiel, Hamburg: Rowohlt 1981.

Ingold, T.: Anthropology and/as education, London/New York: Routledge 2018.

Ingold, Tim: Making. Anthropology, archaeology, art and architecture, London/New York: Routledge 2013.

Ingold, Tim: Being Alive. Essays on Movement, Knowledge and Description, London/New York: Routledge 2011.

Ingold, Tim: The perception of the environment: essays on livelihood, dwelling and skill, London/New York: Routledge 2000.

Ingold, Tim: What is an animal? (= One World archaeology, vol. 1), Milton Park u.a.: Routledge 1994.

IUCN: IUCN SSC guidelines on human-wildlife conflict and coexistence. First edition. Gland, Switzerland: IUCN 2023, https://doi.org/10.2305/YGIK2927.

Jarausch, Anne et al.: 'How the west was won: genetic reconstruction of rapid wolf recolonization into Germany's anthropogenic landscapes', in: Heredity 127 (2021), pp. 92–106, https://doi.org/10.1038/s41437-021-00429-6.

Johnston, Catherine: 'Beyond the clearing: towards a dwelt animal geography', in: Progress in Human Geography 32.5 (2008), pp. 633–649, https://doi.org/10.1177/0309132508089825.

Jones, Karen: 'From Big Bad Wolf to Ecological Hero: *Canis Lupus* and the Culture(s) of Nature in the American-Canadian West', in: American Review of Canadian Studies 40.3 (2010), pp. 338–350, https://doi.org/10.1080/02722011.2010.496902.

Jørgensen, Dolly: 'Rethinking rewilding', in: Geoforum 65 (2015), pp. 482–488, https://doi.org/10.1016/j.geoforum.2014.11.016.

Jürgens, Uta M./Hackett, Paul M.: 'The Big Bad Wolf: The Formation of a Stereotype', in: Ecopsychology 9.1 (2017), pp. 33–43, https://doi.org/10.1089/eco.2016.0037.

Kaczensky, Petra: 'Medienpräsenz- und Akzeptanzstudie 'Wölfe in Deutschland'', Freiburg i. Br.: Forstzoologisches Institut der Universität Freiburg 2006.

Kahl, Antje: Analyzing affective societies. Methods and methodologies (= Routledge studies in affective societies, Vol. 4), London/New York: Routledge 2019.

Kappelhoff, Hermann/Lehmann, Hauke: 'The temporal composition of affects in audiovisual media', in: A. Kahl (ed.), Analyzing affective societies, pp. 120–139.

Keil, Paul: 'Rank Atmospheres: The more-than-human scentspace and aesthetic of a pigdogging hunt', in: Australian Journal of Anthropology (2021), pp. 1–18, https://doi.org/10.1111/taja.12382.

Kirksey, Eben/Helmreich, Stefan: 'The emergence of multispecies ethnography', in: Cultural Anthropology 25.4 (2010), pp. 545–576, https://doi.org/10.1111/j.1548-1360.2010.01069.x.

Kleese, Deborah: 'Contested Natures: Wolves in Late Modernity', in: Society and Natural Resources 15.4 (2002), pp. 313–326, https://doi.org/10.1080/089419202753570800.

Knight, John (ed.): Natural enemies. People-wildlife conflicts in anthropological perspective (= European Association of Social Anthropologists), London: Routledge 2000.

Knight, John: Waiting for Wolves in Japan: An Anthropological Study of People-Wildlife Relations, Oxford: Oxford University Press 2003.

Kolb, Natalie: Akzeptanzstudie zur Wiedereinwanderung von Wölfen nach Rheinland-Pfalz, Unpublished Master's thesis, Oldenburg 2017.

König, Bettina: Die Darstellung des Wolfsbildes im Kontext geschichtlicher Entwicklungsprozesse—eine wissenschaftliche Analyse am Beispiel ausgewählter Printmedien seit 1873. Unpublished dissertation, Freiburg i. Br. 2010.

Kramer-Schadt, Stephanie et al. Habitat modelling and estimation of the potential number of wolf territories in Germany, Federal Agency for Nature Conservation (=BfN-Skripten 556) 2020.

Kruuk, Hans: Hunter and Hunted: Relationships Between Carnivores and People, Cambridge: Cambridge University Press 2002.

Kuijper, Dries P. J. et al.: 'Context dependence of risk effects: Wolves and tree logs create patches of fear in an old-growth forest', in: Behavioral Ecology 26.6 (2015), pp. 1558–1568, https://doi.org/10.1093/beheco/arv107.

Kuijper, Dries P.J. et al.: 'Landscape of fear in Europe: Wolves affect spatial patterns of ungulate browsing in Białowieża Primeval Forest, Poland', in: Ecography 36.12 (2013), pp. 1263–1275, https://doi.org/10.1111/j.1600-0587. 2013.00266.x.

Kulick, Don: 'Human-Animal Communication', in Annual Review of Anthropology 46 (2017), pp. 357–378, https://doi.org/10.1146/annurev-anthro-102 116-041723.

Kurki, Sami/Bisi, Jukka: The wolf debate in Finland. Expectations and objectives for the management of the wolf population at regional and national level, Seinajöki: University of Helsinki, Ruralia Institute 2008.

Landry, Jean-Marc/Borelli, Jean-Luc/Drouilly, Marine: 'Interactions between livestock guarding dogs and wolves in the southern French Alps', in: Journal of Vertebrate Biology 69.3 (2020), pp. 1–18, https://doi.org/10.25225/jv b.20078.

Latimer, Joanna: 'Being Alongside: Rethinking Relations amongst Different Kinds', in: Theory, Culture and Society 30.7/8 (2013), pp. 77–104, https://do i.org/10.1177/0263276413500078.

Laundré, John W./Hernández, Lucina/Altendorf, Kelly B.: 'Wolves, elk, and bison: reestablishing the 'landscape of fear' in Yellowstone National Park,

U.S.A', in: Canadian Journal of Zoology 79.8 (2001), pp. 1401–1409, https://doi.org/10.1139/z01-094.

Lave, Jean/Wenger, Etienne: Situated Learning. Legitimate Peripheral Participation, Cambridge: Cambridge University Press 1991.

Lehmann, Albrecht: Von Menschen und Bäumen: Die Deutschen und ihr Wald, Reinbek: Rowohlt 1999.

Lehnen, Lisa/Mueller, Thomas/Reinhardt, Ilka/Kaczensky, Petra/Arbieu, Ugo: »Gesellschaftliche Einstellungen zur Rückkehr des Wolfs nach Deutschland«, in: Natur und Landschaft 1/2021, pp. 27–33, https://doi.org/10.174 33/1.2021.50153871.27-33.

Lescureux, Nicolas: 'Towards the necessity of a new interactive approach integrating ethnology, ecology in the study of the relationship between Kyrgyz stockbreeders and wolves', in: Social Science Information 45 (2006), pp. 463–478, https://doi.org/10.1177/0539018406066536.

Lescureux, Nicolas/Garde, Laurent/Meuret, Michel: 'Considering wolves as active agents in understanding stakeholder perceptions and developing management strategies', in: T. Hovardas (ed.), Large Carnivore Conservation and Management, pp. 147–167.

Lestel, Dominique/Brunois, Florence/Gaunet, Florence: 'Etho-etnology and ethno-ethology', in: Social Science Information 45.2 (2006), pp. 155–177, h ttps://doi.org/10.1177/0539018406063633.

Lestel, Dominique/Bussolini, Jeffrey/Chrulew, Matthew: 'The Phenomenology of Animal Life', in: Environmental Humanities 5.1 (2014), pp. 125–148, http s://doi.org/10.1215/22011919-3615442.

Liebal, Katja/Lubrich, Oliver/Stodulka, Thomas (eds.): Emotionen im Feld. Conversations on the professional distance to the object, Bielefeld: transcript 2018, https://doi.org/10.14361/9783839445488.

Linnell, John D.C.: 'Beyond wolves: the politics of wolf recovery and management', in Wildlife Biology 11.4 (2005), pp. 393–394, https://doi.org/10.2981/ 0909-6396(2005)11[393:BWTPOW]2.0.CO;2.

Linnell, John D.C. et al.: 'Is the Fear of Wolves Justified? A Fennoscandian Perspective', in: Acta Zoologica Lituanica 13.1 (2003), pp. 34–40, https://doi.or g/10.1080/13921657.2003.10512541.

Linnell, John et al.: The fear of wolves: A review of wolf attacks on humans, in: NINA Oppdragsmelding 731, Trondheim: Norsk institutt for naturforskning 2002, https://www.nina.no/archive/nina/pppbasepdf/oppdragsmeldi ng/731.pdf (accessed 18.06.2022).

Linnell, John D./Kovtun, Ekaterina/Rouart, Ive: Wolf attacks on humans: an update for 2002–2020. NINA Report 1944. Trondheim: Norwegian Institute for Nature Research 2021, https://brage.nina.no/nina-xmlui/handle/1 1250/2729772 (accessed 18.06.2022).

Locke, Piers: 'Elephants as persons, affective apprenticeship, and fieldwork with nonhuman informants in Nepal', in: HAU: Journal of Ethnographic Theory 7.a (2017), pp. 353–376.

Locke, Piers: 'Explorations in Ethnoelephantology: Social, Historical, and Ecological Intersections between Asian Elephants and Humans', in: Environment and Society 4.1 (2013), https://doi.org/10.3167/ares.2013.040106.

Lone, Karen et al.: ' Living and dying in a multi-predator landscape of fear: roe deer are squeezed by contrasting pattern of predation risk imposed by lynx and humans', in: Oikos 123.6 (2014), pp. 641–651, https://doi.org/10.1111/j.1 600-0706.2013.00938.x.

Lopez, Barry H.: Of Wolves and Men, New York: Simon & Schuster 1995.

Lorand, Charlotte/Robert, Alexandre/Gastineau, Adrienne/Mihoub, Jean-Baptiste/Bessa-Gomes, carmen: 'Effectiveness of interventions for managing human-large carnivore conflicts worldwide: Scare them off, don't remove them', in: Science of the Total Environment, Volume 838, Part 2 (2022), pp. 156–195.

Lorimer, Haydon: 'Forces of Nature, Forms of Life: Calibrating Ethology and Phenomenology', in: Ben Anderson/Paul Harrison (eds.), Taking-Place: non-representational theories in geography, Farnham: Ashgate 2010, pp. 55–77.

Lorimer, Jamie: 'Nonhuman charisma', in: Environment and Planning D: Society and Space 25.5 (2007), pp. 911–932, https://doi.org/10.1068/d71j.

Lorimer, Jamie/Hodgetts, Timothy/Barua, Maan: 'Animals' atmospheres', in Progress in Human Geography 43.1 (2019), pp. 26–45, https://doi.org/10.1177/0309132517731254.

Losey, Robert J./Wishart, Robert P./Loovers, Jan P.L. (eds.): Dogs in the North. Stories of cooperation and co-domestication (= Arctic worlds), London/New York: Routledge 2018.

Lübke, Christiane/Delhey, Jan (eds.): Diagnose Angstgesellschaft? Was wir wirklich über die Gefühlslage der Menschen wissen (= Band 51), Bielefeld, Germany: transcript Verlag 2019.

Lubrich, Oliver/Stodulka, Thomas: Emotions on Expeditions. Ein Taschenhandbuch für die ethnographische Praxis (= Edition Kulturwissenschaft,

Vol. 206), Bielefeld: transcript 2019, https://doi.org/10.14361/978383944776 5.

Lübke Christiane/Delhey, Jan (eds.): Diagnose Angstgesellschaft? What we really know about people's emotional state (= Society of Differences, Vol. 51), Bielefeld: transcript 2019, https://doi.org/10.14361/9783839446140.

MacDougall, David: The Corporeal Image. Film, Ethnography, and the Senses, Princeton: Princeton University Press 2005.

Mangelsdorf, Marion: Wolf Projections: Who is suckling whom? On the Arrival of Wolves in Technoscience (= Science Studies), Bielefeld: transcript 2007, https://doi.org/10.14361/9783839407356.

Marchesini, Roberto/Celentano, Marco: Critical ethology and post-anthropocentric ethics. Beyond the separation between humanities and life sciences (= Numanities-arts and humanities in progress, volume 16), Cham: Springer Nature 2021.

Marcus, George E.: 'Ethnography in/of the World System: The Emergence of Multi-Sited Ethnography', in: Annual Review of Anthropology 24 (1995), pp. 95–117, https://doi.org/10.1146/annurev.an.24.100195.000523.

Marshall-Pescini, Sarah: 'Importance of a species' socioecology: Wolves outperform dogs in a conspecific cooperation task', in Proceedings of the National Academy of Sciences of the United States of America 114.44 (2017), pp. 11793–11798, https://doi.org/10.1073/pnas.1709027114.

Marvin, Garry: 'Wild Killing: Contesting the Animal in Hunting', in: The Animal Studies Group (ed.), Killing Animals, Chicago: University of Illinois Press 2006, pp. 10–29.

Marvin, Garry: Wolf, London: Reaktion Books 2015.

McCorristine, Shane/Adams, William M.: 'Ghost species: spectral geographies of biodiversity conservation', in: Cultural Geographies 27.1 (2020), pp. 101–115, https://doi.org/10.1177/1474474019871645.

McFarland, Sarah/Hediger, Ryan (eds.): Animals and Agency: An Interdisciplinary Exploration, Leiden: Brill 2009.

Mech, David et al.: The Wolves of Denali, Minneapolis: University of Minnesota Press 1998.

Mech, David/Boitani, Luigi (eds.): Wolves: behaviour, ecology, and conservation, Chicago: University of Chicago Press 2003.

Mech, David/Peterson, R.: Wolf-prey relations, in: Mech, David/Boitani, Luigi (eds.): Wolves: behaviour, ecology, and conservation, Chicago: University of Chicago Press 2003, pp. 131–157.

Mech, David: 'Is science in danger of sanctifying the wolf?', in: Biological Conservation 150.1 (2012), pp. 143–149, https://doi.org/10.1016/j.biocon.2012.03.003.

Mech, David/Smith, Douglas W./MacNulty, Daniel R.: Wolves on the Hunt, Chicago/London: University of Chicago Press 2015.

Meriggi, A. et al.: 'Changes of wolf (Canis lupus) diet in Italy in relation to the increase of wild ungulate abundance', in: Ethology Ecology and Evolution 23.3 (2011), p. 195–210, https://doi.org/10.1080/03949370.2011.577814.

Merleau-Ponty, Maurice: Nature. Course Notes from the College de France, Evanston, Ill. Northwestern University Press 2003.

Merleau-Ponty, Maurice: Phenomenology of Perception, London: Routledge 2004.

Miller, Jennifer R./Schmitz, Oswald J.: 'Landscape of fear and human-predator coexistence: Applying spatial predator-prey interaction theory to understand and reduce carnivore-livestock conflict', in Biological Conservation 236 (2019), pp. 464–473, https://doi.org/10.1016/j.biocon.2019.06.009.

Mitchell, Andrew: Tracing wolves. Materiality, Effect and Difference. Dissertation, Stockholm 2018.

Moore, Roland S.: 'Metaphors of Encroachment: Hunting for Wolves on a Central Greek Mountain', in: Anthropological Quarterly 67.2 (1994), pp. 81–88, https://doi.org/10.2307/3317363.

Morizot, Baptiste: Wild Diplomacy: Cohabiting with Wolves on a New Ontological Map, Albany: State University of New York Press 2022.

Mounet, Coralie: 'Living with 'problem' animals', in: Revue de Géographie Alpine (2008), pp. 65–76, https://doi.org/10.4000/rga.560.

Mühlhoff, Rainer: 'Affective resonance and social interaction', in: Phenomenology and the Cognitive Sciences 14.4 (2015), pp. 1001–1019, https://doi.org/10.1007/s11097-014-9394-7.

Murie, Adolph: The Wolves of Mount McKinley, Seattle: University of Washington Press 1985.

Musiani, Marco/Boitani, Luigi/Paquet, Paul C. (eds.): A new era for wolves & people. Wolf recovery, human attitudes, and policy (= Energy, ecology, and the environment series, Volume 2), Calgary, Alta: University of Calgary Press 2009.

Nagel, Thomas: 'What Is It Like To Be A Bat?', in: The Philosophical Review 83.4 (1974), pp. 435–450, https://doi.org/10.2307/2183914.

Nancy, Jean-Luc: Being Singular Plural, Stanford: Stanford University Press 2000.

Nancy, Jean-Luc: Corpus II: Writings on sexuality, New York: Fordham University Press 2013.

Niedziałkowski, Krzysztof: Between Europeanisation and politicisation: wolf policy and politics in Germany. Environmental Politics, 32 (2023), pp. 793–814, https://doi.org/10.1080/09644016.2022.2127646.

Noske, Barbara: 'The Animal Question in Anthropology: A Commentary', in: Society and Animals 1.2 (1993), pp. 185–190, https://doi.org/10.1163/156853 093X00073.

Nustad, Karin/Swanson, Heather: 'Political ecology and the Foucault effect: A need to diversify disciplinary approaches to ecological management?', in: Environment and Planning E: Nature and Space, 5 (2022), pp. 924–946, https://doi.org/10.1177/25148486211015044.

Oehler, Alex: Beyond Wild and Tame: Soiot encounters in a sentient landscape, Oxford: Berghahn 2020.

Ogden, Laura: Swamplife. People, gators, and mangroves entangled in the Everglades, Minneapolis: University of Minnesota Press 2011.

Ohrem, Dominik: (In)VulnerAbilities: Postanthropocentric Perspectives on Vulnerability, Agency and the Ontology of the Body, in: S. Wirth et al. (eds.), The Agency of Animals, pp. 67–92, https://doi.org/10.14361/9783839432266 -002.

Ojalammi, Sanna/Blomley, Nicholas: 'Dancing with wolves: Making legal territory in a more-than-human world', in: Geoforum 62 (2015), pp. 51–60, https://doi.org/10.1016/j.geoforum.2015.03.022.

O'Mahony, Kieran/Corradini, Andrea/Gazzola, Andrea: 'Lupine Becomings -Tracking and Assembling Romanian Wolves through Multi-Sensory Fieldwork', in Society & Animals 26.2 (2018), pp. 107–129, https://dx.doi.org/10 .1163/15685306-12341501

Ostrowski, Lea: Die Rückkehr des Wolfs in den Leuscheider Wald: Untersuchungen zu Akzeptanz und naturbezogenen Werten im Bereich der Weidetierhaltung, Master's Thesis, Hochschule für nachhaltige Entwicklung Eberswalde 2022.

Packard, Jane M.: Wolf behaviour: reproductive, social and intelligent, in: D. Mech/L. Boitani (eds.), Wolves, pp. 35–65.

Pates, Rebecca/Leser, Julia: The wolves are coming back. The politics of fear in Eastern Germany, Manchester: Manchester University Press 2021.

Peltola, Taru/Heikkilä, Jari: 'Response-ability in wolf-dog conflicts', in: European Journal of Wildlife Research 61.5 (2015), pp. 711–721, https://doi.org/1 0.1007/s10344-015-0946-0.

Peters, Christian Helge: 'Media Ecology II. What's the point of facts if affects can do it too? Zur Medienökologie des Rechtspopulismus und seinen Strategien der Affizierung', in: Behrendt, Gianna/Henkel, Anna (eds.), 10 Minuten Soziologie: Fakten (= 10 Minute Sociology 2), Bielefeld: transcript 2018, pp. 97–108, https://doi.org/10.14361/9783839443620-008.

Philo, Chris/Wilbert, Chris (eds.): Animal spaces, beastly places. New geographies of human-animal relations (= Critical geographies, Vol. 10), London/New York: Routledge 2000.

Pink, Sarah: Doing Sensory Ethnography, London: Sage 2009.

Poerting, Julia/Marquardt, Nadine: 'Kritisch-geographische Perspektiven auf Landschaft', in: Dies. (ed.), Kritisch-geographische Perspektiven auf Landschaft, Wiesbaden: Springer VS 2019, pp. 145–152.

Poerting, Julia/Verne, Julia/Krieg, Lisa J.: 'Dangerous Encounters. Posthumanist Approaches in the Technological Renegotiation of Human-Wildlife Coexistence', in: Geographische Zeitschrift 108.3 (2020), pp. 153–175, https://doi.org/10.25162/gz-2020-0006.

Pooley, Simon et al.: 'Rethinking the study of human-wildlife coexistence', in: Conservation Biology (2020), pp. 1–10, https://doi.org/10.1111/cobi.13653.

Pooley, Simon: 'Coexistence for whom? ', in: Frontiers in Conservation Science 2 (2021), pp. 1–7, https://doi.org/10.3389/fcosc.2021.726991.

Pörksen, Bernhard: Die große Gereiztheit. Wege aus der kollektiven Erregung, Carl Hanser Verlag GmbH & Co. KG 2018.

Probyn, Elspeth: Eating the Ocean. Durham: Duke University Press 2016.

Reckwitz, Andreas. How the senses organise the social, in M. Jonas & B. Littig (Eds.), Praxeological political analysis, London: Routledge 2017, pp. 56–66.

Reed, Edward: Encountering the world. Toward an Ecological Psychology, Oxford: Oxford University Press 1997.

Reinhardt, Ilka/ Kaczensky, Petra/Frank, Jens/Knauer, Felix/Kluth, Gesa: How to deal with bold wolves – Recommendations of the DBBW (= BfN-Skript 577), Bonn: Bundesamt für Naturschutz 2020.

Reinhardt, Ilka/ Kluth, Gesa/Nowak, Sabina/Mysłajek, Robert: Reinhardt, Ilka et al.: Standards for the monitoring of the Central European wolf population in Germany and Poland (= BfN-Skript 398), Bonn: Bundesamt für Naturschutz 2015.

Reinhardt, Ilka/Kluth, Gesa: Untersuchungen zum Raum-Zeitverhalten und zur Abwanderung von Wölfen in Sachsen. Final report project 'Wanderwolf' (2012–2014), commissioned by the Saxon State Ministry for the Environment and Agriculture (SMUL), 2015.

Reinhardt, Ilka/Kluth, Gesa: Leben mit Wölfen – Leitfaden für den Umgang mit einer konfliktträchtigen Tierart in Deutschland (= BfN-Skript 201), Bonn: Bundesamt für Naturschutz 2007.

Riede, Peter: 'Wolf', in: The Scientific Bible Dictionary on the Internet, WiBiLex, 2009, https://www.bibelwissenschaft.de/stichwort/34973/.

Riedel, Friedlind: 'Atmosphere', in: J. Slaby/C. v. Scheve (eds.), Affective societies, pp. 85–95.

Rinfret, Sara: 'Controlling animals: Power, Foucault, and species management', in: Society and Natural Resources 22 (2009), pp. 571–578, https://doi.org/10.1080/08941920802029375.

Rogers, Lesley J. /Kaplan, Gisela: Spirit of the Wild Dog: The world of wolves, coyotes, foxes, jackals and dingoes, Crows Nest N.S.W.: Allen and Unwin 2003.

Ronnenberg, Katrin et al.: 'Coexistence of wolves and humans in a densely populated region (Lower Saxony, Germany)', in: Basic and Applied Ecology 25 (2017), pp. 1–14, https://doi.org/10.1016/j.baae.2017.08.006.

Rosa, Hartmut: Resonance. A Sociology of the World Relationship. Frankfurt a.M.: Suhrkamp 2016.

Røskaft, Eivin et al.: 'Patterns of self-reported fear towards large carnivores among the Norwegian public', in: Evolution and Human Behavior 24.3 (2003), pp. 184–198, https://doi.org/10.1016/S1090-5138(03)00011-4.

Savalois, Nathalie/Lescureux, Nicolas/Brunois, Florence: 'Teaching the Dog and Learning from the Dog: Interactivity in Herding Dog Training and Use', in: Anthrozoös 26.1 (2013), pp. 77–91, https://doi.org/10.2752/175303713X13534238631515.

Scarce, Rik: 'What do wolves mean? Conflicting social constructions of Canis lupus in 'bordertown'', in: Human Dimensions of Wildlife 3.3 (1998), pp. 26–45, https://doi.org/10.1080/10871209809359130.

Schoof, Nicolas et al.: 'Der Wolf in Deutschland. Challenges for pasture-based animal husbandry and practical nature conservation', in: Naturschutz und Landschaftsplanung 53.1 (2021), p. 10–19, https://doi.org/10.1399/NuL.2021.01.01.

Schöller, Rainer G.: Eine Kulturgeschichte des Wolfs. Tierisches Beuteverhalten und menschliche Strategien sowie Methoden der Abwehr (= Rombach Ökologie, Band 10), Freiburg i. Br. u.a.: Rombach 2017.

Schraml, Ulrich: Wildtiermanagement für Menschen, in: M. Heurich (ed.), Wolf, Luchs und Bär in der Kulturlandschaft, pp. 113–148.

Schröder, Verena: 'Understanding Animal Lifeworlds? Perspectives of More-than-Human Ethnographies', in: Christian Steiner et al. (eds.), More-than-Human Geographies: Key Concepts, Relationships and Methodologies, Stuttgart: Franz Steiner 2022, pp. 317–339.

Schroer, Sara Asu: "The Arts of Coexistence: A View From Anthropology", in: Front. Conserv. Sci. (2021) 2, pp. 711019. doi: 10.3389/fcosc.2021.711019.

Schurr, Carolin/Strüver, Anke: "'The Rest': Geographies of the Everyday between Affect, Emotion and Representation', in: Geographica Helvetica 71.2 (2016), pp. 87–97, https://doi.org/10.5194/gh-71-87-2016.

Scruton, Roger: The Sacred Pursuit: Reflections on the Literature on Hunting, in: Nathan Kowalsky (ed).Hunting Philosophy for Everyone: In Search of the Wild Life, Oxford: Blackwells 2010, pp. 187–197.

Seidman, Steven/Alexander, Jeffrey (eds.) The New Social theory Reader, London: Routledge 2008.

Sheets-Johnstone, Maxine: Body and Movement: Basic dynamic principles, in: Schmicking, Daniel/Gallagher, Shaun (eds.) Handbook of Phenomenology and Cognitive Science, Dordrecht: Springer 2010, pp. 217–234.

Sheets-Johnstone, Maxine: The Primacy of Movement, Amsterdam: John Benjamins 2011.

Sinha, Anindya/Chowdhury, Anmol/Anchan, Nitesh/Barua, Maan: 'Affective ethnographies of animal lives', in: Hovorka, Alice/McCubbin, Sandra/Van patter, Lauren (eds.). A Research Agenda for Animal Geographies, Cheltenham: Elgar (2021), pp. 129–146.

Skogen, Ketil/Figari, Helene/Krange, Olve: Wolf Conflicts. A Sociological Study (= Interspecies Encounters, Vol. 1), New York, NY: Berghahn 2017.

Slaby, Jan: 'Atmospheres—Schmitz, Massumi and beyond', in: Friedlind Riedel/ Juha Torvinen (eds.), Music as Atmosphere: Collective Feelings and Affective Sounds, London: Routledge 2019.

Slaby, Jan/Bens, Jonas: 'Political Affect' in: J. Slaby/C. v. Scheve (eds.), Affective Societies, pp. 340–351.

Slaby, Jan/Mühlhoff, Rainer/Wüschner, Philipp: 'Affective Arrangements', in: Emotion Review 11.1 (2019), pp. 3–12, https://doi.org/10.1177/175407391772 2214.

Slaby, Jan/Mühlhoff, Rainer/Wüschner, Philipp: 'Affektive Relationalität. Umrisse eines philosophischen Forschungsprogramms', in: Undine Eberlein (ed.), Zwischenleiblichkeit und bewegtes Verstehen, pp. 69–108, https://doi.org/10.1515/9783839435793-004.

Slaby, Jan/Scheve, Christian v. (eds.): Affective societies. Key concepts (= Routledge studies in affective societies), London/New York: Routledge 2019.

Slagle, Kristina M./Bruskotter, Jeremy T./Wilson, Robyn S.: 'The Role of Affect in Public Support and Opposition to Wolf Management', in: Human Dimensions of Wildlife 17.1 (2012), pp. 44–57.

Soentgen, Jens: Ökologie der Angst (= Fröhliche Wissenschaft, vol. 117), Berlin: Matthes und Seitz 2018.

Stokland, Håkon: 'Conserving Wolves by Transforming Them? The Transformative Effects of Technologies of Government in Biodiversity Conservation', in: Society and Animals 29 (2020), pp. 1–21.

Stoepel, Beatrix: Expeditionen ins Tierreich: Wölfe in Deutschland, Hamburg: Hoffmann und Campe 2004.

Szanto, Thomas/Slaby, Jan: Political Emotions, in: Thomas Szanto/Hilge Landwehr (eds.), The Routledge Handbook of Phenomenology of Emotion, London: Routledge 2020, pp. 478–494.

Theodorakea, Ilektra T./Essen, Erica von: 'Who let the wolves out? Narratives, rumours and social representations of the wolf in Greece', in: Environmental Sociology 2.1 (2016), pp. 29–40, https://doi.org/10.1080/23251042.2015.1119349.

Theuerkauf, Jörn: 'What Drives Wolves: Fear or Hunger? Humans, Diet, Climate and Wolf Activity Patterns', in: Ethology 115.7 (2009), pp. 649–657, https://doi.org/10.1111/j.1439-0310.2009.01653.x.

Theuerkauf, Jörn/Rouys, Sophie: 'Habitat selection by ungulates in relation to predation risk by wolves and humans in the Białowieża Forest, Poland', in: Forest Ecology and Management 256.6 (2008), pp. 1325–1332, https://doi.org/10.1016/j.foreco.2008.06.030.

Tiralla, Nina/Holzapfel, Maika/Ansorge, Hermann: 'Feeding ecology of the wolf (Canis lupus) in a near-natural ecosystem in Mongolia', in: Mammalian Biology 101 (2021), pp. 83–89, https://doi.org/10.1007/s42991-020-00093-z

Tønnessen, Morten: 'Is a wolf wild as long as it does not know that it is being thoroughly managed? ', in: Humanimalia: a journal of human/animal interface studies 2.1 (2010), pp. 1–8, https://doi.org/10.52537/humanimalia.10090.

Trajce, Aleksander: The gentleman, the vagabonds and the stranger: cultural representations of large carnivores in Albania and their implications for conservation. PhD Thesis, university of Roehampton, UK, 2017.

Tschofen, Bernhard/Heinzer, Nikolaus/ Frank,Elisa: Wolfsmanagement als kultureller Prozess Working Paper zum Symposium 'WOLFSMANAGE-

MENT: WISSEN_SCHAF(F)T_PRAXIS'. SNF project 'Wolves: Knowledge and Practice', ISEK—Institute for Social Anthropology and Empirical Cultural Studies, University of Zurich 2016.

Uexküll, Jakob v.: Streifzuge durch die Umwelten von Tieren und Menschen. Ein Bilderbuch unsichtbarer Welten, Hamburg: Rowohlt 1956.

van Beeck Calkoen, Suzanne T. S. et al.: 'Does wolf presence reduce moss browsing intensity in young forest plantations?', in Ecography 41 (2018), pp. 1776–1787, https://doi.org/10.1111/ecog.03329.

van Dooren, Thom/Rose, Deborah B.: 'Lively Ethography', in: Environmental Humanities 8.1 (2016), pp. 77–94, https://doi.org/10.1215/22011919-3527731

Van Patter, Lauren: 'Individual animal geographies for the more-than-human city: Storying synanthropy and cynanthropy with urban coyotes', in: EPE: Nature and Space 5 (2022), pp. 2216–2239, https://doi.org/10.1177/2514848 6211049441.

Versluijs, Erik/ Eriksen, Ane/ Fuchs, Boris/ Wilkenros, Camilla/ Sand, Hakan/ Wabakken, Petter/Zimmermann, Barbara: ,Wolf Responses to Experimental Human Approaches Using High-Resolution Positioning Data, in: Frontiers in Ecology and Evolution 10 (2022), pp. 792916, https://doi.org/10.338 9/fevo.2022.792916.

Vitali, Chiara: 'A frame-analytical perspective on conflict between people and an expanding wolf Canis lupus population in central Italy', in: Oryx 48.4 (2014), pp. 575–583, https://doi.org/10.1017/S0030605313000276.

von Essen, Erica/Drenthen, Martin/Bhardwaj, Manisha: 'How fences communicate interspecies codes of conduct in the landscape: toward bidirectional communication?', in: Wildlife Biology (2023): e01146, doi: 10.1002/wlb3.01146.

von Essen, Erica/Hansen, Hans-Peter/Peterson, Nils/Peterson, Tarla: 'Discourses on illegal hunting in Sweden: the meaning of silence and resistance', Environmental Sociology, 4 (2018), pp. 370–380, https://doi.org/10 .1080/23251042.2017.1408446.

von Essen, Erica: 'Whose Discourse is it Anyway? Understanding Resistance through the Rise of "Barstool Biology"' in Nature Conservation, in: Environmental Communication 11 (2017), pp. 470–489, https://doi.org/10.1080 /17524032.2015.1042986.

Wam, Hilde Karine: Wolf behaviour towards people. the outcome of 125 monitored encounters, Unpublished Cand. Scient. Thesis, Norwegian Agriculture University, Ås 2002.

White, P. J./Proffitt, Kelly M./Lemke, Thomas O.: 'Changes in Elk Distribution and Group Sizes after Wolf Restoration', in: The American Midland Naturalist 167.1 (2012), pp. 174–187, https://doi.org/10.1674/0003-0031-167.1.174

Williams, Christopher/Ericsson, Göran/Heberlein, Thomas A.: 'A quantitative summary of attitudes towards wolves and their reintroduction (1972–2000)', in: Wildlife Society Bulletin 30.2 (2002), pp. 575–584.

Wilson, Matthew A.: 'The wolf in Yellowstone: Science, symbol, or politics? Deconstructing the conflict between environmentalism and wise use', in: Society and Natural Resources 10.5 (1997), pp. 453–468, https://doi.org/10.10 80/08941929709381044.

Wilson, Matthew A./Heberlein, Thomas A.: 'The wolf, the tourist, and the recreational context: New opportunity or uncommon circumstance?', in: Human Dimensions of Wildlife 1.4 (1996), pp. 38–53, https://doi.org/10.1080 /10871209609359077.

Wirth, Sven et al.: Das Handeln der Tiere. Tierliche Agency im Fokus der Human-Animal Studies (= Human-Animal Studies, Vol. 9), Bielefeld: transcript 2016, https://doi.org/10.14361/9783839432266.

Wolf, M./Weissing, F.J.: 'Animal personalities: Consequences for ecology and evolution', in: Trends in Ecology and Evolution 27.8 (2012), pp. 452–461; https://doi.org/10.1016/j.tree.2012.05.001.

Wörner, Frank: Wölfe im Westerwald: Verfolgt bis in die Gegenwart—Ein Plädoyer für Akzeptanz, Tierpark Niederfischbach e.V., Niederfischbach 2013.

Wörner, Frank: Rheinland-Pfalz erwartet den Wolf: Ein Management soll das Zusammenleben regeln, Tierpark Niederfischbach e.V., Niederfischbach 2015.

Wörner, Frank: Neues vom Wolf im Westerwald: Notizen zu Wolfsnachweisen 2016 bis 2019, Tierpark Niederfischbach e.V., Niederfischbach 2019.

Wörner, Frank: 10 Jahre Wölfe im Westerwald: Notizen zu einer umstrittenen Rückkehr—Eine Zwischenbilanz 2011–2021, Tierpark Niederfischbach e.V., Niederfischbach 2021.

Zbyryt Adam et al.: 'Data from: do wild ungulates experience higher stress with humans than with large carnivores?', Dryad Digital Repository 2017, https://doi.org/10.5061/dryad.p2f4b.

Zbyryt, Adam et al.: 'Do wild ungulates experience higher stress with humans than with large carnivores?', in Behavioral Ecology 29.1 (2018), pp. 19–30, https://doi.org/10.1093/beheco/arx142.

Zimen, Erik: Wölfe (= Was ist was, Band 104), Nürnberg: Tessloff 2010.

GPSR Authorized Representative: Easy Access System Europe, Mustamäe tee
50, 10621 Tallinn, Estonia, gpsr.requests@easproject.com

www.ingramcontent.com/pod-product-compliance
Lightning Source LLC
Chambersburg PA
CBHW070105030426
42335CB00016B/2017